DIVISIONS
THROUGHOUT THE WHOLE

This book explores the connection between the changing social context of colonial New England and the emergence of political unrest in the years before the American Revolution. In doing so it looks not only at the relationship between imperial and domestic politics but also emphasizes the role of common people in making political change at the local level.

Unlike studies that have examined revolutionary activity in major colonial towns, where it was most visible, Professor Nobles's study focuses on the sources of revolutionary behavior in the countryside. He examines the social and political development of Hampshire County from the seventeenth through the eighteenth century and seeks to explain why people who had remained apparently indifferent to the political crisis developing before 1774 became such active participants in a violent political struggle against the established government. In his discussion of a variety of local controversies – religious disputes, sectional controversies, and town divisions – the author shows how common people repeatedly mobilized to act on their own terms for their own concerns. He concludes that these local social and political concerns did as much to shape the colonists' attitudes and prepare them for radical activity in the Revolutionary era as did the actions of the British government.

Western Massachusetts, from a map by J. Reid, 1796.

DIVISIONS
THROUGHOUT THE WHOLE

POLITICS AND SOCIETY
IN HAMPSHIRE COUNTY, MASSACHUSETTS, 1740–1775

———

GREGORY H. NOBLES

CAMBRIDGE UNIVERSITY PRESS

Cambridge

London   New York   New Rochelle

Melbourne   Sydney

Published by the Press Syndicate of the University of Cambridge
The Pitt Building, Trumpington Street, Cambridge CB2 1RP
32 East 57th Street, New York, NY 10022, USA
296 Beaconsfield Parade, Middle Park, Melbourne 3206, Australia

© Cambridge University Press 1983

First published 1983

Printed in the United States of America

Library of Congress Cataloging in Publication Data
Nobles, Gregory H.
Divisions throughout the whole.
Bibliography: p.
Includes index.
1. Hampshire County (Mass.) – Politics and government.
2. Hampshire County (Mass.) – Social conditions.
3. Massachusetts – Politics and government – Colonial
period, ca. 1600–1775 – Case studies.   4. Hampshire
County (Mass.) – Church history.   5. Great Awakening.
I. Title.
F72.H3N63   1983   974.4'2302   82–14674
ISBN 0 521 24419 6

To my parents,
Paul Nobles and Edna Nobles;
and to the memory of my aunt,
Hattie Hight

CONTENTS

PREFACE

Historians may still not be able to explain with certainty – or unanimity – why the American colonists made a revolution, but by
now most would probably agree that the roots of the Revolution
lay not so much in the changes in British policy as in the changes
in American society. This book is a study of local conditions in
one small part of that society, a rural county in western Massachusetts, during the years before the Revolution. Throughout the
seventeenth and eighteenth centuries, Hampshire County remained distinct from both eastern Massachusetts and Connecticut
and in many ways represented a region with its own identity and
pattern of development. By the time of the Revolution it contained
a wide variety of communities, ranging from old, established
towns along the Connecticut River to new, struggling settlements
in the hills or on the frontier.

On the one hand, then, I have chosen to examine the changing
nature of Hampshire County in the belief that this kind of regional
focus provides more complexity and diversity and a generally
broader frame of reference than does the study of one particular
community. At the same time, though, I have chosen to confine
the frame of reference to the county in the belief that it is at the
local level that common people most actively and eloquently express their political values. Then, as now, most people did not
have the opportunity or the ability to participate directly in inter-
national, national, or even provincial politics. The decision-
making process at those levels was remote from common people,
and they remained remote from it. In their own communities,
however, people had the occasion to become much more emphatic
and effective political actors, taking a much more immediate role
in making significant change. By looking at the variety of local

controversies – especially the many religious disputes, sectional conflicts, and town divisions – that erupted in Hampshire County in the middle of the eighteenth century, we can see people acting on their own terms for their own concerns, and in that sense I think we can begin to understand the political consciousness of rural non-elites on the eve of the Revolution.

My point is not to suggest that by exploring this parochial conflict on the local level we can somehow "explain" the revolutionary conflict on the national level. Clearly the Revolution was a phenomenon that transcended and seemingly overwhelmed local concerns. But in order to understand why people responded to the Revolutionary crisis how they did and when they did, I would suggest that it is important to understand how they had responded to their own political crises in the years before.

In more personal terms, I feel it is important for me to respond to those people and institutions who have helped me avoid crises in the years before. If my debts cannot be repaid, they can at least be recorded. This book was once a doctoral dissertation, and the Edward S. Beck and John D. Pierce fellowships from the Department of History at the University of Michigan and a travel and research grant from the Horace H. Rackham School of Graduate Studies provided very important support at the early stages of research and writing. Thanks to Marcia Burick Goldstein and the Hampshire County Bicentennial Commission, I was able to work for a brief period as editor of the Sylvester Judd Manuscripts at the Forbes Library in Northampton, Massachusetts; probably as much as anything else, my work on the Judd papers drew me deeper into the history of the people of western Massachusetts. More recently, faculty research grants from the Department of History and the College of Arts and Sciences at Virginia Polytechnic Institute and State University and a summer stipend from the National Endowment for the Humanities enabled me to do additional research while revising the manuscript. I am also grateful to a number of friends at Virginia Tech – especially Lisa Donis, Carolyn Alls, Connie Aikens, William Mackie, Harold Livesay, and Robert Litschert – for their assistance and support while I was completing the manuscript.

During my research I encountered many librarians and archivists who were generous with their time and advice (as well as a few who were not). Above all, Stanley Greenberg, reference librarian at the Forbes Library, deserves my warmest thanks for his help, especially for the ready access he granted me to the library's resources. Very few town libraries have a historical collection as valuable as that of the Forbes, nor do many have a librarian as knowledgeable and resourceful as Mr. Greenberg. Likewise, Ann Williamson at the Jones Library in Amherst and Ritchie Garrison, Louise Perrin, and David Proper at Historic Deerfield proved to be very helpful and hospitable. I would also like to express my gratitude to Blanche Cooney and the staff of the Neilson Library at Smith College for giving me visitor's privileges – and then tolerating what turned out to be a three-year visit.

I would have had a much worse time as a writer if I had not had help from several readers. Kenneth Lockridge has been with this book from the beginning, and many times he seemed to know which direction it was taking long before I did. In fact, he began talking about "the book" long before I even had enough material for a decent dissertation. He has always been an enthusiastic and encouraging adviser, an incisive and intelligent critic, and a generous and loyal friend. John Shy and Liam Hunt also offered thoughtful questions and helpful suggestions, and since I have benefited from their skepticism, I hope I have also done enough to alleviate it. Robert Gross has had to read the manuscript more often than either professional courtesy or friendship should require. He may decide he cannot read it one more time, but if he does make it at least this far, I want to thank him for the quantity and quality of his comments. I have also been fortunate over the past few years in having become familiar – I would even say friendly – with a number of other people doing research on the early history of western Massachusetts. All of them – Christopher Clark, Nancy Folbre, Kevin Sweeney, Patricia Tracy, and Patricia Wilson – have shared their thoughts with me in correspondence and conversation, and I have been stimulated as much by their own work as by their comments on mine.

Finally, I am grateful to the readers and editors at Cambridge University Press for the intelligence and skill with which they have handled my manuscript. My special thanks go to Steven Fraser for taking the manuscript in the first place, to Frank Smith for seeing it through to completion, and to Janis Bolster for her careful copyediting. To everyone I offer the obligatory absolution for the author's sins.

Perhaps most important of all, I am glad that my work on this book did not interfere too much with what I guess is a normal home life. My wife, Anne Harper, read and commented on a couple of chapters a couple of years ago, and her questions were, as usual, perceptive and to the point. More recently she has been busy with her own teaching and research and writing, but I still consider her my most esteemed colleague and best friend. My daughter Phoebe was born just about the time I began the research for this book, but she has had the good sense to remain largely indifferent to what her father was doing with all the note cards and paper. If nothing else, she got a couple of trips back to Massachusetts out of the deal. Sarah was born just after the manuscript was sent off to the publisher, so she got off, all things considered, fairly easily.

INTRODUCTION

In March of 1774 the people of Amherst, Massachusetts, finally got around to drafting a letter to the Boston Committee of Correspondence. Having ignored the earlier appeals of the urban radicals, the inhabitants of this western town admitted that they had been "Long silent" on the issues surrounding the growing political crisis in the east. Still, they declared that they were "not insensible of the oppression we suffer and the ruin which threatens us or . . . of the Diabolical Designs of our Mercenary and Malevolent Enemies Foreign and Domestic and we are ready not onley to risque but even to Sacrifice our Lives and Properties in Defence of our just rights & liberties." It was a message the Boston Committee of Correspondence could well appreciate. Not only did the Amherst people sprinkle throughout their letter bits of good Whig language about the "Diabolical Designs," "Tironey and Oppression falsehood & Corruption," and "malicious cunning" of "those villens in Exalted Station" in England; they also made a point of thanking "the vigilant and faithfull gardians of our rights" in Boston.[1] In short, the people of Amherst seemed to do just what the Boston Whigs wanted them to do: deny the legitimacy of a corrupted British government, accept the leadership of the Boston Committee, and commit themselves to a growing national movement that would soon reject the authority of the Crown altogether.

Such a letter could easily have come from any number of Massachusetts towns, especially those in the western half of the province. Like Amherst, many towns had been "Long silent" on the question of British oppression, and it took the repeated efforts of the Boston Whigs to stir their fellow provincials to broader political awareness and concerted political action. And yet when the

1

people of the countryside did respond, they generally did so with earnestness and enthusiasm, not just adopting the rhetoric and slogans of the Whigs but eventually taking up arms as the "embattled farmers" celebrated in our patriotic lore.[2] This combination of reticence and radicalism poses an important if somewhat paradoxical question: why would people who had remained apparently unresponsive or indifferent to the political crisis developing in their province before 1774 become such active participants in a violent political struggle, actually carrying through on their promise to "Sacrifice our Lives and Properties in Defence of our just rights & liberties" against the established government of the land? Quite simply, why did rural people become revolutionaries?

This study is an attempt to answer that question, to try to explore the political values of rural people in one part of New England as they entered the Revolutionary era. My interest in political values does not involve only a consideration of the well-articulated (albeit sometimes poorly written) statements that emerged from town after town in response to the Boston Committee of Correspondence, although those statements are of course important and significant documents. The scope is somewhat broader and is not confined to the Revolutionary period itself. I am most interested in the earlier period—roughly, the three decades preceding the Revolution—during which western towns like Amherst appeared to be "silent" on the issues of provincial politics. As John Adams suggested in a now-familiar analysis, the real source of the Revolution lay in a change in the "minds and hearts" of colonial Americans, "a change in the principles, opinions, sentiments, and affections of the people" in the years before the Revolution actually began.[3] The widespread feelings of hostility toward the British government that developed in 1774 and the eventual outbreak of armed conflict were only the culmination of an equally widespread but more gradual process of political transformation among the population at large. Following Adams's lead somewhat, I have attempted to discover signs of political transformation by examining the wide range of local events and activities that occurred during the middle of the eighteenth century, for it is from those local phenomena that I think we can best determine the fundamental political values of the inhabitants of the county. Indeed, I will argue that the political and social concerns that engaged people's energies on the local level did as much to shape their political attitudes in the Revolutionary era as did the alleged tyranny and oppression of the Crown. The people of western Massachusetts may have been in one sense politically silent, but they were by no means politically dormant.

Admittedly, one ought to be a little wary these days about undertaking any sort of study that deals with the American Revolution. By now the whole thing may seem mercilessly overdone. No other topic in American history, with the possible exception of the Civil War, has received so much attention, both in scholarly writing and in popular celebration. The recent Bicentennial provided only the most excessive case in point. On the popular level the commemoration of the Revolution generated a steady flow of words from one end of the country to the other, a national binge of commercialism, boosterism, and plain bad taste. By July 5, 1976, most people no doubt felt they had heard all there was to hear; certainly many felt they had heard enough. For historians, unfortunately, there is an even greater danger than oversaturation. Too great a fascination with the Revolution as the main event in eighteenth-century American history can lead to a tendency to skew all historical analysis toward explaining the Revolution: by looking so hard at the Revolution we can lose sight of more subtle, less conspicuous historical phenomena, or at least misinterpret those we do see. It is bad enough to add to the glut in the present, but even worse to create a distortion of the past.[4]

Why, then, should anyone run the risk of adding to either the glut or the distortion? The only decent answer is that there are still decent questions. Despite the obvious problems of overemphasis and overindulgence in the past few years, some of the recent scholarship on the Revolutionary period has seemed remarkably fresh, generating a lively investigation not just of the nature of the American Revolution, but of the fundamental nature of political and social change. During the late 1960s, for instance, the dominant position belonged to the argument put forth by Bernard Bailyn and his followers, the notion that the Revolution was "above all else an ideological, constitutional, political struggle and not primarily a controversy between social groups undertaken to force changes in the organization of the society or the economy." Throughout the 1760s, so this argument went, American colonists became increasingly alarmed by Crown policies, began to

adopt the old English Whig language emphasizing a devious con-
spiracy against the rights and liberties of the people, and eventually developed a particularly American political identity that
helped them break with England. Bailyn's followers have argued
that this sentiment was common not only to the radical leaders in
the cities but—as the Whiggish language of the Amherst letter
might well suggest—to many people throughout society at large.
In general this ideological explanation stressed a growing unanimity among Americans defined by their growing animosity toward
the Crown and their growing sense of common purpose.[5]

The real strength of such a comprehensive argument, of course,
was that it spurred other historians to challenge or at least refine
it. Rather than portray the Revolution simply as a kind of national
monolith uniting the colonists under a single banner, some have
explored the variety of popular responses, trying to analyze more
clearly the connections between the larger political movement and
the particular conditions that pertained in different parts of the
American colonies. We now know more about the significance of
the Revolutionary movement in numerous towns or regions from
New England to the South; we now know more about the emergence of more clearly articulated political values among people of
different class backgrounds in both urban and rural settings, the
growth of a rather specific "popular ideology" in addition to the
broader, more comprehensive Whig ideology; and as a result we
are beginning to know more about the many meanings of the
Revolution to the American people, even to some of those who
chose not to support the patriot cause.[6] By taking this somewhat
narrow and localized focus, many recent works have offered us a
better appreciation of the Revolution as a social and political
movement among common people, as their struggle to deal not
just with the issues of American rights and independence, but also
with some of the more immediate issues that affected their daily
lives.

To be sure, this emphasis on the local context has done more
than simply revive an interest in Carl Becker's earlier distinction
between the questions of "home rule" and "who shall rule at
home"—although that distinction still suggests a useful line of
inquiry that has by no means been exhausted.[7] Even more important, this emphasis on local social conditions and political values
has helped revise our understanding of the connection between

society and politics. Rather than commit the reductionist mistake of submerging local analysis in an explanation of the Revolution, some historians have taken just the opposite tack, trying to locate the Revolution within a larger process of social change, perhaps especially with regard to the transformation of the comparatively simple, stable, traditional agrarian society of the early eighteenth century to the more complex, unsettled, even more "modern" capitalistic society of the nineteenth century. In that sense the Revolution stands as a heightened historical moment at which social conditions and relationships in a particular era became most clearly outlined, enlarged, and contrasted. The events of the Revolutionary period help reveal and explain the situation of people in the pre-Revolutionary period, not vice versa. If we are now less able than we once were to arrive at a unified synthesis to encompass this variety, it may be just as well. A little complexity and confusion are signs of work in progress.

I would hope that this study adds not so much to the confusion as to our appreciation of the complexity. Hampshire County was a remote, fairly isolated region of New England, distant and distinct from the political world of Boston. For that reason I think it offers a good opportunity for focusing on the nature of political values among rural people. As the subtitle of the study suggests, I assume that "politics" and "society" are closely related; indeed, it is virtually impossible to understand the political values of a given population without having some understanding of the social context within which that population lives. People form certain attitudes on the basis of their personal experience, from their perceptions of themselves in relation to other people and in relation to the ideas and standards of their culture as a whole. Those attitudes are political in the sense that they reflect an understanding of the nature of human society, however limited that society may be. I do not mean to argue for some mechanistic approach dependent on simple economic determinism or, even worse, for a pseudo-psychological analysis of what Bailyn has called "mysterious social strains."[8] I would suggest, rather, that we can best understand those political values by examining what people say and do, especially when they are dealing directly with the conditions they face in their daily lives; in that sense social strains are hardly "mysterious" to the people involved but are very real, concrete, and immediate issues. In eighteenth-century New England, most people were farmers, not philosophers. They may not always have acted in accordance with a coherent ideology—"popular" or otherwise—but they nevertheless acted with an awareness of their own situation and their own goals. If we hope to understand something of their world view, we must keep in mind the limits of the world under their view.

I have chosen the limits of the world under study here fully aware, I think, of both the benefits and the burdens. Studying a county rather than, say, a single community requires certain conceptual and methodological choices, the first of which is the willingness to sacrifice some depth for breadth. As one historian of colonial New England has put it, one can "either deal with many towns, asking few or shallow questions, or . . . deal thoroughly with a single town, running the risk of describing an untypical example."[9] Certainly the rich and detailed information contained in some of the better community studies—the analysis of birth and death rates, household composition, geographic mobility, social mobility, economic stratification, and so forth—would be nearly impossible for one person to produce for each of the forty-odd towns of late eighteenth-century Hampshire County. Yet because several scholars have recently begun to undertake that kind of close analysis for a few Hampshire towns (and here I want to thank them and encourage their future efforts) I have been able to draw on their data as well as my own to provide some of that information for some of the towns when the argument seemed to call for it.[10] In other cases I have relied on somewhat broader measures—totals of net population change, patterns of political leadership, levels of agricultural and economic development, and so forth—derived from provincial census and valuation records as well as from town and county records in order to show comparative figures for a greater number of towns.

In the end, though, this study does not depend primarily on the statistical analysis of quantitative data. It deals instead with popular social and political values, the kinds of human qualities that remain elusive, sometimes difficult to define, almost always difficult to measure. For the most part the evidence derives from a variety of narrative sources—diaries, letters, sermons, petitions, descriptions, depositions, and declarations—that record the attitudes and activities of the people who lived in eighteenth-century Hampshire County. In using such sources I have tried to be fair to the people who created them, tried to understand the particular meaning they attached to their words and actions. But I have also tried, as any historian must, to be sensitive to the implicit meanings of their words and actions in light of a broader historical context.

In that respect I think the regional focus of this study allows for a valuable exploration of the complex social and political relationships that involved the people of the different towns. My earliest reading of both town and county records convinced me that it was very difficult to isolate one town from the others. The history of Hampshire County towns – including their settlement, economic development, political leadership, and ecclesiastical order – reflected a number of regional connections too prominent to ignore. Jonathan Edwards once referred to Hampshire County as a "neighbourhood," and it is that notion of neighborhood, with its suggestion of interrelationships and similarities, that I want to examine here. Though the narrative occasionally relies on an extended anecdote for the sake of example, my purpose is to suggest not so much the peculiarities of one local incident as the pattern of regional trends. In general, by looking at similar events and phenomena in a number of towns at once, I hope to outline the overall pattern of social development and political behavior across the landscape of Hampshire County, and in doing so to offer a better sense of the common experience of the people, perhaps a better understanding of their shared history on the eve of the Revolution.

That history has received little attention of late. Since the 1950s the standard – indeed, almost the only – published work on eighteenth-century western Massachusetts has been Robert J. Taylor's *Western Massachusetts in the Revolution*. Even the most recent studies of colonial social and political history cite Taylor more or less as gospel. In Taylor's view, the distinctive feature of the region's political culture in the pre-Revolutionary era was a pervasive and fundamental rural conservatism. At the top of the social and political structure stood the powerful men called River Gods (John Stoddard, Israel Williams, John Worthington, and a few others) who ruled the county almost without challenge up to the time of the Revolution. The dominance these men exercised over the region derived in large part from their hold on the "confidence of the royal governors . . . [and] an extensive patronage machine" operated by the governors. But at the same time, suggests Taylor, the inhabitants of western Massachusetts themselves seemed to be a rather quiet, politically apathetic, almost docile lot. Within the region as a whole the conservatism of the inhabitants was reflected in a general absence of social or political discord. What disputes did arise over questions of land ownership or religious doctrine, for instance, "were local petty quarrels, of no significance beyond the confines of the town." Moreover, western farmers likewise "tended to be conservative" in their attitudes toward provincial policies and generally "exhibited an indifference to political matters" beyond their immediate sphere. If they chose to send representatives to the General Court at all, and most towns chose not to do so, they repeatedly sent the men who constituted the county's ruling elite. In that sense the continuing political leadership of the River Gods seems to fit reasonably well with the charge of general political inertia among the people. In short, Taylor describes a region marked by the prevalence of hegemony and harmony, by a fundamental sense of agreement between the people and their rulers and among the people themselves.[11]

In the end, argues Taylor, it took the Revolution to break up the local harmony. Only in 1774, when the Intolerable Acts threatened to impose more direct Parliamentary control over judicial salaries, did western farmers become mobilized and militant. Long uneasy about the power of the courts over their lives, they saw the possibility of increased British control as a severe danger. Almost immediately they rose up and closed the county courts, and in doing so they deposed the River Gods, who for years had dominated the bench. At the same time westerners quickly overcame their hostility or indifference toward eastern radicals and even accepted them as leaders in the Revolutionary cause. "The striking fact about the history of western Massachusetts in the eighteenth century," Taylor concludes, "is the profound educative force exerted by the American Revolution. From Revolutionary leaders westerners learned both the technique of revolt and the language of natural rights philosophy."[12] In those towns, then, the Revolution became an agent of sudden and massive political transformation: external events and external leaders caused the people of the region to change both their political allegiances and their political behavior almost overnight.

The purpose of this study is not to flay Taylor's analysis or revise his argument point by point. By all means, there is much to be said for his book, especially for its discussion of the conservative style of rule exercised by the River Gods and the apparent political isolation of westerners from the political world of Boston. But the strength of that analysis also leads to an important conceptual weakness: the attention paid the power and authority of the ruling elites tends to obscure the political role of other people in the region. It assumes rather too easily that the conservatism of the common people – their rural parochialism and general indifference to provincial affairs – formed a harmonious whole with the conservatism of their rulers. Certainly the implied harmony between the rulers and ruled does not suggest a very convincing explanation for the sudden outburst of radical activity in the west at the time of the Revolution. However unintentionally, Taylor's explanation of Revolutionary politics in western Massachusetts – the apparent shift from deference to defiance, the predominant concentration on the issue of the local courts, the sudden acceptance of radical leaders from the east – depicts the people of the west as being politically fickle and perhaps even rather feeble. Like a number of other studies of the Revolution, Taylor's book, in focusing on political leadership, does not allow for a fuller exploration of the complexity of political change among the people at large.

For that reason I think it is necessary to look carefully at the activities of those people in the years preceding the tumult of the Revolution. The picture is in many ways quite different from the one Taylor draws. Indeed, throughout the middle of the eighteenth century Hampshire County was far from being a region marked by peace, harmony, and apathy; communities in all parts of the region became embroiled in a variety of conflicts, and between 1740 and 1775 the county experienced recurring outbreaks of local unrest. In terms of religious life, the years of the Great Awakening brought a number of ecclesiastical disorders, and for years afterward groups of evangelicals and Separates continued to upset the established order of the county. Though the organized clergy of the county, the Hampshire Association of Ministers, attempted to restore some degree of unity after the Great Awakening, throughout the 1750s and 1760s its effectiveness as a source of regional authority deteriorated in the face of repeated challenge. On the secular level conditions were no more stable. I draw special attention to the effects of a dramatic population increase on the social and political life of the county after 1740. In the decades before the Revolution the population of the county more than doubled, and the older towns faced the considerable problems of overcrowding and political instability: almost every one of these older towns eventually had to subdivide into two or more separate towns, and the divisions seldom came about altogether peacefully. At the same time much of the population moved into new settlements on the frontier, and the number of towns in the county more than tripled. The political significance of this dispersal of the population lay primarily in the creation of new and independent political entities no longer directly under the control of the old towns and the old leaders; like the clergy, the established political leaders of the county found their position repeatedly challenged and gradually eroded over the years, and the Revolution served to make that challenge more sweeping and complete.

Just as it would be inaccurate to magnify the unrest far out of proportion, so is it mistaken to suggest, as Taylor does, that each case of local conflict was "of no significance beyond the confines of the [particular] town." Taken together, these "petty quarrels" suggest a broader pattern of political behavior that helps define the conflicting political values of various groups of people in the county. Indeed, this study will argue that the rising level of conflict throughout the middle of the eighteenth century reflected a clash of two fundamentally different attitudes toward social and political order, which could both be described as conservative, perhaps, but which were hardly harmonious. On the one hand there stood, quite unmistakably, the awesome authority of the county elite. By the early years of the eighteenth century the leading ministers and magistrates in Hampshire County had combined power, patronage, and paternalism to fashion an extensive network of regional rule; although they all had considerable influence in their particular towns and churches, their ties of friendship and kinship helped them reach above the community level to develop broadly based organizational structures for governing the county as a whole. In short, the county elite sought to create a source of authority superior to the autonomy of the individual towns.

On the other hand there emerged a widespread movement among common people to maintain—or regain—local control of their political and religious affairs. Especially with the upsurge of religious revivalism and the even more general expansion of the population in Hampshire County by the middle of the century, a growing number of people sought to establish their own independent churches and towns, to recreate the traditional patterns of town life, and in the end to separate themselves from the dominance of the county leadership. This second sort of conservatism, with its emphasis on localism and in many cases on strict religious practices, was almost reactionary in nature, looking back to standards of an idealized past that had been eroded by years of demographic and economic change throughout New England. But in the particular context of Hampshire County this apparent attempt to recapture the past provided the impetus for extreme and almost revolutionary change.

By 1774, then, the growing imperial crisis became superimposed on a pattern of localized crisis in the west. People had been involved in their own political struggles for years. They had of necessity become political actors, gaining immediate experience in organizing and acting on a common principle, gaining perhaps a heightened sensitivity to political rights and ideals. The point is not to argue simply that these local issues somehow represented in microcosm the fundamental issues of the Revolutionary movement. It is important to maintain the distinction between the national and the local movements and not to merge one too easily into the other. It is more accurate to say that the national and local movements remained different and yet contributed to each other. Not only did local events in pre-Revolutionary Hampshire County create a background of political activity and experience that prepared the region's inhabitants for the larger, national struggle, but in turn the Revolutionary years created a context for the continued pursuit of local issues: that is, the outbreak of the Revolution helped accelerate political changes that were already taking place within the region. To be sure, Hampshire County did not experience a radical political or social revolution between 1774 and 1783; neither did any other part of the colonies. But by beginning to understand how local events in the Revolutionary period still reflected certain longer-term local issues, we can get a better sense of the connections people made between concerns in which they had been long engaged and others on which they had been long silent.

Chapter 1

FAMILY POWER AND POLITICAL RELATIONS IN HAMPSHIRE COUNTY

From the beginning Hampshire County represented a sort of frontier paradox: although vast in area, it was still a very limited and restricted universe, almost a world unto itself. In 1636, the year the English inhabitants of Massachusetts Bay established their first college, a small group of white settlers created the first town on the far western end of the colony along the banks of the Connecticut River. The founding of Harvard both reflected and reinforced the dominance that Boston and its surrounding towns had—and would continue to have—in the affairs of the colony. But the founding of Springfield and the subsequent creation of Hampshire County represented the beginning of an alternative focus, the development of a new region of Massachusetts a hundred miles away from Boston. Within the first century of its growth, Hampshire County would become a distinct, coherent political entity governed by its own distinct, coherent political elite. There, probably more than in any other county in Massachusetts, the growth of authority in county institutions, both secular and ecclesiastical, tended to overshadow the local autonomy of individual towns and churches. Moreover, this regional authority also tended to flow through a few selected bloodlines, so that by the early part of the eighteenth century, political power in Hampshire County was defined and divided almost solely according to considerations of paternity and patronage.

When one speaks of the political life of an early frontier region such as Hampshire County, it is virtually impossible to avoid some brief, almost automatic, recollection of the work of Frederick Jackson Turner. As early as 1690, noted Turner, the Massachusetts General Court recognized the inherent isolation of the frontier and designated certain towns as frontier outposts to aid the defense of the colony—among them Deerfield, the "most Utmost Frontere Town in the County of West Hampshire," and North-ampton, Hadley, Hatfield, and Westfield, "not frontiers as those towns first named, yet more open than many others to an attack of an Enemy." Rather than stress the vulnerability that Massachu-setts officials feared in 1690, though, Turner chose to emphasize a more hopeful purpose for those western outposts. Even though the early towns "were hardly more than suburbs of Boston," they still seemed to Turner to be the prototypes of something new, a peculiarly American creation based on innovation and indepen-dence: "Removal from the customary usages of the older commu-nities and from the conservative influence of the body of the clergy, increased the innovating tendency." Whatever their ties to the past, people on the frontier, of whom western New En-glanders were the first group, found "a gate from the bondage of the past" that opened up to them a "freshness, and confidence, and scorn of older society, impatience of its restraints and ideas, and indifference to its lessons." As much as white settlers transformed the American wilderness, suggested Turner, they were in turn transformed themselves.[1]

In the case of early Hampshire County, however, there hardly seemed to be any such restless drive for innovation sown in the landscape of the frontier. Despite whatever appeal one might find in the "freshness, and confidence, and scorn" attributed to Turner's westerners, one cannot overlook a stronger, more funda-mental conservatism in these migrants. When people moved west they simply brought a good deal of their cultural baggage along with the rest of their gear. Isolated in the wilderness, they turned for comfort to what they knew; instead of innovation, western settlers seemed most interested in the recreation of the accepted patterns of life, including the formal institutions and restraints of Puritan society.

The first inhabitants of Springfield, for instance, tied themselves to the "customary usages of the older communities" as faithfully as did the residents of those eastern communities themselves. One of their first acts as settlers was to engage in the traditional Puritan activity of covenant writing, setting down on paper "certayne arti-cles and orders to be observed" for the good order of the town. First on the agenda was the commitment to procure "some Godly

13

and faithfull minister with whome we purpose to Joyne in Church Covenant to walke in all the ways of Christ." A town without an orthodox Congregational minister was not only illegal under the laws of Massachusetts; it was virtually unthinkable. Only after they had made arrangements for their future relations with the Deity, then, could the Springfield people turn to thinking about relationships among themselves. Their next few articles called for limiting the town to "fourty familys or, . . . yet not to exceed the number of fifty familys, rich and poore," and for doling out house lots, pasture, and woodland according to "every ones quality and estate."[2] They may not have deluded themselves into thinking they were setting up some egalitarian backwoods utopia, but certainly they were conscious of both a need and a desire to establish a carefully organized, well regulated, and perhaps even divinely sanctioned community. On paper, at least, they seemed to want what everyone else in Massachusetts wanted.

And for the most part they got it. It would be misleading if not altogether mistaken, of course, to talk in terms of some static, almost idealized model of the New England town. Not all towns were the same, nor did any one town remain the same. Moreover, considering the relatively early settlement of the first few western towns, one can hardly equate "old" towns with the east and "new" towns with the west. The simple truth is that the earliest towns of Hampshire County developed at much the same time and along much the same lines as most of their eastern counterparts, experiencing many of the same processes and problems of growth. The history of a "typical" New England town in the seventeenth century almost invariably reveals change as well as continuity and — no matter what New England Puritans might have written into their initial covenants about unity, harmony, and order — conflict as well as consensus.[3]

Recent historical research has largely undermined the notion of an unchanging and unchallenged Puritan theocracy in any town in New England, either eastern or western. Not only were some people in a sense deviant, violating the standards of personal piety and collective covenant, but many were also defiant, openly challenging their pastor rather than accepting dutifully his guidance and discipline. In fact, precisely because Puritan ministers occupied such a visible and vital position in the structure of the communities, they did not always remain at peace with their people but often became the objects of disfavor and hostility. Even in the early years Hampshire County was not without its ecclesiastical tensions. There was a brief period of disharmony in the Northampton church in the 1650s over both economic and doctrinal matters, and later a minor flap emerged in Springfield over the minister's ownership of his house. In turn, Hampshire ministers were just as likely as their eastern colleagues to take up the lament of Jeremiah and bewail the decline of spirituality and morality among their people. Still, the recurring uneasiness that beset many churches did not necessarily bespeak a radical attack on the church or a widespread movement to break the restraints of religion. Although some seventeenth-century ministers may have had cause to feel personal discomfort and disappointment, they did not really have to face a serious decline in the position of the church in society or even of their own position in the church. Certainly, compared to ministers during and after the Great Awakening, ministers in early western Massachusetts continued to enjoy the dignity, respect, and authority generally associated with their calling.[4]

Likewise, secular authority in the towns generally adhered to the patterns of deference and dependence that seemed to prevail throughout New England. Again, for all their talk of mutual commitment and communality, the inhabitants of early New England towns lived in a world of obvious inequality, both economic and political. On the one hand, the people of seventeenth-century Northampton, for instance, could share common grazing land for their animals and even see to it that every household was provided with a home lot of several acres; yet on the other hand they had already begun to drift further apart in the ownership of property. By the end of the century, as several recent histories of Hampshire towns have pointed out, there was emerging a significant difference between those rich and poor in land in the older communities like Northampton and Springfield.[5]

This economic inequality generally had a clear reflection in town politics as well. Despite the efforts of some earlier scholars to locate the foundations of an idealized American democracy in the New England town meeting, it has by now become reasonably clear that the town meeting offered democracy only of a limited sort. The adult males of a town could choose their own leaders, but they tended to limit their most frequent choices to a fairly select group. They habitually yielded political power in the narrow electoral sense to many of the same men—the occasional merchant or lawyer, the large landowner, the heir to family wealth or position—who held power in a broader economic and cultural sense. Selectmen tended to beget selectmen. A few served many terms in office, as did their sons after them. Most other men were fortunate to hold important office once or twice if at all. Some families had men serving in town office almost constantly, some almost never. Although there was no one rigid pattern of officeholding, in most early Hampshire towns local politics defined a rough middle ground between the basically artificial extremes of fluid frontier democracy and restricted, regimented oligarchy: a core group of long-term leaders generally shared electoral power with a larger pool of short-term officials, all accepting a somewhat uncertain combination of retention and rotation of office.[6]

While such a system offered some chance for new voices and new interests, it also offered a clear opportunity for the continuation of old leadership and old traditions. To be sure, each town had an occasional outbreak of dissent and division, and in at least one case, when a group of Hadley inhabitants sought to break off and form the new town of Hatfield, the level of conflict even became violent.[7] But for the most part the men who governed early Hampshire towns managed to keep local affairs well under control, at the very least within the acceptable bounds of political discourse that pertained elsewhere in New England. In general, a person who left eastern Massachusetts in the seventeenth century looking for a new, freer, less restricted way of life would find little comfort in western Massachusetts: Hampshire towns were changing, of course, but only gradually, almost imperceptibly. To a discontented Easterner they would no doubt have seemed disappointingly familiar.

What, then, was especially significant about the development of early Hampshire County? It is not enough simply to say that Hampshire towns proved in most essential respects to be much like other New England towns, slow to change, governed by traditional considerations of hierarchy and order, bound to the restrictive precepts of Puritan theology and sociology—in short, hardly the hotbeds of social and political democratization Turner claimed to see on Massachusetts's western frontier. The more important focus lies elsewhere, for the full history of the region is greater than the sum of several town histories. In order to appreciate the particular nature of early Hampshire County it is necessary to look beyond the towns to the county itself, the level at which the several towns formed a larger political entity with a governing body of its own. Indeed, the emergence of local political culture at the county level seemed to run counter to Turner's emphasis on rising frontier democracy and to move steadily in quite the opposite direction, back toward a centuries-old tradition of paternalistic authority and elite rule: the whole region became a large arena in which a handful of men ruled in a conservative style that seemed to reflect more the strength of an English inheritance than the transforming power of the American environment.

Almost everywhere in Massachusetts, in fact, the emergence of county government was becoming an increasingly important political phenomenon. Although the first generation of Puritan settlers had expected most immediate authority to rest on the three pillars of family, church, and town, by the second half of the seventeenth century the inhabitants of Massachusetts were also witnessing the increasing consolidation of power in county-wide institutions that represented an alternative and even a threat to the autonomy and power of their particular local institutions. On one hand the expansion of the role of county government had resulted from the conscious design of the General Court in the first decade of settlement. Recognizing early on the difficulties that could arise from trying to govern a growing number of scattered communities that maintained their own secular as well as ecclesiastical independence, the General Court established in 1636 a system of county courts in order to impose some degree of consistency and control over the towns. Without directly attacking or outlawing the autonomy of town governments, the General Court at least intended to provide a separate source of regional authority. And in that respect the plan proved to be reasonably successful. Throughout the seventeenth century the county courts gained in strength and significance because town government began to lose some of its hold on the loyalty and respect of the inhabitants. As towns grew over the years, as new settlers came and old settlers went, and as more people developed social and economic ties with others outside their own towns, the Puritan sense of covenanted communalism began to wane with each passing year. Some inhabitants of

17

seventeenth-century towns became not only increasingly contentious toward their own neighbors but also increasingly unwilling
to accept the arbitration or adjudication provided by their town's
secular and religious leaders. They often turned instead to outside
authorities for relief. As a result, the county courts began to play a
much greater role in dealing with a variety of individual cases and
even in maintaining the general standards of social behavior and
control.[8]

On a different but no less significant level, the strength and
influence of county government came to be increased because of
necessary developments in military organization. With the recurring outbreak of war between English settlers and the native Indian population, the trained bands of the individual towns often
proved unable to defend their own communities, much less to go
on the offensive in the field. The organization of a county militia
thus became vital to the defense of the English settlements, and
like the courts, the militia also represented a base of power that
encompassed all the towns of the region.[9]

In general, then, the growth of county government in seventeenth-century Massachusetts created a number of official positions—justices of the peace, justices of the various courts, officers
of the county militia, and the like—all of which offered a considerable degree of power and prestige to those who held them.
Within each region county government became a framework, as
one historian has put it, that allowed a few prominent men to
develop a new form of elite authority beyond the sphere of town
politics.[10]

The particular situation of Hampshire County, however, proved
to be exceptionally favorable to the growth of this kind of regional
rule, and a few men were able to make the most of their opportunities as no one else in Massachusetts could, eventually turning
the county into their own legal domain and turning themselves
into local deities, or "River Gods," as they came to be called. The
development of their parochial political system derived in large
part from the political realities of colonial expansion. In a sense
Hampshire County remained suspended between Massachusetts
and Connecticut, at once both connected and disconnected. The
Connecticut River offered a natural tie with the Connecticut
towns to the south; trade, communication, and family connections
between Hartford, Windsor, and the early Hampshire towns had

been a common feature of the western region from the times of earliest settlement.[11] Across the Connecticut River and the frontier, however, lay the invisible barrier of provincial boundaries that divided New England politically: quite simply, people in Hampshire County sent both their political representatives and their tax money to Boston. The county's relationship with Boston and the rest of eastern Massachusetts was just the opposite of that with Connecticut. Though political jurisdiction necessarily bound the two parts of the province together, a hundred miles of hills and trees posed a visible barrier between east and west.

Early Massachusetts was not by any means a modern state with established political machinery and an effective civil service to carry out the work of government. Although governors and other administrative officials in Boston held the authority to govern the whole region, they lacked the organization to do so. Throughout the late seventeenth and early eighteenth centuries it was especially difficult for them to penetrate the further reaches of their domain and command the obedience, the respect, and the money of subjects who were far away on the western frontier and essentially out of touch. Moreover, after the tumult Massachusetts experienced in the late seventeenth century – the revocation of the old charter in 1686, the imposition and eventual overthrow of the unpopular Andros regime in 1689, and the arrival of Governor Phips and the new charter in 1692 – the office of governor could command only an uncertain degree of loyalty. Appointed by the king but confronted with a wary General Court, royal governors needed to establish their own political legitimacy within the province, and they came increasingly to rely on regional intermediaries to supply that legitimacy for them. Local leaders in Hampshire County played a role similar to that of favored members of the gentry in England: they were not necessarily official representatives of the royal government, but they were brokers for it, making sure that things got done in somewhat the same way the royal officials planned. Part of their ability to carry out that function depended on their hold on the loyalty and good will of their fellow citizens. As a result they could demand and receive substantial gifts of patronage to bestow locally, thus keeping both themselves and the government in favor with a good number of people.[12]

Even more striking, however, was the way they kept the control of such gifts to themselves. Nowhere else in colonial Massachusetts was regional government more strongly reinforced by kinship ties among members of the local elite. For well over a century political authority in Hampshire County passed through a small number of influential families – the Pynchons, the Stoddards, the Williamses, and a few others related to them by marriage – and the dominant men of each family had a remarkably consistent hold on power and position throughout the region. Hampshire was essentially their private family bailiwick, and they could do much to determine who got what in the county, and when. Even more than in the individual towns, political power at the county level depended on considerations of wealth, kinship, friendship, personal influence, and paternalism. It was a system that relied much on mutual obligation and individual power, not always efficient but usually effective. Moreover, it worked especially well for the favored families in Hampshire County. They had power to begin with, and their role as intermediaries increased that power.[13]

The elitist nature of the local political system began to emerge in the earliest years of settlement. William Pynchon, who led the first group of emigrants west into the Connecticut Valley to establish Springfield in 1636, had come from England in 1630 with the Winthrop fleet, already blessed with both prominent parentage and the title "gent." Upon his arrival in Massachusetts Bay he carried on a lively and apparently quite profitable trade in beaver pelts from his first homes in Dorchester and Roxbury, and while he resided in the east he was repeatedly chosen magistrate and member of the Court of Assistants. By the time he moved west he had behind him a combination of family background, wealth, and political influence that would make him unquestionably dominant among his fellow settlers at Springfield. Indeed, he was the first dominant leader of the whole western region.[14] He and his son John maintained the power of the Pynchon name throughout the rest of the seventeenth century, and in doing so they established in Hampshire County an important and enduring tradition of family rule that would survive well into the eighteenth century, outliving the Pynchons themselves.

The main element in the Pynchons' reign was the vast amount of land under their control, land that in turn would eventually give them control over many of their fellow Springfield residents. At the first division of land in Springfield, William Pynchon received the greatest acreage and the largest home lot in the town, and he and his son took in even more in subsequent divisions. To add to the Pynchon bounty, provincial governors and occasionally the Springfield people awarded them extra tracts of land in grateful recompense for services performed for the sake of the common good. By the time son John had risen to oversee the Pynchon domain in the third quarter of the century, he had at his disposal some two thousand acres.[15]

On the local level the Pynchon wealth in land actually made Springfield something of an anomaly among early Hampshire County towns, and perhaps among New England towns in general. In a recent study of the role of the Pynchon family in seventeenth-century Springfield, Stephen Innes has argued that John Pynchon had so much land that almost everyone else in town had too little. Far from being a frontier town marked by openness and abundance, Springfield under the Pynchons became a town of striking land shortage and increasing stratification, a town becoming "economically and socially polarized . . . divided between rich and poor, creditors and debtors, landlords and tenants." The main creators and beneficiaries of these conditions were the Pynchons. Controlling far more land than could possibly be worked by their own family, they were in a position to rent out land to other men or to hire men to work the land for them. Many of their fellow townspeople had no other alternatives. With relatively small holdings of around seventy acres, on the average, in relatively infertile or remote parts of town, they became Pynchon tenants simply in order to get by. Even if they did not actually rent land from the Pynchons, most townspeople still found themselves involved with them in one way or another. William Pynchon had moved his fur trade west with him, and during the course of the seventeenth century the family added a number of other commercial enterprises; they were the town's chief providers of goods and services, owning stores, mines, sawmills, and gristmills. The Pynchon holdings were not just extensive; for the inhabitants of Springfield they were almost overwhelming. During the last half of the seventeenth century it was virtually impossible for anyone not to have economic dealings with them, and for roughly half the men in Springfield, those dealings resulted in some degree of indebtedness or dependence.[16]

For all the inequality that existed as a result of their power, the

Pynchons did not have to face a town full of openly discontented or hostile people. On the contrary, William and John Pynchon managed to maintain the respect and loyalty of their townspeople throughout the seventeenth century. It was not the style of the Pynchons to exercise their power over their neighbors with undue rapacity or greed. They hardly needed to. There are many forms of indebtedness, and the Pynchons had people beholden to them for more than money. Though some people sank deeper and deeper into permanent economic dependence as tenants of Pynchon land, some others were able to turn their relationship with the Pynchons into a limited means of personal advancement, rising perhaps from indentured servant or wage laborer to a more independent status as husbandman. A man might never quite escape the necessity of renting Pynchon land, but at least he might know that service under the Pynchons gave him an important start; moreover, if he ever wanted more land to work, he knew that they had the best to offer. At times the Pynchons could be flexible about calling in debts or generous in granting special favors, thereby gaining a degree of personal gratitude from particular individuals. In general the sheer economic power of the Pynchons was tempered by a selective tendency toward largesse and leniency. It was no secret to anyone, of course, that the Pynchon fortune made the Pynchon favors possible, for such is the nature of paternalism. But as long as William and John Pynchon refrained from being autocrats, their people refrained from being rebels, and they continued to live under a grossly unequal but generally peaceful arrangement, somewhat like that existing between lords and peasants in medieval Europe. It was, as Innes has suggested, a relationship seventeenth-century Englishmen knew well.[17]

But the Pynchons' network of dependence extended far beyond the town of Springfield itself to encompass all the emerging communities of Hampshire County. In addition to controlling extensive trade operations along the Connecticut River, the family also represented the main political link between Hampshire County and Boston. In a sense, the colonial government depended upon the Pynchons almost as much as their neighbors did. William Pynchon's earlier position as magistrate and member of the Court of Assistants in eastern Massachusetts gave him an immediate claim to political experience and status among his fellow westerners, and in the early years of settlement he became essentially the sole embodiment of provincial authority throughout Hampshire County. He was the main source of judicial power, holding the right to administer all oaths of office, issue warrants, hear cases, render judgment, and in general do "whatever else may fall within the power of an assistant in the Massachusett." He also served as the General Court's main agent in dealing with western Indians.[18]

John Pynchon's collection of offices was even more impressive. In 1652, after father William had published some religious writings unpopular with the authorities in Boston and had subsequently decided to spend his last days back in England, son John still had no trouble assuming his father's position of official power. In the town of Springfield he served as selectman, moderator, member of numerous ad hoc committees, and representative to the General Court; his county offices included magistrate and chief militia officer for the western region. Like his father, John Pynchon did important work for the provincial government out in the west. Not only did he figure prominently in defense and military affairs, but he also took part in negotiations with both Indians and the government of Connecticut, helping to settle Massachusetts's land claims with each. Every new plantation in western Massachusetts in the seventeenth century – Northampton, Westfield, Hadley, Brookfield, Suffield, Sunderland, Enfield, and Deerfield – was settled only after John Pynchon led a committee to secure the land, divide it, and distribute it among settlers. In a few cases he even advanced the money for the purchase of land from the Indians and then sold it himself to individual settlers.[19]

The Pynchons, in short, provided a major source of order and guidance for the settlers and, just as important, legitimacy for the provincial government. Throughout Hampshire County as in Springfield itself, very little went on without their approval and involvement, and the whole western region could hardly have existed as a political extension of the province without the services of the Pynchon family. Both William and John stood clearly above their fellow settlers and squarely between them and the government in Boston – an enviable position, but one few men could maintain. When John Pynchon died in 1703, the Reverend Solomon Stoddard eulogized that he was "honourable and had great influence upon men in authority abroad, and upon the People at home, and had more experience by far, than any among us."[20] In a way, that eulogy pointed to what had become a distinctive feature of Hampshire County leadership in the seventeenth century and would remain so throughout most of the eighteenth: the significance of a single powerful individual, the great man bolstered by wealth and authority, needed by both his neighbors and the colonial government, established as mediator, broker, spokesman, and leader for the people of the west—quite simply, the man on whom the political and economic life of the county seemed to depend.

The man who spoke so respectfully over Pynchon's grave, Solomon Stoddard, was himself already something of a local patriarch, and after John Pynchon's death it was the Stoddard line that would dominate the county for the next three-quarters of a century. If it was true, as the Reverend Stoddard eulogized, that John Pynchon "had more experience by far" than any other single leader in the region, Solomon and his son John eventually combined to share even more between them, bringing the reins of both civil and ecclesiastical authority into the hands of one family. There was no quasifeudal struggle for power in the Connecticut Valley, no need for one clan to wrest power from another. There was simply a political vacuum that John Pynchon's son John seemed unlikely or unable to fill, and the two Stoddards, by the force of personality and ability, were able to shift the focus of local authority up the river to Northampton. From there Solomon Stoddard dominated the county's ecclesiastical order, John Stoddard ruled the political and military, and they both gathered under their leadership other local leaders, most of whom were their kinsmen anyway. Under the Stoddards, and later under the Williams branch of the family as well, there emerged an interconnected regional organization that defined Hampshire County more clearly not just as a scattered collection of towns, but as a distinct political sphere with its own ruling order.[21]

Solomon Stoddard's rise as the dominant force among the valley ministers resulted essentially from his willingness, even eagerness, to challenge the inherited standards of Puritan order and to reshape them according to his own designs. Coming to Northampton in 1669 to replace the deceased Reverend Eleazar Mather, Stoddard not only took over Mather's pulpit but also married his widow—and there ended his commitment to continuing in the ways of his predecessor. Over the next four decades he changed the practices of Mather's church, defied and outraged Mather's more famous relatives in Boston, and eventually forged the leading members of the Hampshire clergy into an organized and active ministerial association under his forceful and confident leadership. In the overall ecclesiastical history of New England, Stoddard's effect may have been fairly limited, but in the developing ecclesiastical order of Hampshire County his impact was little short of revolutionary.[22]

The central feature of Stoddard's prominence was the ecclesiastical order he brought to Northampton and to most of the surrounding churches of the county. Throughout his career, from 1669 to 1729, Stoddard used his pulpit and his pen to attack the old standards of New England Congregationalism. He addressed himself especially to one of the growing problems of New England Puritanism, the inherent tension between individual salvation and collective order. Though his parishioners might indeed feel the workings of the spirit in their souls, Stoddard doubted their ability to express fully the reality of the conversion experience, and he likewise doubted the ability of other church members to evaluate such narratives properly. For that reason, he thought, the traditional Congregational practice of trying to distinguish sinner from saint seemed divisive and even destructive, leading people to look more to their own purity than to their common bonds with their supposedly less pure neighbors. Moreover, the rigid requirements for church membership seemed likely to cut people off from the church just at a time when ministers of New England were needing desperately to keep church membership in line with the rapidly growing population – or, put differently, to keep the population in line through church membership. Breaking with the strict admission practices of Congregational churches in the east, then, Stoddard instituted an open communion in which everyone, saved and unsaved alike, would partake of the sacraments so that the old distinctions among full members, halfway members, and nonmembers would be abolished, and communion would be offered to all but persons of openly reprehensible behavior. Under such an open system it remained the minister's critical responsibility not to allow his people to become lax in their spiritual concerns but to keep them active and inspired through the power of his preaching: the less emphasis he put on the words of his people's conversion narratives, the more emphasis he put on

25

the words of his own sermons. In general, Stoddard's goal was to bring people into the church, not to keep them out; and once they were in, to keep them firmly under his own authority and not let them exercise too much authority over each other.[23]

At the same time, Stoddard sought to extend ministerial control beyond each individual church to encompass all churches of the region. He felt uncomfortable with the idea that each Congregational church stood as an independent community of saints with its own separate covenant with God. In Stoddard's eye, congregations as much as individual Christians needed the guidance of some larger source of discipline. Against the traditions of local purity and particularism, Stoddard argued for bringing all people and all churches together under a common ecclesiastical order, a national synod under which people would recognize their common religious identity with each other and accept not just a common doctrine but a common discipline as well. In challenging some of the basic tenets of seventeenth-century Congregationalism, Stoddard was attempting not to undermine the strength or stability of the church as an institution in New England society but, quite the contrary, to give it added power and influence over what appeared to be an increasingly wavering and wayward population.[24] Not surprisingly, Solomon Stoddard had no shortage of enemies within the Congregational establishment in Massachusetts. His chief antagonists proved to be the two Mathers of Boston, father Increase and son Cotton, whose eminence dominated eastern Massachusetts and almost all of New England. The more they heard from Stoddard, the more they suspected heresy and anathema. His notions of open communion and national synods seemed likely to bring on decline and disorder in the individual churches and the eventual destruction of Congregationalism in North America – in sum, they feared, the failure of the whole Puritan mission. During the first decade of the eighteenth century the Mathers waged a lengthy and famous pamphlet battle against Stoddard, and he took up the challenge with his customary vigor and self-assurance. In the end it would be impossible to say that either side absolutely won or lost.[25] The main point is that the public nature of the disagreement made quite clear a growing split between the orthodoxy of the east and Stoddard's new departures in the west, elevating Stoddard to a position of unquestioned, if somewhat unpopular, prominence in the ministerial circles of Massachusetts.

Most important, of course, was Stoddard's rise to prominence among his local colleagues. Though most of his Hampshire colleagues refrained from taking part publicly in the Mather–Stoddard debates, the ministers of the established churches in the county – William Williams at Hatfield, John Williams at Deerfield, Daniel Brewer at Springfield, Isaac Chauncy at Hadley, and Nathaniel Collins at Enfield – did adopt some form of Stoddard's open communion in their churches.[26] Moreover, they followed him in forming the Hampshire Association of Ministers in the years just following the pamphlet battle. Coming together under a structure of firmly Presbyterian self-government, they agreed, as they put it in 1714, "to be subject to a Council of the Churches of the County, until there be some Superior Council set up in the Province unto which we may appeal." Each minister would be subject to scrutiny and regulation as much by his colleagues as by the members of his church.[27] It was clear to all, however, that Solomon Stoddard was to be their leader, a kind of *primus inter pares* of the presbytery.

The creation of a ministerial association was by no means unique to Hampshire County, and in fact, Hampshire ministers lagged a few years behind their counterparts in other regions in forming such an organization. Ministers in eastern Massachusetts, increasingly mindful of the need to assert ministerial authority in the face of recurring lay resistance, had begun coming together for informal, ad hoc meetings in the middle of the seventeenth century, and Boston area ministers organized a more formal group in 1690; some ministers even sought to gain an official institutional status for ministerial associations in the Massachusetts Proposals of 1705. Despite the failure of the General Court to grant this legal recognition, ministers in several Massachusetts counties continued to meet on a regular basis and to act together as a professional organization, especially with regard to exerting their influence over a particular congregation's appointment of a pastor. Just as secular leaders were beginning to see the necessity – and the benefits – of developing a system of authority above the level of the individual towns, so did religious leaders try to establish some form of collective control over their various churches.[28]

The formation of the Hampshire Association of Ministers, however, added an extra dimension to the nature of clerical organization. Not only did Hampshire ministers define for themselves a place above their people, but they also set themselves self-consciously apart from their fellow ministers in the east. Taking Stoddard's system of open communion as their order, they united under a system of internal discipline that distinguished their churches from the standard Congregationalism common to the rest of Massachusetts. Taking Stoddard as their leader, they united under a man who had challenged the Mathers in debate and who, if he had not won a clear triumph, at least had not suffered a humiliating defeat. More to the point, the main significance of Stoddard's efforts in forming the Hampshire Association lay in achieving regional unity, not in winning an absolute victory. By the end of the first quarter of the eighteenth century, the ministers of Hampshire County could look on themselves as an enclosed community, a clerical network linked as much by practice as by geography. As Stoddard's grandson Jonathan Edwards would later argue, Hampshire County was a distinct "neighbourhood" of ministers who had developed a sense of collective identity they would at times jealously defend against threats from within the county and without.[29]

But whereas Solomon Stoddard made his reputation on a split with Boston, his more secular-minded offspring kept their ties to Boston close and secure. Throughout their political careers, both John Stoddard and his political heir, nephew Israel Williams, relied on their personal influence in the upper reaches of the provincial government to enhance their influence at home in Hampshire County and to extend their local control over both property and position. To be sure, both men were prominent enough in their respective towns to have no trouble getting a start in politics. John Stoddard was first chosen selectman of Northampton in 1705/6, when he was just twenty-four years old. A generation later Israel Williams – like his uncle Stoddard a Harvard graduate and a son of a respected minister, William Williams of Hatfield – had an equally rapid climb to town office, becoming selectman of Hatfield in 1732, at the age of twenty-two.[30] But for both Stoddard and Williams, the real source of power lay beyond the bounds of the town. They became essentially professional politicians at the provincial level, and they pursued their careers with a remarkable degree of success.

From the time of his first election to the General Court in 1716, John Stoddard took away from Boston much more in patronage than he ever brought to it in legislative leadership or skill. He was never reputed to have been an especially effective or even popular member of the House of Representatives, but hardly anyone could question his hold on the favor of provincial governors. To a large degree his unpopularity with his House colleagues and his popularity with Massachusetts's governors stemmed from the same source. During the 1720s and 1730s, a time when most members of the House were challenging the prerogative of the royal governors, especially the power of the impulsive and petulant Jonathan Belcher, John Stoddard remained a loyal governor's man. By Thomas Hutchinson's acount, Stoddard even gave up his seat on the council rather than sit with the other members, who were constant opponents of the governor's prerogative.[31]

In the long run a seat on the council was something Stoddard could do well enough without; he had more to gain simply by serving as representative from Northampton and using his loyalty to the governor as a means of leverage on him. Certainly an unpopular man like Governor Belcher could use any friend he could muster, and he was glad to have Stoddard as an ally. Even a stronger and more effective governor, like William Shirley, Belcher's successor, found it useful to be on good terms with Stoddard. An Englishman by birth, Shirley understood that to avoid the mistakes and animosities that had undone his Massachusetts-born predecessor, he would have to deal effectively with a few important provincials. He maneuvered his way through Massachusetts politics, as Robert Zemsky has put it, "not by echoing abstract defenses of prerogative authority, but by seeking accommodation with local political leaders."[32] Like Shirley, John Stoddard was hardly a man to stand on "abstract defenses," and he too recognized the usefulness of the proper accommodations in nourishing a spirit of political loyalty. Such symbiosis was the very essence of the politics of patronage.

Stoddard gathered almost more plums than he could use. Governor Belcher gladly rewarded his support by raising him from justice to chief justice in the Inferior Court of Common Pleas of Hampshire County in 1725, and he later added a position as judge of Probate on top of that. When Belcher offered yet another judicial post, a seat on the Superior Court of the province, Stoddard had to decline: he clearly had all the judgeships he could use in his home county, and he probably felt no need or desire to accept a position that would require his being away in Boston for more time than he already spent there. By the time Governor Shirley assumed office, then, he wisely chose to add to Stoddard's local military power, elevating him from colonel of the Hampshire regiment to commander-in-chief of the Western Department in 1744.[33] With the New England colonies expecting attack from French Canada, it was of course important for Shirley to have an experienced and respected military leader like John Stoddard to protect his western flank. But Shirley also had his political flanks to protect, and increasing Stoddard's power in the west no doubt helped Shirley feel more secure in that respect as well.[34]

For John Stoddard the main benefit of such gubernatorial patronage was not simply the particular power inherent in the positions themselves, but the more pervasive influence those positions gave him in his home county. On the local level Stoddard directed a patronage operation of his own, dispensing various positions under his direct control and making recommendations on the disposal of other posts controlled by the provincial governors. He took reasonably good care of his family and friends, and everyone – county residents and provincial governors alike – knew that whatever was distributed in Hampshire County came only with the approval of Colonel Stoddard. In 1733, for instance, Governor Belcher had wanted to appoint Oliver Partridge (the nephew of Belcher's "antient friend," Samuel Partridge) to the position of clerk of court, but Stoddard had other ideas. He recommended his own nephew Israel Williams for the post, and Belcher, uneasy but ever mindful of obliging his valuable western ally, had to defer to his wishes.[35] In that situation and in numerous others, Stoddard's role in the patronage system was not just that of grateful recipient; the true mark of his power was his ability to direct the whole operation from the middle, to serve as the conduit through whom favors passed on their way from Boston to the Connecticut Valley. His careful nurture of his relationship with the royal governors had put men in his debt at both ends of the province: those above him in the east rewarded his continued loyalty, while those below him in the west continued loyally to wait for rewards of their own.

John Stoddard died in 1748, just at the apex of his career. The power he had amassed during that career, however, survived well into the next generation. Indeed, it was under Israel Williams, Stoddard's nephew and chosen successor, that the local patronage system in Hampshire County reached its fullest expression. There had been no formal passing of the Stoddard birthright or inheritance, but the colonel's intention must have been quite clear to everyone in the county. Stoddard's own son was still too young to assume his father's role; yet Israel Williams had already proven himself a man of talent and influence in his hometown of Hatfield, and he seemed capable of taking on broader responsibilities. Preserving family power through extended kin networks would do just as well as keeping it tied to direct patrilineal descent. When Stoddard appointed Williams commissary of the Western Forces in 1744, he made his nephew essentially second in command of the military for the western region, and by implication second in command of the Hampshire political domain as well.[36] At the time of Stoddard's death there was no real challenge to keep Williams from becoming first in command, and he stepped rather easily into a position of influence that had been recognized and refined over the course of a century.

In many ways Israel Williams outshone his predecessors. Rather than simply accept his inheritance and make do on its already bounteous rewards, Williams expanded it by adding his own considerable resources. By all means the most significant of these was his family. To a degree unknown to either John Pynchon or John Stoddard before him, Israel Williams had at his disposal an extensive group of family and friends on whom he could depend, and whom he could expect to depend on him. From the first family members to settle in the county in the 1680s–John Williams at Deerfield and William Williams at Hatfield, who were cousins, Harvard classmates, and fellow ministers–the Williams family had branched out along the Connecticut River through Hampshire County and down into Connecticut, forming a wide kinship network through marriage and migration. The Stoddard connection was only one of many.[37] With all its connections throughout the Connecticut Valley, the Williams clan had no equal in western Massachusetts, and with the mark of favor bestowed on him by John Stoddard, Israel had no equal in the Williams clan. During the 1750s and 1760s he was able to fashion a remarkably effective network of regional administration that engaged continually, and rewarded handsomely, his circle of friends and kin.

Not only was Israel himself a grandson of Solomon Stoddard, but he had other strong familial ties among the ministry of western Massachusetts. His father, William Williams of Hatfield, and his uncle, Stephen Williams of Longmeadow parish in Springfield, had been in their respective posts for years, both having been founding members of the Hampshire Association in the early years under Solomon Stoddard. Closer in age to Israel was his brother-in-law Jonathan Ashley, who had the ministry in Deerfield at the northern end of the county. To the south in Connecticut, Israel counted among his relatives brothers Solomon, minister at Lebanon, and Elisha, president of Yale: though not county residents, both men could make their influence felt among the other ministers in Hampshire. Perhaps the only liability among Williams's kinsmen in the clergy was Jonathan Edwards, himself a strong and powerful individual, who in Israel's eyes would turn out to be more trouble than anyone in the Hampshire hierarchy could accept.[38]

In secular affairs, members of the Williams clan were especially powerful at both the town and the county level. Cousin Elijah served as town clerk and selectman in Deerfield for a quarter-century, and nephew William Williams (one of several family members to carry that name) was likewise selectman in Deerfield before moving on to Pittsfield, where he dominated the political life of that frontier town until the Revolution. Like Israel, both Elijah and William also served their respective towns as representatives to the General Court. Among Hampshire's leaders not of the Williams name but connected by marriage were John Worthington of Springfield, Timothy Dwight and Joseph Hawley of Northampton, and Oliver Partridge of Hatfield, each one at various times elected selectman or representative to the General Court, at all times respected as one of the most prominent citizens of his particular town.[39]

The county judiciary was almost completely a family affair. Like his uncle Stoddard, Israel Williams held several concurrent positions, ranging from justice of the peace (1736-72) to clerk of courts (1733-58) to justice of the Inferior Court of Common Pleas (1758-74) to judge of Probate (1764-74). But he also held those positions concurrently with other men of Williams blood. The Inferior Court, for instance, had consisted entirely of Williams's kinsmen during the two decades before Israel himself was appointed: John Stoddard, William Pynchon II, John Pynchon II, Eleazar Porter, Ephraim Williams, and Timothy, Josiah, and Joseph Dwight. When Israel first joined the court in 1758 he sat with the three Dwights, and from then until the early 1770s the justices of the court were almost all named either Williams or Dwight. The Probate Court had perhaps an even tighter family connection. When John Stoddard was judge of Probate, he chose Timothy Dwight to be register of Probate, and when Stoddard died, Dwight ascended to the judgeship. He in turn chose his son Timothy II to be register, a position the younger Dwight continued to hold until Israel Williams became judge in 1764. Williams at first split the register's position between Dwight and John Stoddard's son Solomon, but in 1768 he named his son Israel, Jr., to be register of Probate.[40] Throughout the middle of the century, in short, control of that very lucrative court never left the hands of close relatives.

Powerful though it already was, the family grew in wealth and influence under Israel's careful stewardship. His military authority and his favor with Governor Shirley – both more or less inherited intact from Colonel Stoddard – were enough to guarantee him a ready supply of desirable positions to distribute among his family and friends. During the middle decades of the century kinsmen Oliver Partridge, John Worthington, and William Williams served with him as colonels of the county militia. The Reverend Stephen Williams acted for a while as military chaplain, Dr. Thomas Williams was physician for the western troops, and Elijah Williams, Ephraim Williams, Jr., and Joseph Hawley all held the rank of major. A number of brothers, sons, cousins, and family favorites served in various staff positions somewhat lower on the ladder but nonetheless within the officer corps of the county militia. Almost without exception, the chain of command in Hampshire County followed the bloodlines of the Williams clan.[41]

Like the judiciary, the military offered a ready source of security and status to members of the family. From Israel at the top on down to some of the young eager kinsmen of the rising generation, each partook of the pyramid of patronage, gladly making use of the positions those above them could offer. But besides the obvious honor conferred by military rank, a county commander could also look to gain a decent profit from the perquisites of part-time soldiering. Quite simply, not all the spoils of war had to be stripped from the enemy; some could be scooped rather easily from the provincial coffers. The authority to build, supply, and command a fort along the western frontier, for instance, gave the commanding officer the ability to determine what work was done, when, by whom, and in some cases for whom. County officers could increase their personal wealth by acting as commissaries or suppliers of provisions, thereby getting their hands on valuable bills of credit from Boston. Some could also increase their personal influence by doling out what were essentially low-level defense contracts – repair and construction jobs at the forts, supply orders for food, and so forth – to grateful locals, thereby gaining the good will of many people in the county. Pelf and power helped make the military life a reasonably good one for those with the proper family connection.[42] From his days as commissary under John Stoddard, Israel Williams was no stranger to the possible profit inherent in military positions, and as long as he controlled access to these positions he made sure that no stranger ever held them.

In its fullest bloom, the Williams family tree might strike the present-day observer as a dense tangle of branches, hopelessly complex and confusing. But to Israel Williams it could only have seemed useful and reassuring. There was no part of the county government, from the judiciary to the military to most of the individual towns themselves, that did not include several Williamses or Williams kinsmen among its leaders. As with any group of proud and powerful men, there occasionally emerged personal jealousies that threatened to undermine the overall unity of the family network. More significant, however, was the relative lack of conflict among the individual members of the Williams clan: their collective identity fostered a sense of collective stability, and the bonds of kinship provided a greater degree of cohesion and cooperation than might ever have been achieved in a more formal political organization. As the central and most powerful member of the family, then, Israel Williams became almost automatically identified as the central and most powerful figure in the whole county.

Williams's position of political influence was not only the most important aspect of his own political life, but the crucial point in the political world of Hampshire County as well. The collection of ecclesiastical and secular offices hung on the Williams family tree suggests more than just the obvious advantages of kinship in public affairs; it presents a striking testimony to the persistence of a geographically extensive yet politically restricted type of county government more often identified with England than with the American colonies. During the first century of its history, Hampshire County had developed a stable and fundamentally conservative political system far above the level of traditional New England town government, a system defined by a lively interplay of personal power, patronage, and paternalism. With William Pynchon, John Pynchon, and John Stoddard, the county had first known strong, wealthy, and influential individuals who were able to draw other leaders of the county towns under their sway and to establish themselves as intermediaries between royal authority and the people of their county. Their spheres of influence in the east and west worked out to be complementary: the more indispensable to those in power in Boston the county leaders became, the more power was theirs to dispense at home. It was under Israel Williams's direction that the pervasiveness of that regional power became most imposing.

The power was not, however, absolute or unassailable. In the middle of the eighteenth century, at the very time when the connections of the Williams clan were spread most extensively throughout the towns and churches of the county, there arose repeated challenges to authority in those same towns and churches. Almost everywhere dissident groups of various sorts—some pursuing religious ends, some secular, some both—began trying to overturn or break with the established local order. And almost everywhere the members of the county leadership responded by trying to uphold that order, not only in their particular towns, but in the towns of their colleagues and kinsmen as well. Perhaps the greatest irony surrounding the Hampshire ruling elite was that just when its authority and influence were most widespread, it was beginning to experience its most widespread challenge.

Chapter 2

THE HAMPSHIRE COUNTY MINISTRY AND THE GREAT AWAKENING: FROM REVIVAL TO REACTION

———

The ministers of the county were the first to feel the effects of disharmony and disorder. Throughout the early part of the eighteenth century the Hampshire clergy had seemed a fit counterpart to the county's secular leadership, a well-ordered, unified body led by the forceful personality of Solomon Stoddard. Stoddard had given his colleagues a common organization and a common ecclesiastical practice that bound them together and helped them stand apart from the rest of the New England ministry. Moreover, he had provided an impressive model of the minister as patriarch and evangelist, always able to maintain the delicate balance between institutional stability and spiritual activity. By the 1730s, however, the position of other county ministers became increasingly unsteady. Stoddard was dead, and there was no one, not even his grandson Jonathan Edwards, who could take his place above the rest. Ironically enough, as Edwards led Hampshire ministers in the widespread religious revivalism Stoddard had hoped to achieve, the local clergy experienced an increasing loss of confidence and consensus. The heightened religious upsurge that swept the county in the late 1730s and early 1740s led also to heightened religious unrest, creating disorder in the ministers' respective congregations and division in their collective organization. In many ways the Great Awakening proved to be a rude awakening for members of the Hampshire clergy, and they began to realize just how vulnerable they could be.

In that sense it is important not to confuse the history of the Great Awakening in Hampshire County with the history of Jonathan Edwards. Admittedly, not even Solomon Stoddard could have claimed the intense emotional force and evangelical impact that his grandson Edwards injected into the county. Through his narrative of the "Surprising Work of God" in Northampton and other nearby towns, Edwards brought attention to the early religious revival in Hampshire County in 1734 and 1735, and his work helped prepare the way for the more extensive excitement of the early 1740s. But Edwards was not the only minister in Hampshire County, nor was his the only voice. Too great a focus on him alone obscures the reality and complexity of religious life in the county, perhaps especially in terms of the Great Awakening. Despite his unquestionable influence among the local clergy, there was a minority of ministers who stood quite opposite him during the Awakening. Where Edwards and others saw the work of divinity in the outbursts of religious enthusiasm, some ministers saw sure signs of disorder and even a threat to the position of the clergy itself. This difference of perception was an important one, for it continued to divide Hampshire County ministers even after the Awakening had subsided.

The story of the Awakening and its aftermath in the county is in large part the story of that division. Ministers who had been skeptical about the effects of evangelical religion as early as the 1730s became even more critical during the 1740s. And even some of those who had at first welcomed the revivals began to have doubts during the middle of the decade. As they watched in fear, the Awakening seemed to release energies that defied ministerial control. Gradually during the 1740s the balance among the county ministers shifted away from the religious intensity of evangelicalism toward a greater concern for a stable ecclesiastical and social order. In the face of a popular rising of theological conservatism, the clergy retreated further into a position of social conservatism. By the end of the 1740s the county's leading ministers were trying almost desperately to restore some semblance of collective unity and authority, trying to maintain some hold on their traditional position in society. Their former stance of self-confidence had turned to one of self-defense.

No one had a more abrupt introduction to the effects of the Great Awakening in Hampshire County than John Ballantine, the new minister at Westfield. He first came to the county in December 1740, just two months after the evangelist George Whitefield had made a quick trip through the county.[1] In many respects Ballantine was fortunate to come when he did. Whitefield had spent less than a week in Hampshire County, but in that time he preached daily to hundreds. At Hadley he shook the people from their spiritual deadness and reminded them of their earlier awakening some five years earlier: "It was like putting fire to tinder," Whitefield wrote. "The remembrance of it caused many to weep sorely." Whitefield likewise reduced Jonathan Edwards to tears, and in the Northampton congregation "few eyes were dry." At Westfield he preached four sermons to "a considerable congregation" and apparently with considerable effect.[2] Throughout the county Whitefield brought people to an emotional peak, and when he had gone the tone of religion in the county had changed markedly.

By the time Ballantine arrived to serve as their temporary minister the people of Westfield were anxious to settle a permanent minister and share in the great work of the revival. John Ballantine seemed a good choice. A young man of twenty-four, just five years out of Harvard, he came with a strong recommendation from his own minister, Benjamin Colman of Boston's Brattle Street Church. After a trial period of six months the Westfield congregation voted unanimously to ask Ballantine to settle as their permanent minister, and he accepted with pleasure. He wrote that he hoped that together they could "Follow of the thgs that make for peace & tend to edify – preserved in the present happy union."[3] In this church, at least, the Awakening seemed to be a time marked by a warm harmony and a certain sense of optimism about future relations.

But as John Ballantine looked ahead to his ordination on June 17, 1741, he had another matter to worry about. The state of happy union he found in Westfield was not the overall state of Hampshire County, certainly not of the county clergy. Once the invitations to his ordination were out, the responses that began coming back carried the message that this ordination was likely to be a difficult one. The Westfield people had first written to Ballantine's hometown, asking the Reverends Colman and Welsted from Boston's Brattle Street and Old Brick churches, respectively. The Boston ministers returned their best wishes for the church and for Ballantine but declined the invitation, citing the distance to be traveled and, vaguely, "some special difficulties." Robert Breck of Springfield also declined the invitation. Jonathan Ashley of Deerfield then wrote saying that if Breck's church were not to be represented at the ordination, his church had "no power to act" with the others present. Breck's church, however, thought it unwise that he decline and urged him to go. When Breck changed his mind and decided to attend, it was too late for Ashley to make the long trip from Deerfield. But it was not too late for others to change their plans. On hearing of Breck's acceptance, Jonathan Edwards of Northampton, Stephen Williams of Longmeadow, Samuel Hopkins of West Springfield, and Peter Reynolds of Enfield promptly withdrew; they wished Ballantine well and reaffirmed their consent to his ordination, but went home just the same. Because the churches at Hatfield and Sheffield had not sent representatives in the first place, the ordination took place with only three churches represented, hardly the impressive array expected for the occasion, but a valid ordination even so. Robert Breck opened with a prayer, William Rand of Sunderland offered the sermon, and James Bridgham of Brimfield extended the right hand of fellowship.[4] Ballantine, in taking Bridgham's right hand, probably had cause to question the kind of fellowship he could expect in Hampshire County.

The truth was that, by the time of the Great Awakening, ministerial fellowship was a hard commodity to come by in Hampshire County. The sequence of comings and goings that marked Ballantine's ordination created a confusing and even ridiculous scene, but it was no mere shadow play of protocol and pride. It bespoke a mutual recognition among the county ministers that serious splits had come to exist among them. Over the previous two decades the Hampshire ministry had been a changing group. Not only Solomon Stoddard but several of his colleagues had died, and they were replaced by younger men who had not all grown up under the influence of the valley's "Pope."[5] Stoddard's own successor, Jonathan Edwards, seemed content to carry on in Northampton the traditions established by his grandfather, at least for a while. But some of the others – most notably Breck at Springfield, Rand at Sunderland, and Bridgham at Brimfield – were less willing to fall into line with the dominant theological views of the county clergy, especially with the interest in evangelical religion so fervently preached by Stoddard. The uneasiness that existed soon turned to recrimination and spite. By the time John Ballantine came west, the Hampshire clergy was no longer a single, unified group able to act as a powerful, effective authority; it was, rather, a group of hostile, antagonistic men, many of whom could hardly stand to face each other.

It was with an earlier ordination, that of Robert Breck of Springfield, that the failure of the unity achieved in Stoddard's time had first become apparent. Although most of the county ministers opposed Breck's ordination, their opposition did not prove strong enough to prevent Breck from taking his place among them. Instead, the controversy over Breck provided the clearest starting point for a debate that was to continue for years, regarding the ministers' estimation not only of Breck himself, but of the very nature of religion. In a way, the trouble surrounding Breck's ordination in 1736 was a precursor of the difficulties that would complicate John Ballantine's ordination and the whole religious climate five years later.

Breck had come to Springfield with a questionable reputation, one that neither the people of the church nor the ministers of Hampshire County could ignore.[6] From his days at Harvard he had been branded something of a petty thief, and from his first ministerial job at Windham, Connecticut, something of an Arminian. Thomas Clap, minister of the First Church of Windham, wrote to Samuel Hopkins at West Springfield of some "Erroneous Principles" and "former Immoralities" charged against Breck, and the Springfield First Church thus found itself faced with a serious problem.[7] Breck was not an Arminian in a strict sense, more a theological liberal slurred with a vague but convenient term. He of course denied that his morality was suspect or that his principles were erroneous. But the accusations could not vanish with Breck's claim of purity, and there followed a year of controversy, ill feeling, and intricate maneuverings by Breck's supporters and detractors, during the course of which the Springfield church split into warring factions, the Hampshire ministers met in numerous councils that were either indecisive or ignored, and Breck himself was attacked, defended, examined, arrested, removed, restored, and finally ordained. The whole affair was as nasty as it was complex.

It was also ill-timed. Just as the Breck controversy was beginning, the churches of the county had begun to experience that "Surprising Work of God" which Edwards wrote about. The excitement growing out of increased religious activity and revival in Edwards's own Northampton spread up and down the river, from Massachusetts to Connecticut. With such visible evidence of the seeming power of evangelical, revivalistic religion before them, Edwards and his colleagues may have magnified the evils they saw

40

in Robert Breck, but they could not help but view a supposed Arminian like Breck as a threat and a source of danger to religion in their domain. The evangelical drive for awakening created both hope and fear among the witnesses to the "surprising work" – hope that the revival would last, fear that it would fail and prove false. When the awakened spirit later "appeared very sensibly withdrawing from all parts of the County," Edwards had the good sense to admit that certain excesses, including one case of suicide and many cases of delusion, had helped cool the religious passions of the people; but at the same time he attributed part of the blame to the dissensions caused by the controversy over Breck.[8]

As Breck later wrote in a letter to the Springfield church, he had quickly become well aware of the "uneasyness of some of the Neighbouring ministers." The ministers of the county had come to see their Hampshire Association not just as a source of ministerial fellowship, but as a source of regional orthodoxy as well. In 1732, several years before Robert Breck even became an issue, the local clergymen met to establish "What rules [we are] to observe in admitting Candidates to the work of the ministry." Initially the standards they set emphasized the fairly common professional attributes expected of ministers throughout New England: that is, new ministers had to have "knowledge in the Learned Languages," had to be "well skilled in Divinity" and able to "Common-place upon any Scripture that is assigned to them," and in general had to be "Persons of regular Conversation" willing to "devote themselves to the Work of the Ministry both publick & private." The Hampshire ministers also made a point of insisting that newcomers assent to an orthodox confession of faith and "be members in full communion with some particular church."[9]

Within a few years, however, just on the eve of the Breck controversy, the members of the Association began to express more caution about the possible danger of outsiders in their midst; in 1734 they added to their earlier rules the stipulation that there be "thorough care taken to know the Qualifications of Candidates for the ministry particularly as to their orthodoxy."[10] At about the same time a council of six Hampshire ministers recommended that the Springfield church "not make further application" to Breck until local clergymen could meet and reach some clear position on him. These six represented the main churches in the southern half of the county, and they were the ministers most likely to be in close association with Breck.[11] There was, to be sure, a small handful of Hampshire ministers who apparently felt more comfortable with Breck and, as later events would indicate, probably agreed in general with his liberal views. But they were still a minority, mostly younger men new to the county who had not yet made clear to their colleagues any of their own disagreements with the theological standards of the county. No one rose vocally to Breck's defense, and at his ordination in 1736 Breck had so little support from his neighboring colleagues that he decided to invite ministers from Boston to perform the ceremony.[12]

Perhaps as much as anything else, Breck's appeal to Boston ministers to certify his orthodoxy and ordain him in the ministry galled many of the western ministers, annoying them almost beyond reconciliation. Jonathan Edwards, in defending the opposition to Breck, wrote angrily of the intervention of outsiders. He cast his argument in terms of the distinctness of Hampshire County as a region or, to give a greater impression of closeness and interdependency, a "neighbourhood" that had its own sense of values and order. Not only was the appeal to Boston a "manifest neglect, and slight of neighbouring Churches," it also seemed "unjust and disorderly, and tending only to Confusion," a threat to the integrity and orthodoxy of religion in the county. The local churches, he said, knew their situation best, and therefore could know how best to act respecting each other when circumstances required it; by being tied together by geography and habitual dealings with each other, the churches

> will above all others partake of each others Prosperity, and feel each others Diseases. And especially, is this a case wherein the interest of neighbouring Churches is concerned; for the Settlement of an heterodox Minister in a Church wou'd be likely not only to hurt the Souls of those that are of the Church, but to be an occasion of a great deal of mischief in the Neighbourhood.

When interlopers from Boston – "those that live an hundred miles off" – came and spread their diseased theology in the west, the people of the neighborhood should have every reason to feel threatened, for if "they are the means of Heresies being established amongst us, 'tis we that must rue the Consequences of it, while they sleep at home in their whole Skins."[13]

Breck himself had first been the main issue, but as the controversy around him developed, it became clear that there was more than just the personality and principles of Robert Breck at stake. Whatever unity of doctrine and mutual support the ministers of Hampshire County had been able to establish seemed threatened by a new element, both foreign and dangerous. By admitting Breck to their county, they would be admitting to themselves that questionable religious ideas could be allowed the legitimacy of ministerial fellowship. The majority of Hampshire County ministers were hardly ready for such a degree of toleration. For Edwards and the other ministers who opposed Breck, Hampshire County should exist as a separate, organic entity, independent of Boston, a neighborhood secure in its spiritual health, yet one that had to maintain its isolation in order to survive. When Jonathan Edwards pointed out to the Boston clergy of the 1730s that "we have from the beginning till now, always managed our ecclesiastical affairs within our selves," he was only reminding them of what they knew to be true, and what the westerners had maintained both out of necessity and out of a sense of independence.[14] In the matter at hand, their aim had been to keep themselves free of the potential sickness they saw in Robert Breck.

As it turned out, of course, they were not successful, and Breck was ordained without the assistance or the approval of the Hampshire Association. But even after the initial fervor died down, a number of disturbing problems still remained. Perhaps most troubling was the very fact that the Association had not been able to block Breck's ordination. Though the county clergymen claimed the authority to pass judgment on candidates for local pulpits, the people of Springfield, or at least the dominant faction in the church, had ignored the Association's opinion. In the first real test of its power, then, the Association had failed. Moreover, it had begun to lose its sense of solidarity. On one hand stood the evangelically inclined majority, reaffirmed in their belief in the power of a spirited ministry and an awakened and enthusiastic people, both given to outward physical and emotional expressions of inner salvation; when asked to confirm Edwards's account of the late revival, this majority responded unequivocally.[15] On the other hand stood Robert Breck, a symbol of a different style of religion, one inclined to skepticism and coolness toward emotional excess, reliant instead on good works, good learning, and good order. During the battle over Breck's ordination several ministers quietly dissociated themselves from the anti-Breck hostility of their county colleagues, and for several years they tended to remain aloof from their brothers in the Hampshire Association.[16] From 1736 on, it was clear that the regional unity developed under Solomon Stoddard was at an end. Where once there had been relative harmony, the county clergy now lived in a state of tension, increasingly divided by matters of doctrine, style, and even personality.

Such was the world John Ballantine entered in 1741. Even in the calmest of times this sort of division among the local ministers would have made for a troubling situation: the spiritual leaders of society could not really lead their people if they were pulling in different directions. But 1741 was hardly the calmest of times. The turbulent background of the Awakening, with its sudden rush of renewed revivalism, made the crisis of the clergy even more severe. Although the county ministers may have avoided each other at Ballantine's ordination, they could not avoid the growing intensity of religious feeling that made their divisions sharper and more immediate, both for them and for their people. The Awakening years would push those divisions to the extreme and in the end create a theological reassessment that would shape the future of the Hampshire clergy for several decades to come.

Among Hampshire County clergymen, perhaps the best eye-witness account of the Awakening comes from the Reverend Stephen Williams, minister at Longmeadow and the oldest minister in the county. He had occupied the same pulpit since 1716, had known the powerful preaching of Solomon Stoddard, had seen the effects of the Awakening of 1735 in his own town, and by 1740 was waiting for revivalism to come again.[17] Early in 1740, after hearing of the growing revival spirit from Eleazar Wheelock, he prayed that God would make such spirit more general throughout the area. Later that year he read Whitefield's journal approvingly, saying that the evangelist "Seems to have much of ye presence of God – & he has been instrumental of doing Great things." Hoping that Whitefield could be preserved from "running into any Extreames yt may disserve ye interest of [Christ]," Williams invited him to preach at Longmeadow. Whitefield instead wound up preaching close by, at Westfield, and Williams went to hear him, only to be personally confirmed in his estimation of Whitefield's "inimitable faculty of touching ye affections and passions."[18]

In his own town Williams began to see the work of revival among the people: he recorded with approval the prayer meetings some women in the town were having, and noticed the increasing numbers of people holding meetings, attending lectures in nearby towns, and coming to him to seek spiritual advice. He traveled to Enfield with Jonathan Edwards to hear him preach the electrifying sermon that would later be published and made famous as *Sinners in the Hands of an Angry God*, and he remarked at the amazing outpouring of emotion, wishing he could preach as effectively. Even in his own family, his wife became possessed of the spirit and stayed awake all night speaking in an "Unusuall & (to me) Surprising man[ner] of Divine things."[19]

But even as he recorded and relished the wondrous things he saw around him, Williams was troubled by doubts. He had no cause to believe the ecstasies of religion altogether false, but occasionally he felt uncomfortable about the possibilities of excess. He did not look with favor on the disruptive activities of his brother-in-law, the enthusiastic itinerant James Davenport, who went from town to town attacking the spiritual health of the established ministers and turning their people against them. Nor was Williams altogether pleased when his own son took to the streets of Longmeadow as a lay exhorter; the elder Williams did not condemn his son, but neither did he praise him.[20] As he saw supposedly awakened spirits challenge the traditional position of the office he held, his earlier doubts about the potentially damaging effect of Whitefield's preaching continued, and though he rejoiced at Whitefield's work, he did so "with trembling."[21] In a sense Stephen Williams embodied the ambivalence of those who watched with joy as the revival spirit spread throughout the land, but who also watched with concern as success turned to excess. "I am full of fears," he wrote in his diary at the height of the ecstasies in June of 1741; "ye Ld be pleasd to direct to Duty – & Give to know ye truth."[22]

Part of the truth, at least, was that the Awakening proved to be a highly disruptive event, in Hampshire County as throughout the colonies. The main importance of the revival lay in the fact that it was a movement of tremendous popular force, a movement in the pews as well as in the pulpits. Throughout the American colonies

the sudden and widespread release of religious energy was a remarkable phenomenon that swept through whole congregations at
once. To a great degree ministers became as much observers as
participants. Those who tried consciously and earnestly to excite
the spiritual passions of their people often watched in wonder as
their congregations went almost wild with both joy and agony.
Other ministers watched simply with disgust. Everywhere people
seemed to have pushed the normal relations between pastor and
flock beyond their traditional bounds, and the desire for salvation
that gripped many led them to want more and demand more from
their ministers. It remained for the ministers to try to understand
this intense activity, to give it some meaning, and above all, to try
to keep it under some degree of control.[23] In the latter task they
were not always successful.

Edwards and the other pro-revivalist ministers in Hampshire
County seemed pleased by the events of the Awakening. The
increased interest in religion, the surge of admissions into the
churches, and the seemingly constant demand to have ministers
preach both in their own pulpits and in those of others stood out
as sure signs that something of a divine nature had touched
Hampshire County, just as it appeared to have done in the rest of
the colonies. The Awakening, they believed, represented no false
fit of passion, but a true stimulation of the spirit. By 1743, when
the peak of the Awakening had passed, nine of the ministers of the
county testified that they had perceived a "blessed Out-pouring of
the Spirit of God in this County," and then went on to say that in
their particular churches they had been fortunate to witness a
"happy Revival of Religion."[24] Jonathan Edwards, in his *Thoughts
on the Revival of Religion*, could point to an alteration in the
behavior of the people, toward Bible reading, prayer, serious conduct, and reform, and away from luxury, idleness, debauchery,
and other weaknesses of the flesh. "The work is very glorious," he
said, "in the great numbers that have, to appearance, been turned
from sin to God, and so delivered from a wretched captivity to sin
and Satan, saved from everlasting burnings, and made heir of
eternal glory."[25] Under such circumstances ministers could only
be pleased and gratified.

At the same time they were conscious that "there has been,
especially in some Places, a Mixture of Enthusiasm and false Religion, and some have run into great Errors in their Conduct, and

some have fallen away, and there is a Declension in others, that is to be lamented." By mistaking passion for piety, professing Christians could allow their affections to get the best of them and degenerate into ungodly behavior. For the clerical supporters of the Awakening the outbursts of enthusiasm and emotional excess – especially lay exhorting, spiritual pride, and extreme censoriousness – diverted attention from the substance of religion to the form: it was the kind of thing, they admitted, that was giving the Awakening a bad name. But even after acknowledging the errors, all could still insist that on balance "the Effect has been such, and still continues to be such, as leaves no Room reasonbly to doubt of God's having been wonderfully in the midst of us."[26]

Some ministers, however, began to be quite worried by the possibility of disorder, both personal and social. The renewed interest in the importance of spiritual conversion, of being "turned from sin to God," as Edwards put it, created an even stronger emphasis on an individual's spiritual condition. Those who felt themselves blessed with the spirit often gave marked physical and verbal expression to their awakened state. Whether it consisted of staying up at all hours immersed in Bible reading or of walking the streets exhorting others to repent and be saved, the outward behavior of the saved could sometimes be, at best, unpredictable. As Stephen Williams learned, even the family of a Harvard-trained minister might begin to act in ways that he himself could not always understand. Moreover, the crucial distinction between salvation and damnation could lead almost imperceptibly to an equally important distinction between the saved and the damned. Spiritual considerations could form the dividing line between people, replacing the more common distinctions of wealth and status.

Feelings of hostility between rich and poor, for instance, gained a new coherence with the onslaughts of Awakening sermons and exhortations. Ever since the seventeenth century, New England society had been growing increasingly prosperous overall, but also increasingly stratified in the distribution of that prosperity: in town after town the early struggles for collective survival gave way to individual struggles for personal enrichment; and as some people took self-interested advantage of economic opportunity, they set themselves further apart from their common bonds with their neighbors.[27] Yet however much ministers might have decried the evils of materialism before their congregations, they failed to stop the apparently widespread transition from communal to commercial values. In the late 1730s, in fact, the ministers of Hampshire County took anxious note of the problem, expressing their uneasiness if not outright displeasure with the cultural implications of economic self-interest. Asking themselves how to explain "the Voice of God to us in the Late Frowning Dispensations of his Providence," they pointed their fingers at "Worldlyness, or an Idolizing of the World," and singled out especially the "abundance of Fraud, Injustice, and Oppression In mens Dealings, . . . Lawsuits for Small Matters," and in general a rising level of contention among their people, most of it economically motivated.[28]

A few years later, at the height of the Great Awakening, Jonathan Edwards very pointedly asked the comfortable "middle aged" of his town if they found themselves too encumbered with material and worldly concerns to be "disposed to mind the affairs of your soul." He was not simply commenting on the stages of life and the concerns of fathers; he was also making clear to all the differences between material and spiritual success. Even if the two were not explicitly opposed, the immediate rewards of the former could still make men forget the rewards of the latter. "And now lately," he reminded them, "God has revived his work here again, and has revived the work of conversion amongst us, and some have been brought to Christ; but you are still left behind."[29] No longer a sign of God's approval of man's faithful fulfillment of his calling, the accumulation of wealth – or the striving after it – became a visible sign of an imbalance of material and spiritual priorities. In this respect the message of the Awakening stood one point of Calvinism on its head. One's acceptance and performance of a chosen calling should show its good results not in wealth but in service to others: wealth became a sign of "selfishness" that separated a man both from his neighbors and from God.[30]

Armed with such a reversal of traditional Calvinist dogma, then, awakened lay people did not find it difficult to turn against their wealthier neighbors as embodiments of self-centered worldliness and pride. Admittedly, the revival was an event with extremely complex roots and varied results, and it would be far too inadequate an explanation to suggest simply that it represented some early form of class conflict. It did, however, provide a means of expression for people who felt a vague uneasiness about the

48

changing nature of their society, especially about the growing significance of wealth and an apparent decline in the significance of equality and community. The emphasis on spiritual purity created both a standard and a language for criticism. Where money had once brought some degree of deference, it could now earn its owner an equal amount of defiance.

Status in society could not keep individuals free from attack, and neither could status in the church. During the Awakening even the ministry – perhaps especially the ministry – came under intense criticism. Those who were charged with the care of other people's souls soon found themselves charged with showing too little care for their own souls. When Whitefield and others preached against the evils of unconverted ministers, they attacked not only individuals but the whole institution of the ministry itself, for where conversion became the standard of measurement, the unconverted could make no claim to enlightenment, leadership, or authority. A course of study at Harvard or Yale mattered little if it were not attended by proof of grace, and it could even be considered a liability:

> I make no Doubt but the Colleges pour forth Swarms of young Men, who have spent their Days in diverse Lusts and Vanities; – and these unhappy Men come forth to serve the Churches (but really to serve *themselves*) and after a Life spent in Pleasure, Pomp, and Worldly-mindedness, go down to the dead, and to the *Damned*, and *their People with them*.[31]

The unconverted minister could thus appear as a real threat to his congregation, whose hopes for salvation could be ruined by the weaknesses of their spiritual leadership. By implication, a converted member of the congregation could feel actually superior to such a hopeless minister, and refuse to accept his guidance or discipline.

In short, the Great Awakening brought a heightened sense of individual and collective purity to bear on the traditional standards of social stability, and it became an especially menacing movement to those who stood at the top of the social order. The Awakening made some people concerned not only about the state of their own souls, but about the state of others' souls as well. Just as they might joyously express their own salvation, so might they vigorously attack someone else's apparent damnation. When the unfortunate sinner occupied a high place in society, the regenerate saint knew both whom to attack and how. Small wonder, then, that when a man like the Reverend Williams looked around him at the extreme behavior of the recent converts, he tempered his hopes for their spiritual success with fears of their possible excess.

He was hardly alone. While Williams confided his doubts to the privacy of his diary, his colleague Jonathan Ashley came to express his quite openly in public. The young Deerfield minister had earlier seemed to be generally comfortable with the evangelical emphasis of the county clergy, and like others whose churches had felt the happy effects of the first revival in the mid-1730s, he had been apprehensive about the ordination of the liberal Robert Breck. When the Great Awakening came in full force to Hampshire County in the early 1740s, however, Ashley gradually became one of the leading critics of its results. Despite the effects of the Awakening in increasing the numbers in his own church, he never allowed himself to be overly impressed by the results of enthusiasm. By late 1741 Ashley began to speak out with increasing criticism against the disorder and emotional excess he saw around him, seeking first to find a point of balance between the demands of the congregation and the abilities of the minister.[32]

Bowing to the popular demands of the time, he admitted that the minister could not be lethargic in his concern for either his own soul or the souls of his people: he had to "strive and even be in agony" until he became assured of his own conversion, and at the same time he had to deliver himself of fiery and awakening sermons, not dull and coldly academic ones. The minister should make it his business to be a true source of revival. But in turn, the people should not become excessive in their demands on him. If their minister remained unconverted, they should still pray for him – and pay him – rather than attack him and leave him materially impoverished as well. He also had to be able to continue to read and study and prepare himself for the work of the ministry. Here Ashley reminded his audience of the dangers he saw in the recent emphasis on enthusiastic exhortation, for "However men of such a Stamp who despise humane Learning and Study may be admired and followed when Men are over heated with Zeal; it is certain they cannot last long; and in a little time their Folly will be known to all Men." Above all, the people had to try to live in peace rather than contention. If the excitement of the Awakening were, as Ashley suspected, a temporary phenomenon, there should

be something left when the furor was over. The state of the church could not be sacrificed for the uncertain state of the minister's soul. Indeed, it was of critical importance for the church to maintain its own order and authority throughout, for during a period of excitement and controversy like that accompanying the Awakening, "we are in the utmost Danger of falling into the wildest Confusion in our religious Affairs." And as Ashley pointed out in a slap at the evangelical majority in the valley, *"We can't have any Help from Councils of Churches."* [33]

Within another year Ashley no longer made any pretense of evenness in his judgment of the Awakening. Taking the pulpit in Boston's Brattle Street Church in November 1742, he attacked the effects of the Awakening in a sermon that his colleagues in the west could not hear but, with its publication a few months later, could certainly read. Ashley made no attempt to hide his sentiments. He chose for his main image the early church at Corinth and the disorders it suffered during a period of spiritual excitement, and in drawing the comparison between past and present he offered one of the briefest yet clearest catalogues of ills and errors that came out of the anti-Awakening backlash. In general, Ashley saw in the effects of the Awakening a destruction or inversion of the good order of church and society: the intense interest in religion had not set people's hearts to God as much as their hands to each other's throats. Churches were breaking up into antagonistic sects and parties, and religious debates were bringing contention into the daily lives and conversations of the people. They began to engage in "uncharitable Judging and Censuring one another," treating each other with offensive "Stiffness and Unyieldableness." Even the family bond began to come apart as converted wives refused to respect their obligations to unconverted husbands.[34]

Worst of all, in Ashley's mind, was the distortion of the relationship between pastor and people. Some ministers — Ashley must have had Jonathan Edwards in mind — had come to be held in too high admiration, far beyond their positions as preachers and teachers. At the same time, other ministers were suffering the disdain of their people, being starved and reduced to lowly circumstances by a lack of financial support, "as tho' an extraordinary Degree of Zeal excus'd People from supporting their Minister." This lack of respect for the ministers culminated in the rejection of established ministers for "Novices" and "illiterate Teachers" that had "thrust themselves into the Church." The final image Ashley summoned of the church at Corinth—where "several taught and exhorted at the same time . . . [and] Women laid aside their female Modesty, and set up to be Teachers in the Church"—was an image of chaos and disorder, the image of a world out of balance. For Ashley that was the world of the Awakening. "Who is so blind," he wrote, "that he cannot see our Disorders described as in a Glass by the Apostles in this *Chapter*."[35]

Ashley had to look no further than his own church for signs of such disorders. Despite his own coolness toward enthusiastic religion, the Deerfield church had experienced awakenings in 1735 and 1741, and doubtless there were awakened members in the church who feared that his dim view of their recent revival could threaten to put out the new light in their souls. By the end of the Great Awakening Ashley could see that his authority as a minister was by no means beyond challenge. In January of 1743 he asked the church to vote on whether persons called to come for consultation with the minister should be considered disobedient if they refused to come. The majority of church members voted affirmatively, but the vote did not guarantee obedience: during the next two years several persons called by Ashley still refused to come, defying the threatened discipline of the church. And despite his earlier warnings against the dangers of a poorly supported ministry, by 1745 Ashley was having to write the townsmen assembled at their meeting that he could not get by if they continued paying his salary in depreciated bills of credit rather than silver. Ashley's position in the town remained relatively secure despite these inconveniences, and there is no indication that more than a small minority dared oppose him openly; this minority, however, continued in its hostility toward him, and after several years of increasing disdain and defiance, broke away and joined the neighboring New Light church at Green River.[36] If Ashley's enemies eventually retreated into a nearby district, he still came to know firsthand of the disturbances and disrespect that could follow in the trail of religious revival.

He had even more compelling examples of ministerial vulnerability to cite when he looked beyond Deerfield to other towns in the county. Three other ministers—Benjamin Doolittle of Northfield, Grindall Rawson of South Hadley, and William Rand of Sunderland—had faced even more serious attacks, and in their situations a worried minister like Jonathan Ashley could see his worst fears coming true: the people were rising up vehemently against their spiritual leaders, and the former respect accorded the ministry was turning to outright insult.

To some extent the hostility directed against the unfortunate ministers stemmed from complaints about their ability to perform their pastoral duties properly. Grindall Rawson, for instance, was accused of being personally dishonest and professionally incompetent, lax in providing his people with adequate spiritual direction; some people even said that the minister did not write his own sermons but cribbed them from other sources.[37] At Northfield the dispute seemed initially to center on the Reverend Doolittle's attempts to maintain himself materially. In the late 1730s Doolittle had expressed dissatisfaction with the payment of his salary, even to the point of taking the town to court in order to extract payment; and perhaps worse, he also held part-time jobs on the side. His practice as a doctor and as proprietor's clerk for the town of Winchester, some felt, cut into the time he should have been spending on his ministerial duties.[38] Certainly, at a time of growing popular antipathy toward seeking after wealth, a minister had to be especially careful not to engage in any unseemly economic behavior.

At the same time, though, all three of these clergymen aroused even greater disfavor for doctrinal reasons. Unlike Jonathan Ashley, Doolittle, Rawson, and Rand had not joined in the earlier opposition to the ordination of Robert Breck, and as a result they came to be tainted with supposed Arminianism. During the late 1730s Rand had begun to achieve the reputation of being a man of liberal theology and had published several sermons to give weight to the charge; he had, for instance, preached to his own people at Sunderland the somewhat Arminian position that Christ "will at last judge every man according to his works."[39] In Doolittle's case the leaders of the movement against him had close familial ties to Northampton, and Doolittle's failure to close ranks with Edwards and the majority of Hampshire County ministers in 1736 must have made his position suspect in the minds of his own people. By 1739 Doolittle was confronted with a paper charging him directly with Arminianism and pointing out further that because the "uneasiness" of some of the people had existed for a long while, the time had come to submit the matter to an ecclesiastical council of valley ministers. When Doolittle refused to respond, the unhappy church members appealed to the Reverend William Williams of Hatfield and eventually to the May 1739 meeting of the Hampshire Association, which happened to be taking place in Northfield.[40]

The calling of a clerical council to deal with these local disputes created a paradoxical problem for the Hampshire Association. The majority of local ministers may have had their disagreements with Doolittle on matters of doctrine, and they may have been even more displeased by his position in the Breck controversy. But at the same time they must have been hesitant to undermine his position as an established minister: it was one thing to try openly to keep a prospective candidate like Breck from coming into the region, yet quite another to help unseat a man like Doolittle who had been in his pulpit for years. Especially as long as a good number of Doolittle's parishioners still supported him, it would have been touchy for the Association to intervene on the side of dismissal. If the anti-Doolittle faction expected quick action from his colleagues, then, they were wrong. The Association counseled "calm conversation" between the two sides and refrained from becoming more directly involved in the matter.[41]

Doolittle's opponents made a further appeal to the Association and even a call to the county court, but both bodies proved unwilling to take decisive action, and the church remained divided. Finally, in 1740, Doolittle insisted that those people who had been making "a great noise about my Principals" confront him personally and discuss particular points of doctrine, "to see if I can satisfie them." The church voted to support his call for conversation, and it appeared that by defying his opposition from the pulpit, Doolittle had won.[42] He had the majority on his side and managed to keep them there until his death in 1748. But like Ashley, he had also been made aware of the presence of a disaffected minority that was not afraid to attack him for the life he lived and the doctrine he preached. He could go on to speak out strongly against the errors of enthusiasm, and he did so openly in print, knowing that many in his own church held him in error for his lack of it.

Less fortunate was Grindall Rawson of South Hadley. In February of 1740 the people of the precinct voted to call for the dismissal of Rawson, and they chose a committee to inform him of the fact. They elaborated on their disaffection a month later, pointing out that Rawson had refused to have any more to do with thirty-three people in the church and in so doing had effectively cut himself off from the majority of church members in the precinct. By the following year the people of South Hadley had voted to deny Rawson his salary and firewood, and eventually to deny him the pulpit. At that point both sides agreed to call upon the Hampshire Association of Ministers to resolve the dispute. Recognizing the extreme unwillingness of the people to have Rawson preach, the Association council did what it had been reluctant to do in the Doolittle case and in May of 1741 recommended that a peaceful separation might well be in order. Soon thereafter, however, a council of the Association members met a second time on the Rawson case and had a change of heart. Perhaps again overlooking their own antipathy toward a particular minister in favor of preserving the honor of the ministerial office, the ministers on the council decided that the charges against Rawson had not been sufficiently substantiated, and that therefore they could not argue for his dismissal.[43]

Rawson's people were irate. They rejected the advice of the second council and stated emphatically that "we have wholly done with Mr. Rawson as a minister & if you endeavour to restore him to his place it will (instead of promoting our peace) have a tendency to end in our utter disturbance." They soon had an opportunity to prove their point. Feeling vindicated by the action of the second council, Rawson attempted to regain his pulpit. Feeling equally violated by the action of the second council, the people of South Hadley formed a committee to keep Rawson out. At one point Rawson was pulled forcibly from the pulpit, roughed up a bit, and ejected from the church. Extralegal means accomplished what the normal procedures could not: even though Rawson stayed in town for another year or so, he never came back to preach.[44]

The vehemence and violence of the people of South Hadley speak clearly of the level of popular passion aroused during the Great Awakening. Controversies had existed before, sometimes lingering for years until the unhappy brethren perhaps found some means of reconciliation with their minister, perhaps learned to live with his unsettling habits or doctrine, or at least waited until he died. Before Rawson, most ministers in Hampshire

55

County had managed to maintain themselves through divisions and disputes in their churches, relying to some extent on the eminence of the ministerial position or the support of their colleagues, and most had enjoyed relatively long tenure. But during the Awakening Rawson provided the model for what was to become an increasingly common phenomenon: he was the first Congregational minister in Hampshire County to be dismissed from his job because of the growing popular desire for religious passion and purity.[45]

William Rand was the second. In 1742 his people apparently wanted to share more directly in the exuberance of the Awakening and asked to have itinerants come and preach from Rand's pulpit. Rand would have nothing to do with the enthusiasm of itinerants and refused, whereupon the people showed both their annoyance and their determination by formally recording in the town records their desire to have itinerant preaching. For his own part, Rand made his position clear at the ordination of the Reverend Abraham Hill at Road Town (Shutesbury) in October of 1742:

> There are some persons at this Day, that cry out against the ministers of Christ, reproach them, and treat them with Contempt, who pretend to justify themselves herein, because, as they pretend, they are not lawful Ministers; they are unconverted, dead, carnal, etc. And those persons that are so very forward to slight and reproach Ministers, do, many of them, discover a great Inclination to intrude themselves into the ministerial office.

This thoroughly anti-Awakening minister in a town anxious for a burst of enthusiasm could not hope to last. By 1745 he was gone, dismissed, and on his way to Kingston, Massachusetts, where the congregation had just dismissed its pastor for his support of George Whitefield.[46] Rand had found a good home.

But for all the ministers who still called Hampshire County home the problems of the Great Awakening lingered on. After the revival itself had passed, the power of ministerial authority continued to seem uncertain. Above all, the experiences of Ashley, Doolittle, Rawson, and Rand had shown just how vulnerable that authority could be. Others likewise had been attacked by itinerant preachers or by people of their own congregations. In a few towns groups of Separates were beginning to form their own churches, standing defiantly apart from the established church. In general, the last few years had been difficult ones for the county's ministers, even for some of those who had welcomed the Awakening in the first place, and the threats to the authority and good order of their churches had been too recent and too real to ignore.

By the mid-1740s, then, a growing number of local ministers began to speak out against the Awakening and its effects. Although Ashley, Rand, and Doolittle contributed the most significant publications by Hampshire County ministers, there were others who also made clear their anti-Awakening sentiments. John Ballantine at Westfield, Abraham Hill at Road Town, and Noah Merrick at Springfield's fourth parish were among a number of new ministers settled in the county since 1741, and in 1743 they joined Breck, Ashley, Rand, and others in subscribing to Charles Chauncy's famous blast against the errors of the Awakening and its leaders, *Seasonable Thoughts on the State of Religion in New England*. Whereas only nine ministers in the county had put their names to the 1743 *Testimony and Advice* defending the Great Awakening, no fewer than thirteen appeared on the list of subscribers to Chauncy's document.[47] Two years later, when sentiment for and against George Whitefield seemed to be running high, sixteen Hampshire ministers joined ministers in Connecticut in wishing him away. To defend the "Peace and Purity" of their churches they urged Whitefield to stay away from them, lest they be deeply offended. They accused him of preaching false doctrines, of being "deeply ting'd with Enthusiasm," and of exhibiting "a very censorious Spirit by slandering the Ministers and Colleges in this Country . . . [and] having caus'd Divisions and Offences contrary to the Doctrine which we have learn'd of Christ."[48] In speaking so against Whitefield they were at the same time addressing themselves to the evils they had seen come out of the Awakening; the disorder they had either feared or experienced could no longer be allowed to grow, and by blocking Whitefield they hoped to shut out at least the most visible and vocal symbol of the problem.

There had become evident a new balance in the county, and it was not just that new men had come in to tip the scales heavily toward the anti-Awakening side: like Ashley, some of the other established ministers had begun to change sides. Samuel Hopkins of West Springfield, for instance, who had joined Edwards and the others in opposing Breck's ordination in 1736, did not join

Edwards and the eight others in signing the *Testimony and Advice* of 1743. In 1743 Hopkins signed Chauncy's *Seasonable Thoughts* instead. His signing this document did not in itself indicate a radical shift or a violently hostile view toward the Awakening or its results; it did suggest, though, that by 1743 he was one of those who could no longer be considered a staunch supporter of revivalistic, enthusiastic religion. Perhaps like Stephen Williams (who signed the *Testimony and Advice* even as he expressed his doubts in his diary), most local ministers had become uncertain and a little fearful of what would come from the excesses of religious excitement. By 1747 Jonathan Edwards claimed still to be working hard on the Arminian question and was "so deep into this controversy, that I am not willing to dismiss it, till I know the utmost of the matter."[49] But most of his colleagues did not share his concern: Arminianism seemed rather a tame enemy in comparison to the disruptive energies of an awakened people.

When theological disputes spread beyond the established clergy to become contested by lay exhorters, itinerants, and divided congregations, the established ministers had to realize that they themselves could ultimately be the ones to suffer. Certainly their main source of collective identity, the Hampshire Association of Ministers, had experienced a steady decline in power over the past few years. To some extent they had weakened it themselves by allowing doctrinal differences to stand in the way of ministerial collegiality, unity, and authority. But even more serious had been the threat from below. Rather than recognize the authority of clerical councils to exercise some degree of control over ministerial positions, people in some congregations were beginning to challenge, reject, or simply ignore the voice of the Association, ordaining one minister against the Association's wishes and, even worse, dismissing two others. Having witnessed the surprising and sometimes appalling events of the 1740s, even some former evangelicals in the Association became more cautious.[50]

Chapter 3

THE REVIVALIST REMOVED

It eventually took a bitter dispute between a minister and his congregation for the Hampshire County ministers to demonstrate fully their growing concerns over the effects of revivalism and its attendant disorders. Ironically enough, in this case they came down against the minister. The celebrated dismissal of Jonathan Edwards from his Northampton church in 1750 not only supplied one of the most colorful and complex examples of ecclesiastical conflict in a single town; it also provided a means of realigning and reassessing local ministerial opinion in the post-Awakening years. The Edwards controversy was something no Hampshire County minister could ignore. When it was over Edwards was gone from the valley, banished to the remote Indian village of Stockbridge on the far western frontier. With him went the most vigorous mind and eloquent voice for evangelical religion in western Massachusetts. Remaining behind were the advocates of a more liberal theology and conservative sociology, most notably Robert Breck, who assumed a place of almost unchallenged leadership among the majority of ministers in the county.

There is hardly any need to go into great detail here about the complexities of Jonathan Edwards's controversy with the people of his own town. The story has been told repeatedly, and told very well.[1] It may be accurate enough to say that by the mid-1740s the people of Northampton were growing disenchanted with their minister, and he with them. Edwards was by no means the easiest man to get along with. More comfortable with his own thoughts in the privacy of his study or on the long solitary rides he took than in the company of others, Edwards lacked the easy amenities and conversational familiarity a country minister so often needed in his parish duties. In his late years he even described himself as having a constitution "in many respects peculiarly unhappy . . . and a low tide of spirits; often occasioning a kind of childish weakness and contemptibleness of speech, presence, and demeanor, with a disagreeable dulness and stiffness, much unfitting me for conversation."[2] Whatever his earlier successes in preaching to his people from the pulpit, he increasingly managed to offend, anger, and annoy them in his day-to-day dealings with them. Edwards always acted out of adherence to strict principles and high standards, but apparently he also acted without much tact.

It was the question of standards, in fact, that finally provided the overt reason for Edwards's dismissal. Edwards had begun his ministry in Northampton in the final years of Solomon Stoddard's pastorate, and when the grandfather died and the grandson took over, it was with the implicit understanding that things would remain as they had been. The Stoddardean system of open communion would continue to be the norm. But rather than let open communion be an invitation for halfhearted concerns over personal conversion, Edwards relied, as had Stoddard before him, on the power of his preaching to bring in fresh harvests of souls. During the religious excitement of 1735 he had been especially successful, and during the Great Awakening his Northampton church had shared in the general glory of the revival. But increasingly Edwards came to feel that he might not have been as successful as he had thought.[3] No less than the Awakening's most skeptical critics, Edwards knew that some of the apparent converts were not sanctified at all, but were deluded, demented, or downright fake. There were others who gave salvation too little thought, and that to Edwards was a troubling thought:

> I have had difficulties in my mind, for many years past, with regard to the admission of members into the Church, who made no pretense to real godliness. These gradually increased, and at length to such a degree, that I found that I could not with an easy conscience, be active in admitting any more members in our former manner, without better satisfaction . . . And by reading and study, I found myself more strengthened in my reasons to the contrary. On which I came to this determination, that if any person should offer to come into the church without a profession of godliness, I must decline being active in his admission; which, I was sensible,

60

would occasion much uneasiness and public noise and excitement.[4]

Not only could he no longer accept the Stoddardean position on communion, Edwards decided, but neither could he accept the Halfway Covenant. If church membership were to be open only to converted saints, baptism should be offered only to their children. In order to purify the Northampton Church, Edwards would have to break with the recent past of Stoddardean standards and return to an even more distant past in which visible saints stood apart from their fellow townspeople. What Edwards wanted to do, in short, was to recreate the strict Congregational standards of the early seventeenth century.

Such a reversion to the practices of the past would necessitate obvious changes in the church and might indeed cause "much uneasiness and public noise and excitement." If people were to give adequate testimony to the experience of conversion, someone would have to judge the truth of their words; no matter what Edwards might say about inner assurances, some outer standards had to apply. Edwards perhaps assumed that as minister, he alone would be the one to apply those standards in order to maintain the decorum and discipline of the church. He certainly had no intention of encouraging his parishioners to create the sharp separation between sinner and saint that had been so destructive to church harmony during the Great Awakening. But with the widespread disorder and occasional chaos still fresh in people's memories, many Northamptonites had good reason to fear that the practices of the previous century would create problems in the present: after so many years of enjoying apparent spiritual equality under the Stoddardean system, people would unavoidably be put in the position of judging each other, of wondering whether their friends or enemies were saved or damned along with them. The Awakening had cast such judging in an altogether new light. Moreover, even if some people could continue to live in an unconverted state, they would not be content to leave their children in an unbaptized state. Here again the standards of the seventeenth century clashed with the practices of the eighteenth, and as Edwards himself admitted,

> The greatest difficulty of all relating to my Principles is here respecting *Baptism*. I am not sure but that my People, in length of Time, and with great difficulty, might be brought

to yield the Point as to the Qualifications for the Lords Supper (tho' that is very uncertain;) But with respect to the other sacrament there is scarce any Hope of it. And this will be very likely to overthrow me, not only with Regard to my upperness in the work of the ministry here, but every where.[5]

Still he pressed for change. The only way to correct a backsliding people was to push them, even if they were unwilling, into a new spirit of religious revival.

His people did not agree. Perhaps if Edwards had been on better personal terms with the members of his congregation, he might have had more success in convincing them to follow his leadership in ecclesiastical terms. But the strained relationships that had emerged between Edwards and the Northampton people in the post-Awakening years served only to make them more resistant to doctrinal departures. Whatever peace existed in the church was only of a tenuous nature in the late 1740s, and Edwards avoided a confrontation with his people only because no one actually sought admission to the church under the new standards he sought to impose. In 1748, however, when a young man declared himself ready to join the church on Edwards's terms, no one could pretend to avoid the issue any longer. Rather than allow Edwards the chance to establish an important precedent and force the church to accept his standards, the people chose to fight him.[6]

Almost from the beginning Edwards realized that this fight would assume exceptional proportions and would not be simply a doctrinal disagreement between a pastor and his flock. By 1749 the controversy had been taken over by the precinct meeting, and the leading members of the precinct committee – "many of them some of those that were most violently engaged in this Controversy" – were trying to move toward a separation between minister and people. Angered by this intrusion of secular powers into his business, Edwards "told them what I thought of the Precinct's taking the Ecclesiastical affair in their hands." The members of the committee were unmoved by Edwards's opinions, and after offering a fervent justification of their position, "went away without concluding anything, after long continued uncomfortable disputing, and some harsh Reflections & injurious Charges."[7] By the end of 1749 Edwards could only write in disgust that the people of Northampton had talked much but listened little:

There have been abundance of meetings about our affairs . . . society meetings & church meetings, & meetings of Committees, of Committees of the Parish & Committees of the Church, Conferences, debates, Reports, & Proposals drawn up, & Replies & Remonstrances. The people have a Resolution to get me out of Town speedily, that disdains all Control or Check.

Throughout all the sound and fury, Edwards complained that they had really rejected all sensible discussion and seemed to be "determined that the argument for my opinion shall never be publickly heard."[8]

Whatever he could have said in defense of his principles would no doubt have been useless anyway, because nothing could have kept him in the Northampton pulpit for long. The immediate dispute over the doctrines of admission and baptism did not in itself cause his dismissal; it simply provided the moment for bringing together a growing number of disagreements, both doctrinal and personal, the sum of which proved too much for Edwards to fight all at once. Despite his later complaints about the role certain outsiders took in the affair, he must have known that there was enough local hostility to ruin him, and after the death in 1748 of his influential uncle, John Stoddard, Edwards had too few supporters in his own church to hope to survive.

Still, for the sake of understanding the Edwards affair from a broader regional perspective, it is important to examine its meaning in the context of the county as a whole. Edwards was too influential, both as a theologian and as a preacher, to be considered only within the limited realm of his own church or even in strictly theological terms. Certainly the decision by Northampton leaders to deal with him in the precinct meeting rather than in the church gives some indication of the implicitly secular nature of the controversy in their eyes, and to a large degree the exceptional measures taken in Northampton served only to underscore the significance of the case throughout the region. If Edwards felt that he was suffering unusual and unfair treatment at the hands of a few powerful men in the town, he would have cause to feel even more injury when the leading political and ecclesiastical figures of the county added their weight to the opposition.

One of Edwards's chief antagonists, for instance, proved to be his cousin Joseph Hawley, a rising political leader in Northampton and in the wider sphere of the county as well; in a sense he defined an important link between the local and regional aspects of the affair. Just a few years out of Yale, Hawley was young, able, ambitious, and well-educated, altogether a likely candidate to take his place among the county elite. His father and grandfather, both likewise named Joseph Hawley, had been leading men in Northampton before him, and local prominence came almost automatically with the name. More important, perhaps, his uncle was John Stoddard, who could help him gain positions of influence beyond the town. By the late 1740s young Joseph Hawley was still in his mid-twenties but already a Northampton selectman and member of the Hampshire bar, and he clearly had no reason to doubt that he would gain even more political prestige in the near future.[9]

Hawley had many personal reasons for opposing Edwards, but as much as anything else he seemed intent on using the Edwards controversy as a convenient vehicle for his upward political mobility.[10] The trait that emerges most clearly from his behavior throughout the affair is his almost blatant ambition. Edwards wrote that Hawley had become "the most leading man in town . . . bold in declaiming and disputing for his opinions." As Edwards chided, and as Hawley later admitted, "you made your Self greatly guilty in the sight of God, in the part you acted in this affair; becoming . . . very much their Leader in it; & much from your own forwardness, putting your Self forward as it were, as tho fond of intermeddling & Helping."[11]

To charge Hawley with political ambition or even personal spitefulness, of course, is not necessarily to charge him with absolute hypocrisy. He did consider himself a man of serious religious convictions – he had earlier even toyed with the idea of becoming a minister, and he actually did serve as chaplain with the Hampshire troops involved in the Louisburg expedition in 1746 – and though Edwards perceived him as "a man of lax principles, falling in, in some essential things, with Arminianism," the young lawyer nonetheless seemed quite effective in presenting his "notions" to the people of Northampton.[12] The point, simply, is that Hawley became outspoken in his religious leanings only when it seemed safe to do so. As long as his uncle Stoddard remained alive and continued to support his nephew Edwards in the pulpit, Hawley apparently kept to himself whatever negative opinions he may have had of his cousin. When Stoddard died, however, Hawley had no further need to be circumspect and quickly emerged as one of the most vocal leaders of the anti-Edwards faction. Above all, he must have recognized the degree of authority that suddenly devolved upon John Stoddard's other nephew, Israel Williams, a man who like Hawley himself was a cousin of Edwards but hardly a friend. By challenging one kinsman in the Northampton pulpit Hawley could firmly ally himself with another kinsman whose power was much more calculable and almost tangible.

The extent of Williams's personal involvement in the Edwards case—especially his influence on his young cousin Hawley—remains uncertain, but the available evidence, however circumstantial, seems clearly to implicate him. Williams's antipathy to Edwards was hardly a secret. Like Hawley, Williams may not have been an Arminian in the strictest sense, but he certainly had little tolerance for the enthusiastic evangelicalism he witnessed in the Awakening. As early as 1740, when Williams learned that George Whitefield was on his way to the area, he reputedly forbade Whitefield to preach in his hometown of Hatfield, even though a good number of people wanted to hear the evangelist.[13]

Throughout the years just after the Awakening, Williams had enough to do in his new military position as commissary, and he probably bothered himself little with religious issues. By the time of the Edwards affair, however, Williams was no longer simply John Stoddard's heir apparent but firmly in control of the county political apparatus. No doubt he recognized, as did others, the potential for renewed religious enthusiasm and extremism implicit in Edwards's new doctrine, and he therefore felt the need to deal with the possibility of ecclesiastical and social disorder before it once again got out of hand. Though he remained somewhat in the background, Williams obviously followed and apparently helped direct the move to oust Edwards and his doctrines. In writing about the controversy later, Edwards complained that his opponents in Northampton had been "assisted and edged on by some at a great distance, persons of note; and some men in civil authority have had a great hand in it." He especially pointed the finger at Israel Williams, saying that Williams had "called me a Tyrant &c . . . He has great Influence on many of the neighbouring ministers: and his thus appearing will doubtless greatly embolden my People; and will have Influence on many of the Principal men in neighbouring towns."[14]

Edwards's nineteenth-century biographer, Sereno Dwight, also wrote of the "personal hostility of the —— family, residing in an adjoining town, [as] another cause of exciting opposition to Mr. Edwards." Dwight may have been reluctant to name names, but his discretion covered little. He could only have been referring to Israel Williams when he mentioned one particular "near relative of Mr. Edwards, . . . strongly biassed" toward Arminianism, who "came often to Northampton, to advise with some the leaders of the opposition, and threw his whole influence into that scale." This "individual . . . [had] various members of the family . . . residing in more distant parts of the country" on whom he could count to add to the pressure against Jonathan Edwards. One brother, for instance – presumably the Reverend Solomon Williams of Lebanon, Connecticut – became the "confidential friend and adviser of Mr. Edwards's enemies." Early in the fight, when the anti-Edwards faction at Northampton sought to have some learned minister write an attack on Edwards's *Humble Inquiry*, Solomon Williams willingly took on the job.[15]

It was the Hampshire clergy, of course, that ultimately played the most prominent role in the drama. Far from being considered intrusive outsiders, they seemed to be indispensable insiders, crucial figures in the larger neighborhood defined by the county. Although Edwards's colleagues may not have been the prime movers in his dismissal, they were for the most part active accomplices, providing a valuable stamp of legitimacy to the proceeding against him. At the same time, however, the ministerial council that came to Northampton to preside over Edwards's dismissal cannot be seen simply as the agent of Joseph Hawley and Edwards's other hometown enemies. Neither can the council, loaded though it was with members and allies of the Williams clan, be seen simply as the tool of Israel Williams. Although Edwards's fellow ministers undoubtedly acted in concert with his secular enemies, they also acted on their own in defense of their own particular position. Perhaps even more than the people of Northampton or the political leaders of the county, the Hampshire ministers saw in the doctrine that Edwards had lately espoused a threat to themselves, both collectively and individually. For them especially, then, the Edwards controversy represented an opportunity to demonstrate forcefully their rejection of the last vestiges of the Awakening and the first signs of a dangerous outgrowth.[16]

There had been some attempt to turn to outside ministers almost from the beginning of the crisis. Edwards himself first suggested calling a council of ministers to help judge the controversy because his people seemed so unwilling to listen to his opinion. All he asked was that he be able to choose half the members of the council. A committee of the church agreed in the beginning but then backed off when one dissident member warned that any such plan offered by Edwards was "some snare laid to entrap The People."[17] The Northampton precinct did turn to a few ministers for advice, however. Not only did they ask Solomon Williams to draft his reply to Edwards, but they also wrote to the Reverend Peter Clark of Salem Village and the Reverend Thomas Prince of Boston, hoping in each case for a condemnation. Clark at first suggested in his reply that Edwards's ideas seemed absurd, but later he admitted that he could not judge the matter competently. He, like so many of the people of Northampton, had not actually read Edwards's *Humble Inquiry*, nor had he even talked to anyone who had read it. Moreover, he said, he could not get to the matter as quickly as the impatient townspeople seemed to want. When Clark finally did get around to reading the book, he wrote Edwards that he could not understand why so much controversy had come to exist, because the differences between Edwards's ideas and those of Stoddard were not so great. Clark, in short, did not say what the anti-Edwards forces in Northampton had wanted him to say. Neither did Prince, who likewise expressed surprise at the existence of such an apparently irreconcilable conflict. He said that he basically agreed with Clark's sentiments.[18]

But if ministers in the eastern part of the province proved to be of no help to the Northampton people, the majority of clergymen in Hampshire County gave them all they needed. By the end of November 1749, the people of the town had decided to call in a council of ministers, and from the beginning they insisted on inviting only local ministers to attend. Everyone, including Edwards, could be fairly sure how such a council would act. Quite simply, the Northampton minister could expect little or no support from his colleagues.

Exactly why Edwards found himself so cut off from the rest of the county ministry is a matter with roots in both personal and doctrinal questions. Robert Breck of Springfield certainly had his own reasons for opposing Edwards, and the Northampton council offered him the opportunity for sweet revenge. Now that his nemesis of fourteen years back was himself the subject of clerical scrutiny, Breck could help make sure that scrutiny was sharp and intense. Others may have had less obvious personal reasons for wanting to get rid of Edwards; some, like Timothy Woodbridge of Hatfield and Chester Williams of Hadley, may have felt the pressure of the Williams family helping push them toward a vote for dismissal.[19] But for all of them there still remained the disturbing question of Edwards's recently enunciated views on the sacraments. Just about all the churches in the area were Stoddardean and had been for years. Despite any differences in personality or style that existed among the ministers, they shared a common view of ecclesiastical polity. Now Edwards seemed on the verge of disrupting that unity. If nothing else, the Stoddardean practice of open communion allowed a church to exist without clear distinctions between the saved and the unsaved and – of special importance in the relative quiet of the post-Awakening years – without the sometimes rancorous judging of sinner by saint. Edwards, of course, tried explicitly to dissociate himself and his doctrines from the censorious practices of the extremists of the Awakening, and no one really accused him of being such an extremist. But perhaps more than the Reverends Clark and Prince, the ministers of the west saw danger in the differences between the ideas of Jonathan Edwards and those of his grandfather Stoddard. If the Northampton people wanted to dismiss Edwards because he had "separated and departed from the principles which the great Mr. Stoddard brought in and practiced," then the county ministers would do nothing to dissuade them.[20]

From the beginning, then, Edwards knew that his only chance for a fair hearing, or a hearing of any sort, lay in his bringing in ministers from outside. At first he had agreed, somewhat reluctantly, to accept a council made up of those ministers who lived closest by, in the immediate neighborhood of Northampton. It was not by any means a very sympathetic group, but at least in John Woodbridge of South Hadley and Edward Billing of Cold Spring Edwards had two supporters. But the Northampton church insisted on choosing representatives from all over the county, so that some of Edwards's greatest detractors could be among the invited. If such were to be the case, argued Edwards in return,

It would be a very unjust proceeding. The neighbouring ministers, on whom you first insisted, have indeed much to prejudice them against me in those affairs. But it is well known that many of the ministers of the County, who are out of the neighbourhood, have had much more to prejudice them . . . [It] is well known, that four or five of them have heretofore had the reputation of Arminians. Some others of them are known to have been strenuous opposers of the late revival of religion, for which I have been so public an advocate . . . There are no less than six of them, who have either had a particular difference with me thereupon, or have in times past openly manifested towards me a personal hostility or aversion for the part I have taken therein. Another of them, one of the senior ministers of the County, has shown a strong prejudice, in this particular controversy between you and me, in something which he has said to two of the brethren of the Committee of the Church, as I have been well informed. Another of them has an own father in the town, who is one of the Commitee; and several of his brothers are greatly engaged in the controversy.[21]

It was Edwards's clearest statement of the isolation he was beginning to feel. Throwing out accusations of injustice, prejudice, personal hostility, and even Arminianism, he dropped any remaining shreds of ministerial delicacy and told the Northampton people what he thought of most of his colleagues in the county. He knew that he was no longer a leader in the region, and that his enemies were ascendant. The problem was essentially that, as the main voice of discord breaking the religious harmony of the county, Edwards knew he could not be treated fairly. Disagreement over principles, no matter how trivial, has a "powerful tendency to prejudice the mind, not only against the doctrines which are opposite to those we embrace, but against the persons who introduce and maintain them."[22] In the context of the post-Awakening years, Edwards was speaking an unfortunate truth that his hearers knew only too well. With the cards so stacked against him, Edwards insisted that he have the right to go even further, to pick men from beyond the county.

It proved to be an interesting and even ironic debate. In April of 1750 the Reverend Stephen Williams wrote the Northampton church committee that, years before, when Solomon Stoddard was pastor, the Northampton church had agreed to settle internal differences by calling in a council of county churches. As far as the county ministers were concerned, said Williams, that rule should still apply, and "We See No Reason for your Departing from that Vote."[23] Edwards, however, did see a reason. He replied to the first council just assembled at Northampton that he could

> freely own that it is a good general rule, that Councils, which are to judge of difficulties arising in particular churches, should be constituted of neighbouring churches. But to say, that this is a rule so established by the word of God, or the reason and nature of things, and made so universal, that it never will or can admit of any exception, and never, in any case whatsoever, ought to be dispensed with, is carrying the matter to such an unreasonable length, as no one of the members of this reverend Council would sanction.

He insisted that his position in the Breck controversy – "That the affairs of Religion are not confined to single churches, properly belonging to the neighbouring churches" – was intended as a good general rule, but that even he allowed for "exceptions in extraordinary cases."[24] His case, of course, should be so considered.

Edwards claimed that his was not just a case of local importance to be decided by a local jury; in his own eyes what happened to him had far-reaching implications. It was not just that he, like any other dismissed minister, would suffer damage to his reputation and might have trouble getting another job – although for a man of forty-six, that was an important consideration. There was something more. What happened between him and his Northampton church, he argued, would be "an event of great and extensive influence on the interests of religion, and the Church of God."

> Northampton having been a place much heard of, and extensively observed by the church at large . . . the report of our separation must needs produce an extensive and great effect . . . People at a distance have been more ignorant of our former imperfections, and have been ready to look on Northampton as a kind of heaven upon earth. The result of the Final Council will undoubtedly be published to the world, and will be regarded with deep attention by many, not only in New England, but in the other provinces of North America, as well as by some perhaps in England and Scotland.

Taking such a global view of his personal problem, Edwards insisted that "some of the wisest and ablest men in the country, should have an opportunity to look into our affairs and give us their advice, and use their wisdom if possible to prevent this calamity." Whatever the church had said in Stoddard's day about submitting disputes to councils of county ministers, this present matter seemed far too important to be "confined to the limits of this particular neighbourhood." Edwards said he did not feel himself necessarily bound "by the determination of our forefathers," and he thought it much more important that he have the right to appeal to a "Council or Synod from larger limits." The story of his struggle in Northampton had to be "given to the world by men whose characters are known and respected in other parts of the world," not simply by a handful of local ministers.[25]

These were fine words from Edwards, who only fourteen years before had chided the Boston ministers for their intervention into the Hampshire "neighbourhood" during the Breck affair. Now embroiled in a struggle for his own job, Edwards had developed a rather flexible if not patently inconsistent definition of what that neighborhood actually was. Distrustful of most of his Hampshire colleagues, he first tried to narrow his definition to encompass only those ministers who lived in close proximity to Northampton; when that ploy failed, he rejected the whole notion of regional autonomy and turned outward. What had once been an enclosed neighborhood had suddenly become an area of concern to the whole world. Edwards's argument left him in an ironic spot, and though he tried to extricate himself as best he could, it was not a terribly convincing performance.

As it turned out, Edwards was able to choose half the council, or almost half. He brought in two outsiders, David Hall from Sutton and William Hobby from Reading, and for more local support, Peter Reynolds from Enfield and Robert Abercrombie, the Presbyterian minister from Pelham. Against Edwards stood Jonathan Hubbard of Sheffield and some of the more powerful ministers of the county: Breck of Springfield, Joseph Ashley of Sunderland, Timothy Woodbridge of Hatfield, Chester Williams of Hadley. Each minister brought along a lay delegate from his church; so there was a total of eighteen men to sit in judgment on Edwards. At Edwards's request, the council added one more minister, Edward Billing of Cold Spring, who was known to be a

71

friend of Edwards. But Billing came only under the protest of his own church, and the Cold Spring church refused to send a delegate along with him.[26]

That missing delegate proved to be the deciding factor. All the other lay delegates voted along with their ministers, but Billing had only his own vote to offer. In the end the decision had ten men against Edwards, nine for him; indeed, the vote would not even have been that close had it not been for the presence of the men from outside Hampshire County. The report of the council, issued on June 22, 1750, found Edwards and his congregation "diametrically opposed to each Other" on the question of sacraments, and considering the state of affairs in the Northampton church, recommended a separation between pastor and people. To underscore their point, the majority of the council further recommended that the separation take place immediately. With a weak bow in Edwards's direction the council noted that there was "no other point against him" than the question at issue: "And altho we dont all of us agree with Mr. Edwards in our Sentiments upon ye Point," they went on, they would certainly recommend him to any church for a future position – any church, that is, that would agree with him on principles.[27]

Despite some futile words of support from a minority report of council members, it was all over for Edwards in Northampton.[28] It was pretty much all over for him in Hampshire County. He knew, as certainly the members of the council knew, that there were few churches in the area that could in fact agree with him on principles. His rather awkward reversal on the question of the ministerial neighborhood gave perhaps the clearest indication of just how isolated he was in his position by 1750. Where in 1736 he had been the most influential voice in the neighborhood, perhaps the only one who could defend it so forcefully against outsiders, by 1750 he was an outcast, facing only the prospect of moving away.

In a sense he and most of his brethren in the clergy had been drawing apart for some time. All of them had been somewhat disturbed and worried by what they had seen during the Awakening, especially the emotional excess, the censorious bickering, the false religion of rampant enthusiasm. Edwards sought to cure those evils by taking Stoddardean revivalism one step further and making converts be certain of their salvation. He wanted to return to the old distinctions between the saved and unsaved, to make people painfully aware of the differences, and to use that awareness as a means of bringing them to the point of conversion. Most of the other ministers were leaning in the other direction. They wanted to maintain the old local traditions of open communion developed under the leadership of Solomon Stoddard, and most of all they wanted to maintain order in their churches. The evangelical excitement of the 1740s may have brought new life into their churches, but it also brought in new problems. For the converted saint, the line between assurance and arrogance was a thin one; the language of salvation could also become the language of attack. For the ministers, making that assurance an important part of church polity could leave them and their churches divided, constantly involved in trying to make judgments, trying to winnow the pure from the impure. Life could become especially difficult if the minister himself were judged to fall into that latter category. In short, what Edwards represented was not just a threat to local tradition, but possibly a threat to local ministers themselves. If they had survived the earlier threats of the Awakening, they were not about to follow Edwards in creating others. By helping force him from his Northampton pulpit, then, they might well have been preserving their own.

There was a brief postscript to the Edwards affair, a kind of coda that restated the basic position of the county clergy by the early 1750s. Edward Billing, who had dared to come to Northampton to sit on the Edwards council despite the wishes of the Cold Spring congregation, was himself dismissed. Like Edwards, Billing had come to feel that the old Stoddardean practices were not really valid, and that a profession of grace must precede each individual's admission to communion. And like the Northampton people, the people of Billing's church disagreed and insisted that he change his position; there was no doubt here, too, that considerable ill feeling between Billing and his people helped make the controversy much more unpleasant. When a council of local ministers convened at Cold Spring in early 1752 to judge the matter, the affair seemed to Stephen Williams to be "much Entangled – heat & warmth." At one point in the proceedings two of those who had opposed Edwards, Timothy Woodbridge and Chester Williams, apparently thought they had got Billing to admit that he could accept the church's position, and the council recommended reconciliation and peace. But when Billing emphatically repeated his opposition to the Stoddardean principles and to the Halfway Covenant, the council quickly reconvened. Facing the inevitable and probably disgusted with the whole affair, Billing asked to be dismissed from his pastorate. On April 17, 1752, he was.[29]

By the end of the Billing affair the Hampshire County ministers had known division and turmoil for over fifteen years. It was almost paradoxical that they could define a new sense of unity only by taking action against two of their fellow ministers. But it was the moment of crisis raised by Edwards's situation in Northampton and later by Billing's in Cold Spring that forced the county ministers to declare a common sentiment among themselves, and by 1752 they seemed more able to act as a group than they had been for some time. Their earlier attitudes toward the revivals of 1734-6 and 1740-1 became almost unimportant by 1750, somewhat beside the point. They had witnessed the revivals with different expectations, but most had gradually come to similar realizations about the inherently dangerous effects of enthusiastic religion. What they saw in Edwards's new position on admission standards they especially feared as likely to exacerbate those effects. Acting with a consensus they had not known in years, they were able to help drive both Edwards and Billing to small and relatively insignificant churches in new towns where they would be less likely to have a great influence on the ecclesiastical order of the county.[30] In doing so the county ministers increased the likelihood that they would be able to maintain common standards of governance within their own churches. But as they were to find out in the succeeding years, their new sense of ministerial unity did not necessarily create a new ministerial authority, and the problems of religious division and turmoil did not necessarily vanish from their midst. The next quarter-century would offer new challenges almost as severe as those the ministers had so recently overcome.

Chapter 4

THE LEGACY OF RELIGIOUS DISSENT

After Edwards and Billing had been dismissed from their churches, the ministers of the Hampshire Association may have hoped to enjoy the future years in peace, free from divisive debate over doctrine. The churches of Northampton and Cold Spring had both found suitable replacements for their departed ministers, and neither John Hooker at Northampton nor Justus Forward at Cold Spring could be considered at all friendly to evangelical or enthusiastic religion or to stringent standards for church admission. Likewise, during the 1750s, a number of other congregations in the county apparently decided to settle for a little less religious excitement, and they filled vacancies in their pulpits with orthodox, well-trained young men, many of whom were openly opposed to Edwards and the principles he had lately espoused. At West Springfield, for instance, Edwards's former supporter Samuel Hopkins died in 1755 and was succeeded by Joseph Lathrop, who had lived and studied for two years with Robert Breck after graduating from Yale. And at Hadley, a younger Samuel Hopkins, son of the West Springfield minister, took over the pulpit when Chester Williams died, but the new minister must have seemed almost as dead as the old; his preaching style was, according to later accounts, "dull and languid." Moreover, even though he was Jonathan Edwards's nephew, he was reputed to be "in opposition to some of the distinctive points in the system of his uncle," and there was certainly little of the revivalist about him. In general, the ministers who had helped usher Edwards and his principles out of Northampton could feel assured that the new crop of ministers coming into the established churches was much of their opinion in matters of doctrine and decorum; none seemed likely to endanger the fragile peace in the region by reviving the extreme religious passions that had only recently abated.[1]

But their peace of mind could never be complete, because the comparative calm in the county did not prove to be universal or even especially long-lasting. The Great Awakening had done much to stimulate public energy and undermine ministerial authority, making it almost impossible for ministers to restore that authority fully in later years. Despite whatever agreement may have come to exist among most local ministers with regard to the evils of enthusiastic, evangelical religion, there still remained people both inside and outside their churches who did not share their willingness to put the spirit of the Awakening so quietly to rest. For some it was primarily a question of individual purity, the agonizing struggle for personal conversion and the enduring concern over one's prospects for salvation or damnation. Yet others expressed a desire to redefine their sense of religious community, to come together with those whose purity seemed certain and to draw apart from those whose spiritual state seemed questionable. This insistence among some parishioners on clear spiritual distinctions continued to pose a threat to the established clergy in the established churches, as some of their people set increasingly stringent standards, tolerating less and demanding more. The attacks on ministers that had become so prevalent with the heightened religious emotions and expectations of the Awakening years proved to be not just a passing phase, not just the product of spiritual anxieties run temporarily wild; they continued to crop up in church after church long after the initial excitement of religious revival had passed away.

In the years after the Awakening, then, the established ministers of Hampshire County found that a good deal of their time and energy had to be turned to protecting each other from such abuse and effrontery. Many suffered as individuals, and they all suffered as a group. Though the Hampshire Association of Ministers still claimed to represent a source of regional authority above the individual churches, the recurring, and largely successful, lay challenges to ministerial authority in particular churches tended to undermine the credibility of the Association as a whole. By the time of the Revolution it had long since become reasonably clear to everyone, ministers and lay people alike, that the clergy's claim to collective authority rested more on pretense than on actual power.[2] If people sought outside help in resolving their religious disputes, they increasingly began to call upon higher secular, rather than religious, authorities. More often, however, they simply chose to settle their own affairs by themselves, ignoring or openly rejecting the intervention of outsiders altogether. Even those who no longer chose to call themselves Congregationalists still insisted on their right to determine their particular religious standards at the local level.

Perhaps the most striking testimony to the powerful effect of the Great Awakening was the way the spirit of religious revival continued to be a vital part of some people's lives, even for a few who had not been touched by the Awakening in the first place. When the Awakening swept Hampshire County, Seth Coleman was still an infant, probably more aware of the commotion he caused in his parents' household than of the commotion in the community at large. His family moved from Hatfield to Amherst in 1742, just as the intensity of the Awakening was beginning to die down and religious life in the region was beginning to return more or less to normal. But though young Coleman grew up in these somewhat more placid times, he did not miss out on the revival experience altogether. In the winter and spring of 1753, around the time of his thirteenth birthday, he became aware of "some special attention to the things of religion in Amherst," when once again people began holding extra meetings to discuss spiritual matters. "In the early part of this season of the Spirit's visitation," Coleman later wrote, "my mind was arrested to the concerns of my soul, and my anxiety arose much higher than ever before." Full of both doubt and hope, he began to seek counsel with the town's minister, David Parsons, and he continued to visit Parsons periodically throughout his adolescent years. By 1761, when Coleman was about to leave to matriculate at Yale, he had still not overcome his spiritual agony but "Continued to hunger and thirst after holiness."

> I had a peculiar dread of being left to the abusive sin of using what few talents God had been pleased to entrust to me with, in the service of an opposing kingdom and not in his service . . . The idea of committing one sin, pierced my heart with many sorrows; and yet I was conscious of being guilty of committing them every hour.

When he unburdened himself in a long conference with David Parsons, the minister gave him no definite reassurance about his self-doubt other than to remind him that "That is the temper of a Christian."[3]

Coleman's individual struggle was in many ways no different from the struggles of countless Christians in Puritan New England. Like his forebears a century before, Coleman turned inward to probe his heart and try to discover the true nature of his soul, always living with the unsettling awareness of his own sinfulness. What makes Coleman's ordeal noteworthy in the context of the post-Awakening years is that he did not undergo the experience alone but apparently partook of a general movement among many of his fellow townspeople, all of them under the guidance of their minister. Indeed, when Coleman came home from Yale on spring vacation in 1765, he again

> found the Spirit of God operating upon the minds of many of the inhabitants. Many were in great anxiety for their souls, and some "rejoicing in the hope of the glory of God" . . . In the evening [I] attended a singing meeting at Mr. P——'s, which was turned into the most solemn religious meeting I had ever seen.
>
> After the exercise of singing, Mr. P—— addressed the meeting, in a very solemn manner upon the subject of religion. Every one present seemed deeply affected; there was scarcely a dry eye in the room. Many were in deep distress for sin, ready to cry out, "What shall I do to be saved?" Some were so debilitated by their distress for their souls, that they were unable to walk, or stand . . . The meeting was closed with prayer. I returned in agony of soul.[4]

Parsons, of course, had been one of Jonathan Edwards's local supporters both during the Awakening and at the time of Edwards's dismissal, and one might expect him to have been favorably disposed to a revival of the spirit among his people. It seems equally significant, however, that his people responded so immediately and so emotionally to this revival, whether because of his encouragement or not. Over twenty years after the Awakening had passed into memory—and even into some disrepute—"deep distress for sin" could still become manifest as a collective experience marked by shared excitement and expressive participation. Though now exceptional, such a phenomenon was hardly extinct.

The "Spirit's visitation" that affected people in Amherst apparently touched at least one person across the river in Northampton. Joseph Hawley, who had taken such a prominent role in the dismissal of Jonathan Edwards in 1750, spent the next few years after the controversy watching his town suffer the consequences of its actions. Unable to procure an immediate replacement for Edwards, the people of Northampton found themselves in the embarrassing position of having to ask their former minister to stay and preach to them for a few months. Then, becoming unhappy with that uncomfortable arrangement, they let Edwards go for good and suffered through three years of making do with temporary preachers, some of them serious applicants for the job, but some of them only second-rate itinerants. Writing from his new home in Stockbridge, Edwards noted that his former parishioners "are in sorrowful circumstances, are still destitute of a minister, and have met with a long series of disappointments." Only in 1753, after local inhabitants had become increasingly exasperated and contentious, and after several candidates had refused to accept the job because of the existing tension, did the people of Northampton unite in their choice of Thomas Hooker, the man who would be their minister until his death in 1778.[5] Hawley no doubt shared in the relief that came with Hooker's acceptance, but he also felt himself burdened with a growing sense of personal guilt for the trouble he had helped create. Though the church had found peace, Hawley had not, and in 1754, as he later wrote, "God began to shake me."[6]

His spiritual remorse first led him to write Edwards, apologizing for his actions and words, which he admitted were "Irreverent immodest derisive magisterial & savouring of haughtiness & levity." More chastened by Edwards's rebukes than pacified by his eventual forgiveness, Hawley struggled with his conscience for a few more years until, in 1760, after Edwards was dead, he wrote to the Reverend Hall of Sutton, one of the ministers from outside Hampshire County who had come to lend his support to Edwards. Hawley's letter was remarkable not so much for its further admission of guilt as for its tone of almost utter self-loathing and abasement. "I appear to myself vile," he wrote, "and . . . abhor myself, and repent sorely . . . I am most sorely sensible that nothing but that infinite grace and mercy, which saved some of the betrayers and murderers of our blessed Lord, and the persecutors of his martyrs, can pardon me." He went on to add that the people of the Northampton church needed to consider whether the "odious and ungodly" words spoken against Edwards left them all "guilty of a great sin [and] lying under great guilt in the eyes of God."[7]

If ever a sinner felt himself in the hands of an angry God, it was Joseph Hawley. However haughtily he may have clung to his Arminianism during the Great Awakening of the 1740s, his personal awakening in the 1750s left him speaking the language of sin and repentance his cousin Edwards had spoken years before. In purely personal terms, Hawley's inner struggle with guilt would be one of the main factors contributing to the recurring melancholia that plagued him throughout the rest of his life. Moreover, this agonizing reappraisal of his past would provide at least one reason for his growing antagonism toward his other cousin, Israel Williams, in the future. For Joseph Hawley as for Seth Coleman, the spirit of the Awakening may have come long after the mass movement had dissipated, but the impact it had on his perceptions proved to be substantial and sustained.

Still, the spiritual transformations of several people in Amherst or even of one especially prominent person in Northampton might not themselves seem greatly momentous or disturbing to the members of the Hampshire clergy. Quite the contrary: most ministers would generally be glad to see people turning increasingly to religion as long as they did so within the proper bounds of ministerial guidance and church discipline. Certainly David Parsons seemed to maintain harmony with the most spiritually intense members of his Amherst congregation, and likewise John Hooker, Edwards's replacement in Northampton, was able to establish a strong and lasting relationship with Joseph Hawley, even though Hooker was not the sort of minister to push personal repentance and revival to extremes.[8] What worried local ministers were more disruptive manifestations of religious zeal emerging throughout the county at about the same time. The old problems of the Awakening years – especially the stringent standards of personal purity and piety imposed upon ministers by members of their congregations – repeatedly resurfaced to create crises in a number of churches, dividing the people and eventually driving some ministers from office. Moreover, even those ministers who did not suffer serious challenges themselves still had to be sensitive to the implied threat they all faced in common. Lay disaffection and dissent could never be taken for granted by any minister.

The most striking sign of this danger recurred with disturbing frequency in the years after the Awakening. Not many ministers in Hampshire County had been dismissed before, but between 1746 and 1776 over a dozen lost their jobs, and a few others just barely managed to keep theirs.[9] The cases of Jonathan Edwards and Edward Billing, in which the majority of the other ministers worked almost as accomplices in helping get rid of the ministers, were quite the exception. More often the members of the Hampshire Association had to step in to defend their fellow ministers — usually without success. Pelatiah Webster of Quabbin, for instance, found his ability to serve capably as minister "very much Impeded if Not wholly frustrated & Cutt off... by the Great Disaffection & Ill will of Sundry Inhabitants who keep up contention, Endeav[or] to disaffect others." He wrote to Breck and the other members of the Hampshire Association in 1754 complaining that the "reflections & Slurs which are cast on the Moral character" were keeping about two-thirds of his people away from services, and he wanted some outside help. When a council of ministers went to Quabbin to look into the matter, they tried earnestly to bring about some degree of reconciliation, urging the people to submit to Webster and Webster, "by all the arts of tenderness, Gentleness, and Ministerial Fidelity to endeavour to regain the Love & Esteem of them who are so offended." As the council so ominously pointed out, "the Dismissing Ministers purely for popular Disaffection is a [thing] of dangerous consequence, and like to have an extensive bad Influence."[10]

Indeed, the bad influence seemed to be spreading, and a few years later John Ballantine refused even to attend such a council called at Blandford because he felt the council had been too hastily summoned by only one party, those people who wanted to dismiss their minister, James Morton. "I know no reason in a controversy between equals, that one party set up a Judicature and the other party be obliged to submit to it," Ballantine wrote. "These disaffected persons did not want advice as they pretended, they wanted a council to come and execute a sentence against Mr. Morton." Although some ministers refused to sit as executioners for their unfortunate colleagues, that did not stop the executions from taking place. Morton was dismissed from his post at Blandford in

1767, just as his predecessor had been in 1747 and his successor was later to be in 1772. And despite the conciliatory advice of the council at Quabbin, Pelatiah Webster lost his job too.[11] In a number of cases the attacks on ministers "purely for popular Disaffection" may have been as unfortunate and unfair as the Hampshire Association's council at Quabbin had suggested, but there seemed little the defending ministers could do. Especially when there seemed to be no complex doctrinal issue at stake, but instead a public question about the morals and reputation of a minister, or even worse, a refusal to pay him his salary, outside ministers could only urge the town to reconsider. And among themselves they could only lament the shabby treatment men of their profession were having so often to face.

The fall of one was a warning to all. To be sure, most of the dismissals took place in some of the smaller, newer towns in the county, where in many cases a growing, changing body of recently arrived settlers had not yet developed a sense of spiritual harmony and ecclesiastical stability. Except for Edwards none of the ministers in the major towns along the river faced any serious threat to his job—at least before the Revolution. But even the well-established ministers were not immune from open opposition and occasional abuse from those who questioned the standards and practices of their pastor. At Robert Breck's church in Springfield a member of the congregation named Joseph Ashley became openly critical of the minister in 1764 for refusing to invite George Whitefield to preach when the evangelist once again passed through the region. Two years later one Jedediah Bliss, a tanner who apparently objected to the practice of singing in church, once began to read aloud during the singing of a hymn. Bliss, described as "an eccentric man . . . lacking in judgment, and rather coarse fibred withal," was duly rebuked by Breck and eventually made to apologize for his effrontery. Rather than allow Ashley or Bliss to break away from the church in protest—which might actually have been the more agreeable solution for Breck as well as for the two unhappy parishioners—the minister made sure he kept them under his personal discipline.[12]

The Reverend Samuel Hopkins of Hadley faced a much more troubling problem with Charles Phelps, a prosperous farmer who had recently served a term on the town's board of selectmen. By the late 1750s Phelps had reached the conclusion that he could no longer go along with Hopkins's Stoddardean practices, and in January of 1760 he "appeared and declared himself of different sentiments from this Chh. in respect of the Qualifications of such as are to be admitted to full Communion." Apparently now inclined to favor the stricter standards that Edwards had espoused years earlier, Phelps insisted that the "difference between him and ye Chh. herein [was] a Point of such Importance that He could not in conscience hold Communion with a Chh. of different Sentiments from him." The Reverend Hopkins, in turn, had good reason to be torn in his sentiments. On the one hand he had to recognize the possibility that if an influential figure like Phelps were to reject the church's standards, others might soon follow his example. And yet at the same time he could not easily surrender his authority to this challenge and reopen a divisive debate that had long since been laid to rest in his church. In Charles Phelps the Reverend Hopkins clearly had a much more powerful voice of dissent than, say, Breck had in Jedediah Bliss, and he no doubt realized that he could do little to mollify or control him. In the end, then, trying to preserve his congregation's peace and his own job, he decided that Phelps had essentially already cut himself off from the church's jurisdiction, and he let the unhappy Edwardsean break away from the church.[13]

On a somewhat lesser scale, Westfield's John Ballantine, surely one of the more moderate ministers both in theology and in personality, suffered a string of disturbing incidents throughout the 1760s. In 1762, for example, when he held the wedding of his niece at his house, he knew that it might cause offense to invite some townspeople and not others, so rather than invite everyone he invited no one. He thereby offended everyone. There was some disparaging talk in the town, and Ballantine took it personally as a threat to his position as minister. "How watchful is Satan for opportunities to alienate people from me," he fretted. A few years later he was insulted by one of the town's leading citizens because of "a plain sermon delivered last Sabbath against idleness." "May none of these things move me," he cautioned himself, but it was clear that these things could hardly help but move him.[14] He had seen enough trouble in the other towns to make him understand how serious even these apparently minor rebukes could be.

In the sensitive atmosphere of the post-Awakening years, a slur against the minister could well grow into a more general feeling of dissatisfaction among his people, and his people might be much less willing than before to overlook his mistakes, whether theological, social, or otherwise. If some became upset over certain conditions in the church – say, as was later the case in Ballantine's church, over the seating arrangement or the introduction of hymn singing[15] – they might walk out and threaten never to return. The ideal of harmony and mutual toleration that had always been so important to the governance of a church seemed repeatedly challenged by a growing willingness of some people, sometimes even whole congregations, to take action against their ministers for any number of reasons. For Ballantine the appearance of such rapid alienation between a pastor and his people might be explained as the work of Satan; but in the context of the times, it might be more accurately described as the work of the Great Awakening.

Ballantine, like any number of other ministers in the county, had yet another, equally troubling, problem left over from the Awakening, one that lay not inside his church but outside it. In April of 1753 he recorded in his journal the ominous note, "Seperates raised a Meeting house." For about five years there had been a small band of Separates living in Westfield, and now they seemed prepared to stay. By the end of the year, in his annual tally of Westfield families, Ballantine noted that there were thirty-eight adult Separates residing in town, not a terribly large total perhaps, but large enough to be disturbing. For the next few years he carefully kept track of the Separates in town, counting their numbers, looking over his shoulder to see what they were up to. Even some of the people in his congregation became concerned and asked him how they should act regarding people who "walk disorderly." He assured them that they had best keep away from the Separate meeting, and he no doubt wished the Separates would keep away from his people as well. Separates were "grievous wolves," Ballantine wrote. "They do not spare ye flock when ye shepherd is with them."[16] For Ballantine and other ministers who had so recently lived through the Great Awakening, the Separates were the worst thing to come out of it.

Separates posed a danger because they rejected the commonly accepted standards of order. Like Charles Phelps of Hadley, they too chose to break with the established churches rather than tolerate religious standards they thought to be too lax. But unlike

Phelps, an individual who apparently lived quietly apart from his former church, groups of dissenters organized into Separate congregations had the reputation of being a defiant, disruptive force, a real menace to the ministry. Dissatisfied with the halfhearted evangelical efforts of the established ministers, they seemed often to follow the example of enthusiasts like the itinerant James Davenport, indulging in the excessive behavior that caused so much worry during the Awakening: the physical and emotional expressions of supposed salvation, the insistence on judging the saved and the damned, and most of all, the willingness to assign established ministers to that latter category. It was not just what they said that was a problem; it was as much how they said it. They not only stood outside the bounds of normal governance, at least as far as the county's leading ministers were concerned, but they seemed exceedingly proud of that stance. In forming their own churches these dissidents accepted no authority other than the authority of their collective religious experience, and no council of ministers could bother them in the least.

That independence was what bothered established ministers most. Such a defiantly independent "come-outer" stance had a long history in the traditions of Protestant Christianity, and it had long posed a serious problem to both church and state. Small wonder, then, that "disorderly" was the word so often used to describe the Separates: in a world where the church mattered so much in directing both spiritual and secular concerns, to stand brazenly outside the established order was essentially to upset and threaten that order. Ballantine and his fellow ministers had good reason to keep track of what the Separates were doing.

Massachusetts and the rest of New England had certainly known religious dissent before, almost from the first years of settlement. From Anne Hutchinson and Roger Williams to Baptists, Quakers, and Anglicans, dissenters had generally been persecuted and harassed. But by 1728 the worst of the official persecution was over, and the Massachusetts General Court had even extended a degree of toleration. Accepting the fact that many Baptist dissenters refused to pay taxes to support Congregational ministers, the General Court gave formal exemption to those "who alledge a scruple of conscience as the reason of their refusal to pay any part or proportion of such taxes . . . *provided* that such persons do usually attend the meetings of their respective societys assembling upon the Lord's day for the worship of God, and that they live within five miles of the place of such meeting."[17] The Standing Order could tolerate them, albeit somewhat grudgingly, as long as they kept to themsleves and conformed to the standard practices of having a distinct, organized, and regularly gathered church body. If the General Court could not enforce orthodoxy, it could at least encourage order.

In some cases the early Baptists were as socially conservative as their Congregational neighbors. During the Great Awakening many of them were outspoken in their criticism of the religious disorders sweeping the land, and in Hampshire County the Reverend Edward Upham of the Baptist church at Agawam joined the majority of local Congregationalist ministers in endorsing Chauncy's *Seasonable Thoughts*. At nearby Brimfield a Baptist church formed in the 1730s existed relatively peacefully without causing any apparent disruption to the Congregational church there during the years of the Awakening.[18]

In one rare case, in fact, the Baptists at Agawam actually came together with the Congregationalists to form a single congregation. Upham had left to go to Newport, and the Reverend Sylvanus Griswold united both groups under his leadership. He agreed, for instance, to perform both infant and adult baptisms, thereby placating everyone. Following Griswold's ordination in February 1762, the Boston *News Letter* applauded the show of harmony:

This people have with a truly Catholic Spirit, united and agreed to worship and sit down at the Lord's Table together, allowing to each other without offence full liberty to follow the Dictates of their own Private Judgement, with respect to Baptism.[19]

John Ballantine was present at the ordination ceremony, and he too came away impressed with the "rare instance of Catholicism" he saw there:

I was well pleased with it. It appears to me quite reasonable that we should hold communion with those with whom we hope to live in heaven, though they differ from us in some non-essentials, as the subjects and mode of baptism. All true Christians are members of Christ . . . So should Christians deal with each other. Perhaps some things are left obscure by God to exercise the charity of his children. It is arrogance in any man to set himself up as the standard, and condemn or approve others according as they appear when measured by their standard. I disclaim infallibility in myself and will not allow it in others.[20]

Ballantine's ruminations on the meaning of the day offered a good indication of what was the utmost concern in his mind, and probably in the minds of other ministers as well. It was not so much the substance of religion as the style. Within certain limits he could tolerate Baptist doctrine, suspend judgment over minor particulars, and even hope someday to join Baptists in heaven. He could not tolerate, however, the arrogance and infallibility with which some people upheld their own standards. The distinction between belief and behavior, in short, was the line that divided acceptable Baptists from deviant Separates. Ballantine was willing to live in harmony as long as he did not have to live under attack.

But by 1760, Ballantine must have realized that the prospects for harmony were hardly promising. During the years after the Awakening, the line between Baptists and Separates came to be less clear in the minds of many people, including some Baptists and Separates themselves. In their search for a position of purity outside the regular Congregational churches, various Separate groups rejected the Congregational practice of infant baptism along with other supposedly loose sacramental practices, and they chose rather to adopt the Baptist practice of adult baptism. They also rejected the notion that they should pay for the support of the unconverted, uninspiring, unsaved, and deadly dull Congregational ministers they so strongly detested. With these dissenting congregations claiming the right if not really the true identity of Baptists, there came to exist a wide range of groups outside the regularly established, tax-paying order. As a result, the official toleration extended to Baptists since 1728 became extremely fragile. By 1753 the General Court was changing its exemption laws to try to exclude Separates from the privileges offered true Baptists, to catch these unruly people who dared to break away from their regular churches and to refuse to pay for their support.[21] But despite the restrictions and tests thus created, it was not always easy to tell a Separate from a Baptist. To many Congregationalists in the post-Awakening years, both types of radical dissenters had a similar effect on society, and they looked about the same.

Nothing offers a better indication of the growing concern over the threat of religious dissidents than the increasingly vigorous and often indiscriminate attacks on Baptist and Separate groups in the 1760s and early 1770s. In a sense the persecution and anger may have stemmed as much from the heightened fears of Congregationalists as from any real actions taken by those outside the regular churches; but still, the growing numbers of such groups and their very existence as distinct and even competing alternatives gave some foundation to the perceptions of Congregationalists. No one could be quite sure what the separating groups had in mind, and no one could be quite sure of keeping them under control.

At Brimfield, for instance, the old Baptist community came under attack and was saddled with much of the blame for a dispute that created a split among Congregationalists. In 1762 an outlying part of the town, where both Baptists and Congregationalists lived, split off from the parent town and became an independent district called South Brimfield. As might be expected, the separation of the new district called for the construction of a new meetinghouse, and the construction of a new meetinghouse called for a good deal of disagreement and debate over the site. The new district quickly fell into eastern and western factions – the east inhabited by most of the Congregationalists, the west by a mixture of Baptists and Congregationalists – each wanting the meetinghouse built on its side of town. After a number of failed attempts to find a site acceptable to both sides, the majority on the east went ahead and began building a meetinghouse, hoping that the Congregationalists on the west would hold to their promise and "never make any more trouble than for peace sake." But, predictably, the westerners were quite unhappy with the meetinghouse and, as the east-siders complained, "will not come to Hear preaching in it but are still striving to make contentions amongst us."[22]

It was bad enough that so much ill feeling had come to exist, but even worse that the Baptists seemed to be working behind the scenes to keep the parties split. Exempt from taxation for the new meetinghouse, settled in a meetinghouse of their own, the Baptists ostensibly had neither reason nor right to interfere in the squabbles of the Congregationalists. But the people on the east accused them of sinister motives, arguing that "the annebaptice for the sake of their own privat intrest" were working with the west-siders in the conflict, and they warned that the Baptists were out to "manage things so as to make a great Deall of trouble." To

avoid being identified with the forces of disorder, however, the
west-siders reversed the charge and responded that it was really
the eastern party that was getting help from the Baptists. A few
Baptist assessors, they accused, were helping pad the valuation
lists in favor of the easterners, giving the east an unfair majority of
voters. Beyond that trickery with the voters' list, the Baptists
posed an even greater threat in the eyes of the westerners:

> We further beg Leave to Enform this Honbl Cort that one of
> those baptists (& the seinor of them all) who Joyn with the
> East party in all their voteings Respecting building their
> meeting house & granting of money for the same: We are
> Credably Inform'd, & it can be proved that he said that he
> would have a Baptist minister settled in that meeting house
> in the East part of the Destrict with the Space of two years.

But if the people on the west side thus raised the specter of
Baptist subversion of the east, in the end they were the ones
subverted. Frustrated by their failure to stop the construction of
the meetinghouse on the east side, the westerners eventually
threw in with the Baptists. The Baptist minister in town was a
"good Regular Preacher," they explained to the General Court,
and they insisted that they would rather share services with the
Baptists for the time being than have to worship with their antagonists in the east.[23]

It was a curious turn, but it provided an interesting ending to
the affair. In the beginning both sides warned the General Court
that the other was up to something in league with the Baptists.
Each side tried to slander or undermine its opponent by identifying it with the uncertain but apparently unhealthy motives of the
Baptists. Whether the charge was fixing the lists of voters or
working to bring in a Baptist minister, the Baptists were accused
of scheming for "their own privat intrest." The fact that those
interests remained indefinite was the main strength of the slander.
Certainly, as a rhetorical device, the threat of devious machina-
tions by the Baptists was designed to put the officials in Boston on
guard and to put the opposing party on the defensive.

In actuality, of course, the Baptists were probably something
less than disinterested innocents in the affair: they may well have
done some of the deeds ascribed to them, and a few Baptists may
have expressed some desire of putting a Baptist minister into the
new South Brimfield pulpit. At the same time, though, the west-

side Congregationalists were not their captives, but joined them with some apparent willingness. The truth of the matter may well have been that what the Baptists really did was provide an alternative for the alienated Congregationalists, a way for them finally to break with their old church. For the disaffected members, the existence of the Baptist church offered them a refuge and may have made the decision to separate less difficult. For the remaining Congregationalists in South Brimfield, however, that Baptist refuge no doubt provided proof of their worst fears. The presence of Baptists in town did in fact cause trouble. It may not have cost the Congregationalists their meetinghouse, but it cost them some members. If nothing else, they – and worried Congregationalists elsewhere – could look at the situation in South Brimfield and feel even more strongly that Baptists could do Congregationalists no good.

No matter what some people might say about the virtues of a catholic spirit and the evils of doctrinal arrogance, Baptists and Congregationalists were indeed different. It was not just a question of dissimilar practices and beliefs; it had as much to do with a difference of standing within the religious context of New England. For Baptists especially, their minority status in a larger Congregationalist society probably heightened their sense of group identity and made them aware of how important these differences were. They stood outside the theological mainstream precisely because they were critical of certain aspects of it, and to give up that critical stance was essentially to give up the meaning of their beliefs. They might not always engage in the kinds of extreme behavior exhibited by some groups of Separates, but neither could they hope to exist for long as loyal allies of the Congregationalist majority. Even the catholic spirit so widely admired at Agawam lasted only about a decade, and by the early 1770s the Baptist and Congregationalist factions there had fallen into a dispute that dragged on into the Revolutionary era.[24]

Perhaps, had Baptist congregations existed far apart from the Congregational churches, the problem they posed might not have seemed so great. But, as was the case in South Brimfield and Agawam and almost everywhere else, dissenters in the same town eventually had a generally unsettling effect on religious peace. And as a result, Congregationalists responded to the threat in kind. If Baptists were going to be the source of religious controversy and local wrangling, then most towns felt it best to get rid of them. They would cause the same unhappy consequences as Separates. Years of quarreling could only upset the good order of the town, throw the church into confusion, draw members away, even increase the tax burden and depress land values. Given the choice, most people would choose to avoid the problems and live in peace. Given the chance, they would do what they could to make the religious dissidents pack up and leave. In the quarter-century after the Great Awakening, peaceful coexistence and mutual toleration in religious affairs had simply not yet become a workable pattern of life. As long as the Standing Order did in fact stand for order, those standing outside it had some real cause for concern. As long as they were perceived as a threat to it, it remained a threat to them.

In the town of Ashfield the Congregationalist residents and nonresident proprietors made it fairly evident that their goal was total defeat of the Baptists. Actually, a group of Baptists had settled there first, and in 1762 the Baptist settlers had gathered a church and ordained a minister, Ebenezer Smith. Because he was the first established minister in town, they thought he should rightfully receive the land reserved by law for the minister and the support of the church. But by the mid-1760s the town had also been settled by a growing number of Congregationalists, and they soon became the majority. Rather than accept the Baptists' claim to the minister's lands, they joined with the nonresident proprietors and voted instead to make the Baptists pay for the support of the Congregationalist minister, Jacob Sherwin. When the Baptists refused to pay their assigned taxes, the proprietors sold their lands at auction and, so the Baptists claimed, destroyed their orchards, laid waste to their fields, and even took over the Baptist burying grounds. The Congregationalists seemed in no mood for conciliation or toleration.[25]

Indeed, the Ashfield case reveals most tellingly the underlying suspicion among supporters of the established order, namely, that most recent Baptists were in reality Separates who had taken the name of Baptist in order to assume the appearance of social and legal legitimacy. Certainly no other group was as emphatic on that point as the Ashfield proprietors. In 1771 they had to respond to Baptist charges of unfair treatment, and the letter they wrote the General Court was a remarkable piece of invective, sarcasm, and

91

accusation directed against their neighbors. Probably as much as any other contemporary document, the Ashfield letter provides a revealing summary of the fears and hostility generated against the apparent Baptist menace. The Congregationalists' words were as harsh as their earlier actions, and they intended their letter to be the final and fatal blow.

"These people," wrote the proprietors, "who have assumed the name of Baptists were originally Separates, so called." That charge in itself was intended to be the most damning, designed to undermine the very legitimacy of their opponents' calling. Rather than allow them any sense of identity with the established and recognized Baptist churches of the early part of the century, the proprietors tried to lump them together with the unruly elements of the post-Awakening years. In Ashfield as elsewhere, Congregationalists were unwilling to accept these post-Awakening Baptists as true Baptists, protected and exempted by law. To bolster their case the proprietors accused the Ashfield Baptists of committing all the sins of Separates: claiming the right to be teachers, holding their former ministers and congregations in contempt for supposed impurities, attacking the established churches, and refusing to accept church discipline for their own offenses. The petition took especially close aim at the leaders of the Baptist church. By destroying the credibility of the leaders, the proprietors could hope to destroy the credibility of the whole group and make its claim to land and legitimacy ridiculous. The Baptists' pastor, Ebenezer Smith, could hardly be taken seriously as a truly qualified minister, for instance, because he possessed one great flaw: "He is ignorant." The petition recounted an incident wherein Smith had been teaching from a passage that mentioned "the thick bosses of God's buckler," and he persisted in saying "God's butler" even when questioned by one of his hearers. The proprietors concluded wryly, "We do not think he has any supernatural light."[26]

For Ebenezer Smith's father, Chileab Smith, the leading lay member of the Baptist society, the proprietors had nothing but ridicule and scorn. They said that when the elder Smith, who had formerly lived at South Hadley, had once attempted to make some dental instruments, one of his neighbors had started the rumor that Smith was trying out the tools on his own children's teeth. Smith was outraged at the slur, but the South Hadley church refused to back him in his quarrel with the neighbor. Smith finally withdrew in anger. Only then, according to the Ashfield Congregationalists, did he begin to question the purity of the South Hadley church, and only then did he become a Baptist. By extension the experience of Chileab Smith was imputed to more or less all the Baptists at Ashfield. Their religious identity, argued the petition, derived more from their own frustration and arrogance than from any commitment to doctrine or belief:

> For a number of years they did not pretend to be baptists, nor thought of refusing to pay taxes with us, but acted and voted with us in the affairs of the propriety. Their conduct then and since has savored more of a high kind of Quakerism than anything else, in religion. For some time they knew not what they were . . . it became impossible for persons so holy as they & who held such friendly correspondence with heaven, to return to their first station. They remained anonymous until they happened upon the lucky name of Baptists.[27]

In short, cautioned the petition, Separate meetings in Ashfield and in fact everywhere had become

> a receptacle for scandalous & disorderly christians, & may be considered as a sink for some of the filth of Christianity in this part of the country . . . Thus pride, vanity, prejudice, impurity, & uncharitableness seem to have originated & supported a sect so pure they cannot commune with ordinary Christians . . . It has been found that these people have no stability, and their covenents no perpetuity.

It was an attack based not so much on theological as on sociological distinctions: quite simply, those people who became Separates or Baptists did so because they were in some ways social deviants, ungovernable, unpredictable, and unstable. They used their religion as a means of expressing their disorderly notions of other people's impurity. Certainly the General Court must know, warned the Ashfield proprietors, that such behavior could not "answer in any tolerable sense the valuable ends of religion to the Community."[28]

In a sense the Ashfield proprietors may have been right. Although the untempered and vitriolic cynicism of their attack was undoubtedly a little out of line, they had some justification in arguing that "Baptist" and "Separate" had become convenient and almost interchangeable designations for a wide range of religious dissidents. There were, of course, still a few Baptists like Edward

Upham, people who could trace their religious identity back to the Baptist church of the pre-Awakening era. But there were also Baptists of a more recent vintage, hundreds of Chileab Smiths scattered about, people who took the name Baptist primarily as a result of sometimes very particular, yet sometimes rather general and only vaguely defined feelings of dissatisfaction with the spiritual and moral standards of their society. In becoming Baptists or Separates they did not embrace any one coherent, carefully articulated doctrinal position; rather, they adopted a stance. The "pride, vanity, prejudice, impurity, & uncharitableness" the Ashfield proprietors complained of were all elements of that stance, at least as viewed by irate Congregationalists from outside.

From the inside, from the viewpoint of the Separates themselves, everything could be reduced to a single word: purity. It was a notion of the impurity of the established religious and social order that set them apart; it was a conviction of their own purity that bound them together. If there was anything central to the theology underlying that stance, it was not so much the tenets of the pre-Awakening Baptist church as the post-Awakening position of Jonathan Edwards. The issues that had torn the Northampton church in 1750 – Edwards's rejection of the Stoddardean system and the Halfway Covenant, his insistence on proof of grace, his requirement of greater sacramental purity – became the main identifying marks of most of the new Separate and Baptist churches of the 1760s and early 1770s. Though Edwards might have denied and disavowed any link with the Separate movement, it drew on him. To be sure, no dissenting church could properly be called Edwardsean in the sense that it adopted his theology fully, with all its complexity and subtlety. Separates adopted instead the basics, the standards of purity that set the saved apart from the damned. Edwards certainly had no intention of making these distinctions so clear that people could no longer coexist, let alone take communion with each other, but among the Separates that came to be the result. Especially in the religious context of Hampshire County in the years after the Awakening, people who insisted on such strict standards could not find a home in the established churches. Call it arrogance or assurance, the question of purity drove some people outside the regular order and left them angry, unhappy, and unruly.

The other, rather vicious, charge – that Separates were "some of the filth of Christianity in this part of the country" – implying as it did both social deviance and low social status, seemed much more out of line. To be sure, exactly what sorts of people became so disenchanted with the apparent impurity of society is difficult to determine from the surviving records. Given the impermanent and transient nature of many small Separate congregations, historians have been largely unable even to determine the total number of Separates, much less to offer a comprehensive collective profile. The two leading students of the Separate movement have argued that in general the movement "was not just an uprising of the rabble," but that Separates tended to reflect "a fair cross section of the community." Other local studies have suggested similar conclusions, and indeed, with some qualification much the same can be said about the groups of Separates or Separate-Baptists in Hampshire County.[29]

The Baptists at Ashfield, for instance, were by no means the poorest members of the community. Thirteen of the eighteen signers of their 1768 petition to the General Court appeared on the town's 1771 valuation list, three of them in the top quintile of taxpayers and another five in the second quintile; only three had no taxable property at all.[30] At the same time, however, the question of their social status needs to be considered in a somewhat broader regional perspective. A town like Ashfield – and in fact most of the other small agrarian villages where the majority of organized Separate groups lived – had nowhere near the degree of economic development or social stratification that pertained in some of the older, more established towns: even the top taxpayer in Ashfield owned property worth less than nine pounds annual rent, whereas some of the leading men in nearby Deerfield owned property worth ten times as much.[31] The point is that by and large the people who called themselves Separates or Baptists in Hampshire County were comparatively small-scale farmers – not dirt poor, perhaps, but still far from wealthy. Certainly Separatism was not a movement that appeared to have much appeal among the county's elite.

Indeed, the Separate movement generally developed a defiantly antielitist point of view. One did not have to be a social deviant to feel some degree of disaffection for those who governed the social order. As had been the case at the height of the Great Awakening, the vision of a purer, more spiritually oriented society in the past came into conflict with the awareness of the worldly, unworthy state of society in the present, and the growing concerns generated by this conflict could quickly focus disapproval on established religious and secular leaders: ministers because they seemed too comfortable and complacent, unsaved and therefore incapable of saving others; and prominent laymen because they seemed more concerned with earthly wealth and power than with the more important rewards of eternity. Though Separatism cannot be reduced simply to a class-based form of discontent, it did confront clerical and political elites with a clear challenge from below.[32] Perhaps most important, the challenge came not only from disruptive individuals who cut themselves off from church and community, but from groups of like-minded dissidents who joined together to organize their own bases of mutual support. More than anything else, it was the creation of these alternative institutions that made the Separate movement such a disturbing source of dissent.

Probably no single case points up the continuing challenge posed by these standards of purity more effectively than the experience of another minister named Smith, this one Jedediah Smith, the Congregationalist pastor at the small town of Granville. During the 1750s and 1760s Smith became involved in a dispute with a handful of people in his town, and the contention remained unsettled until well into the 1770s. In the end the issue of ecclesiastical purity overwhelmed both him and his church. If nothing else, his experience showed that the fears of the established county ministers were not mere paranoia, not just the products of nagging anger and irritation over their inability to rid their territory of a bothersome theological issue. As the rest of the county ministers looked helplessly on, the actions of a few dissidents led to a crisis that ultimately cost Smith his church and, indirectly, his life.

In 1756, when Smith first came to Granville, he entered an already difficult situation. Two years earlier, in 1754, the members of the church had drawn up "Some general rules," and they had made it clear then that theirs was to be a church of a decidedly Edwardsean stamp. They agreed that evidence of grace was "of absolute necessity in order to a right Receiving the Lords Supper," and they determined to establish an examining committee to help the minister decide exactly who should be eligible.

Anyone who tried to argue the Stoddardean position that the sacrament could be a converting ordinance would "not be admitted into our Fellowship or communion." Lest there should be even the slightest doubt about where church members stood, they took pains to make themselves as clear as possible: "As for that that is called the halfway covenant we see no Scriptural warrant for it neither do we admit it into our Chh . . . As for the Stodarian Principal we will have nothing to do with it." Perhaps more clearly than any other church in the county, the Granville church rejected the theological and ecclesiastical norms that governed throughout the area.[33]

But by the time Smith was ordained at Granville things were changing. Granville was a fairly new and rapidly growing town, and as more and more people entered the town and the church, the Edwardsean faction evidently began to be overtaken in numbers. In 1756 the church voted to change its principles, to adopt the Stoddardean system and the Halfway Covenant. Indeed, the ordination of Jedediah Smith, a minister openly committed to these policies, was in itself no doubt a clear sign of the new direction the church was taking.[34]

Not everyone agreed with the changes, however. By October of 1757 the members of the church had to wait through three adjourned meetings to consider the complaints of five dissidents who protested the late reversal. "Although we Covenanted together to walk according to the Platform," wrote the unhappy members, "now we think you have warpt off in Some Points." They went on to list several grievances, chief among them the lax method of admission that had been recently adopted by the church. Because the Granville congregation had so obviously broken the covenant of 1754, the writers felt that they could no longer be bound by any obligation to the church. Two other specific complaints, however, had less to do with the new practices of the church than with the special concerns of the most extreme sort of evangelicals. Thomas Gillet, one of the five dissenters, had his questions about the church's admission policies, of course, but what bothered him as much was the fact th t "the Chh Suffers not the Brethren to use their gifts in Publick.' Gillet doubtless was something of a lay exhorter, and he felt constrained by the church's unwillingness to hear him. And if his special talents were not enough, his wife

97

Elisabeth testified that "she had heard a Voice which Seised her mind as the Voice of Christ making such Discoveries to her that She was perswaded that the Separates or those so called was of Christs Choosen Number."[35]

In short, though there were only five outspoken dissidents in the Granville church, there seemed to be crystallized among them the basic elements of the revivalistic spirit. They certainly felt themselves spiritually saved and therefore deserving of sacraments that they would not extend easily to other questionable church members. And for at least two of them, the issue went beyond salvation to a form of personal expression; Thomas Gillet thought he should speak, Elisabeth thought she could hear, and both thought the established church was no longer the place for them. Though it could offer communion and baptism to the unsaved, it could offer them neither understanding nor hope. If the dissenters did not immediately adopt the label of Separates, they certainly adopted the position.

These five unhappy people posed a problem for the Reverend Smith and the people of his church, perhaps even more of a problem than anyone could see in the beginning. They had directly challenged church policy, and two of them seemed on the verge of challenging and usurping the role of the minister. Still, there were only five of them causing trouble, and in order to bring them back under the good governance of the church, a committee went to "take Some further Pains" in talking with them.[36] Indeed, compared with the sharp criticism they directed at the church, the response was at first remarkably conciliatory, full of kind words and gentle reminders of Christian duty. The latest covenant of the church had bound the members to avoid "Sinfull Stumbling Blocks & Contentions," and in light of that agreement the separating members were urged to "return with meekness humility faith & true repentance." In a surprising admission of guilt, the Granville church even accepted blame for "so much Coldness deadness Slothfulness & Ereligion among us." Their past conduct may have been "Sensurable," but they asked the absent members only to be tolerant and show a "Spirit of meekness tenderness watchfullness & faithfulness Endured with all Long Suffering Patience & Exhortations."[37]

By making explicit the tension between censoriousness and tolerance the church seemed to go to the heart of the problem posed by the emphasis on spiritual purity. For those remaining in the church the unity of that body must have precedence, and a covenant denouncing "Sinfull Stumbling Blocks & Contentions" only served to underscore the importance of maintaining order. But for the separating members it was quite another question. Faced with an institution marked by religious deadness and falling standards, they could see salvation only outside the church. If they had been inclined to tolerance they would not have separated in the first place. In their terms, any conflict between personal and institutional standards would have to be considered irreconcilable. They did not return to the church.

The church, however, returned to them, but this time with a much less conciliatory tone. Having been spurned in its first effort, the church wrote a second letter that avoided any mention of guilt on its own part and issued a truculent warning to the Separates. They should ask forgiveness, argued the letter, for their "Sins of Ignorance Error & Ereligion" and return to their "lot & Standing" in the church. "We do also Give it in Charge," they concluded, "that you Deseist from all Contempt Discord Debate rangling & Dispising your Brethren." Once again, in much stronger language than before, the church pressed its main attack on Separatism and the threat it posed to corporate church unity. Although the letter warned of "Strong Delusions & . . . false Doctrines with all Deceivableness of unrighteousness after the working of Satan," explicit questions of doctrine were not precisely the point. Here again it was essentially the Separates' arrogant sense of self-righteousness that caused them to reject their fellow townspeople and remain a visible, critical faction outside the good order of the church. Because the dissidents still resolutely refused to be brought back in, the church finally decided to keep them out, formally and for good. In May of 1763 the five separating members were excommunicated.[38] Probably nothing could have bothered them less.

But even for those who still continued to go to hear Jedediah Smith in the regular church, the questions the Separates had raised could not be altogether shut out by the meetinghouse doors. The whole controversy over the Separates and their eventual expulsion from the church caused many to begin to examine

99

more closely the state of affairs in their church. Some did not like what they saw. A group of church members drafted a statement of remorse for

> our Conduct and Dealings with our Christian Brethren call'd the Seperates in not giving Sufficient heed to their reasons and in Destreining their Estates to Support a worship which they could not Profit by . . . and in Censuring and excommunicating them . . . without Sufficient grounds.

As became incresingly evident throughout the 1760s, there were people in the Granville church who actually agreed with the "Brethren call'd the Seperates." The excommunicated members, insisted the writers of one complaint, "we concienciously believe to be more eminently in the truth & order of the Gospel than their censurers . . . and according to our abilities we think it our Duty to Join with to Assist Strengthen and build up in the cause of Jesus Christ with them."[39] If the Reverend Smith and the majority of church members had thought that the Separates were merely outrageous deviants who could be dispensed with and forgotten, they quickly learned how strong a force these dissenters could be as they stood apart from the church.

Moreover, several unpleasant rumors had begun to filter in from outside regarding one of the deacons and leading citizens of the town, Luke Hitchcock. Accused of some devious and possibly dishonest business dealings with people in other towns, Hitchcock became tainted with one of the worst sins of worldliness, personal corruption for the sake of personal gain. No matter how much he denied the rumors, the doubts about his character persisted. In a community of small farmers who took their living from the soil, suspicions of questionable commercial practices could take on a moral significance far beyond the technical legal issues at hand. Indeed, though Hitchcock was apparently never brought to court to face the discipline of secular authorities, the people in his own town used the church as the forum in which to express their sentiments: in order to underline their antipathy toward the defamed deacon, some began to refuse to take communion with him, and others at least suggested that he surrender his position as deacon. Smith, hoping to bolster Hitchcock's standing, invited a council of neighboring ministers from the Hampshire Association, but even their efforts proved futile. Hitchcock remained deacon only amid low rumblings of protest. Some of his chief antagonists, in fact, were those same people who had been most upset by the expulsion of the Separates.⁴⁰

If the animosity directed toward Luke Hitchcock suggested any one thing, it was that there still existed within the Granville church a group of people for whom the purity of their sacraments was an important issue, and the purity of their ecclesiastical leaders perhaps equally important. At the very least, these people had adopted the notion of purity as a means of expressing their discontent with their leaders. Even though the recent policy of the church under the leadership of men like Smith and Hitchcock had been to leave such strict standards to the Separates, other people began to feel that perhaps the Separates had a point after all.

In November of 1769 the church made a remarkable reversal. The members gathered in a meeting, and "after some debate the Chh voted that all Baptised Persons only outwardly Clean & Doctrinally taught may not own their Covenant & have their Children Baptised." The vote, that is, was to give up the Stoddardean open communion and Halfway Covenant and return to the Edwardsean standards spelled out in the 1754 covenant. Several months later the church made its position even clearer when it denied admission to a man and woman recently moved to town "because he was of the Stodinarian Principles." Finally in August of 1770 the church reaffirmed its objections to the Stoddardean principles by voting to reject the doctrine of the Lord's Supper as a converting ordinance; it also voted to reject the application for admission of anyone who believed differently.⁴¹ There is no certain evidence that the Separates had any direct involvement in forcing such a significant shift in church policy. They still remained apart from the church and took no part in its problems. It is likely, however, that they had an indirect influence, primarily because they did remain apart. Seeing the Separates and their apparent standards of purity on the outside, and seeing Deacon Hitchcock and his questionable purity on the inside, a growing number of people evidently began to weigh the differences and feel the need for a change. If they would not be Separates themselves, they would follow to some degree the Separates' example.

Such a change, of course, was an open slap at Jedediah Smith, the minister who had upheld Stoddardean practices ever since he had come to Granville. He had entered with a change in the doctrines of the church in 1756, and now a majority of the church members had turned full circle against both him and his principles. When he refused to change with the church, he began to feel increasingly the weight of hostility and religious conviction pressing against him. The wrongs charged against him had very much to do with doctrinal differences and a feeling that his public sermons seemed "to many of the Chh as they receive them as not Sound & too much Crouding upon the Chh . . . & further Some things that he may have Said more Privately . . . may be Matters of uneasiness." He, along with other members of the church – and Luke Hitchcock was certainly included among these – had "so departed from the Congregational Platform & their Covenant with this Chh as that they are worthy of Discipline & rejection from the Chh upon non repentance."[42] As Jedediah Smith should have learned in 1756, the covenant could be a changeable thing. In effect his people had gone back to their earlier position, the one that had existed before the Separates became an issue. And in the new light of an old doctrine, Smith's actions of the past years, his opposition to the Separates and his support of Luke Hitchcock, left him open to suspicion.

After 1769 or 1770 Smith never again lived in peace with his church. Life had never been easy throughout the 1760s, and it continued to get worse. During the early 1770s he barely managed to hang onto his position, occasionally having to turn to his colleagues in the Hampshire Association of Ministers for support. By 1776 the growing dissatisfaction with his doctrinal beliefs was matched by an equal dissatisfaction with his political beliefs. Smith was reputed to be a Loyalist, and that proved too much for his people to bear. The delicate balance he had maintained tipped against him; he was dismissed, and by April of 1776 he was on his way out of town. Given the temper of the times, or, perhaps, given the frustration he had had to endure, Smith decided to get far away, completely out of Massachusetts and New England. He booked his family on a ship headed south for the Mississippi River, where they would be part of a new colony of settlers near Natchez. But during the trip south he became delirious with fever, jumped overboard, and almost drowned. Soon after the family reached Natchez, in September of 1776, he died, never quite recovered from his fever, perhaps never quite recovered from the painful events of the past few years in Granville.[43]

The case of the unfortunate Reverend Smith was certainly

unique in its eventual tragedy, but it was hardly unique in its general circumstances. No less than Jedediah Smith, a number of Hampshire County ministers faced hard times during the years between the Great Awakening and the Revolution. They suffered severe challenges from within their churches and without, from their own unhappy parishioners or from nearby Separate or Baptist congregations. Despite the efforts of the county clergy to maintain common standards among themselves as a group, different people had different standards that they were not at all unwilling to proclaim. Rather than standing as the main source of sound doctrine and ecclesiastical discipline, the ministers found themselves questioned on doctrine and subjected to the judgment of others. Their collective judgment in matters of dispute was quite often unsolicited by lay people and, more important, went almost always unheeded. By the early 1770s, the ministers' position, as individuals, as an organization, and as a kind of distinct social caste, was no longer as strong and secure as it once had been.

Looking with concern at the situation in 1773, Jonathan Ashley of Deerfield spoke pointedly to remind his congregation of the sacred place of the ministry in New England society. Ministers, he argued, derived both their office and the power of that office from "the mediate agency & authority of God." The people of the congregation could only offer their consent. Gaining the power to appoint and ordain a minister under their own authority would give them by implication the equal right to dismiss their minister—a right that, Ashley concluded, "would be impious and absurd."[44] It was a kind of divine right of ministers Ashley claimed, certainly an extreme reading of both the theology and the history of Puritanism. But the extremism of his words bespoke the underlying desperation in them. Long hostile to assertions of popular authority over the ministry, Ashley had watched such challenges continue strong and disruptive during the years after the Awakening; now faced with a social reality in which ecclesiastical disorder seemed almost painfully commonplace, he used the strongest terms possible to try to reassert the authority of the minister's position.

But the words would prove to have little effect. The subjection of ministerial authority to popular regulation, however "impious and absurd," had become a fairly common phenomenon, almost too common to reverse. During the early years of the Revolution several Hampshire ministers would become prime targets of popular abuse and not so gentle attempts at political persuasion. Some would suffer humiliation at the hands of their people, some even the loss of their pulpits. But despite the immediate political context of the Revolution, these attacks also had their roots in the religious context of the preceding quarter-century. This is not to say simply that certain ministers who had been Old Lights or theological liberals necessarily became Tories, although in a number of cases they did. Rather, a certain continuity ran through the actions of the people. If people could dare challenge their minister in the Revolutionary period, if they could subject him to strict political standards and perhaps drive him from office, they did so with the precedent of earlier cases behind them. Whether a minister was being judged by doctrinal or by political standards, or even by both, the important thing was that he was being judged at all, and that the judgment might be followed by forceful action. As much as anything else, the power of such judgments was the legacy of the Great Awakening and its aftermath.

In an even broader sense, that legacy extended far beyond the ministry to encompass society as a whole. The problems of particular ministers in particular churches—the strict standards of popular judgment and the attendant ills of discord, division, separation, and subversion—could become problems for secular leaders as well. To be sure, some officials tended to pass over the whole issue rather lightly. Looking at Hampshire County's religious unrest from the vantage point of Boston, for instance, a man like Governor Thomas Hutchinson might well have found it difficult to appreciate the importance of these local ecclesiastical controversies. Indeed, after the dispute in Ashfield had been dragging on for a few years and Israel Williams had become personally involved in it by sponsoring legislation in favor of the Congregationalist proprietors, Hutchinson wrote to Williams in 1773 that the issues there "require more thought than I am now able to afford. I have no other interest in them than as the Publick is interested & am open to any beneficial measure."[45] Hutchinson, deeply embroiled in the increasingly hostile political struggles in pre-Revolutionary Boston, simply could not comprehend how a doctrinal disagreement between two groups of settlers in a western frontier village could be worth all the bother, especially the concern of a man like Israel Williams, who certainly must have had other, more pressing, matters on his mind.

On one level, of course, Williams and most of the other members of the political elite in Hampshire County could not spend too much time worrying over fine theological distinctions purely for the sake of theology. Like Hutchinson, they had much more pragmatic interests. Of all the leading figures in the network of secular authority, only Joseph Hawley of Northampton and Charles Phelps of Hadley seem to have been personally wrenched in the soul by the question of purity the Great Awakening had injected into the religious life of the county – and perhaps partly for that reason both Hawley and Phelps had fallen out of favor with Israel Williams and his allies in the county elite. Unlike Hawley, who became, as a nineteenth-century historian has put it, "a Puritan in the staid style of his deportment, as well as in the religious complexion of his mind and life," most of the others came closer to the same author's description of Hawley's colleague, John Worthington of Springfield: "a man of liberal attainments . . . less profound and more facile . . . a scholar and a gentleman, accustomed to the usages of polite society."[46] As much as possible, the men who ran the machinery of politics and patronage in Hampshire County generally remained willing to exercise some degree of tolerance and leave the subtler religious issues to their colleagues and kinsmen in the ministry.

At the same time, however, these leaders knew better than to draw too sharp a distinction between religion and politics. Beyond the strong familial ties that bound together many of the ecclesiastical and secular leaders of the county, there remained a more fundamental connection in their respective social roles. The members of the clergy represented an important source of order and authority, both in their particular towns and at the county level. As the events of the Great Awakening had shown clearly, disorder in the church could easily spread to create a much more general disorder throughout society at large. Though religious dissent might appear to be a mere curiosity or annoyance from afar, within the close context of the region it represented a kind of contagion that Williams and other Hampshire leaders could not dismiss easily. Even if they rarely used their secular authority to intervene directly in religious controversies – as Williams did in the dispute at Ashfield – they at least had to be sensitive to the problems that their brothers in the ministry were facing. A few dissident people could upset the harmony of a single town, and the contagion could spread from town to town throughout the county. As Williams and others had learned only too well in the years after the Awakening, the most dangerous precedent was less one of particular doctrine than one of a more pervasive disorder.

Chapter 5

NEW SETTLEMENTS
IN AN UNSETTLED SOCIETY

It was not just a movement of human souls that shook the order of Hampshire County, but a movement of human bodies as well. During the middle of the eighteenth century New England became a society marked by a sharp increase in geographical mobility, and a large number of the migrants pushed into western Massachusetts. In discussing migration in colonial New England, most historians have tended to emphasize its significance for the older towns the migrants left: out-migration represented, for instance, a necessary response to the growing land scarcity that resulted from population pressure and overcrowding or, put perhaps more accurately, from the unequal distribution of land and wealth.[1] Useful though these analyses are, they tell only half the story. We know less about the effect of migration on the region receiving large numbers of new migrants. In the case of Hampshire County it proved to be quite dramatic. Between 1740 and 1775 the flood of migrants sweeping into the county created a rapid surge of growth and expansion, a sharp increase in both the population and the number of towns. People soon came to live up in the hills as well as down in the valley, in new towns as well as in old ones, in poor towns as well as in prosperous ones. As they did so they transformed the limited universe of the older Hampshire towns into something very different from what it had been on the eve of the Awakening—not only more crowded, but also more complex and divided. Certainly the traditional leadership of the county, already suffering from the disruptive effects of religious dissent, found its effectiveness eroded even further by the rapid spread of the population far beyond its established network of influence. By the time of the Revolution, Hampshire County had experienced a gradual regional transformation that helped

107

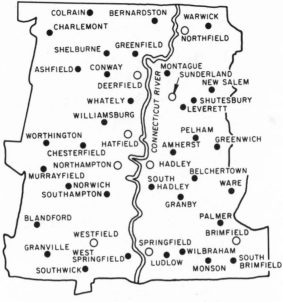

○ Towns Incorporated Before 1740
● Towns Incorporated 1740–1774

Map 1. Hampshire County in 1775.

prepare the way for a subsequent and rather sudden revolutionary change.

Throughout the first century of white settlement Hampshire County remained a vast area inhabited by only a relatively small number of people. As late as 1740 there were only fourteen incorporated towns in the county, and though Springfield was a good-sized town, with almost two thousand inhabitants, the rest ranged in size from a few hundred to around a thousand. Over the years the towns grew steadily but hardly rapidly, with no real evidence of overcrowding. For one thing, there seemed to be little population movement from outside to make the situation any worse. Up until the middle of the eighteenth century the rate of geographic mobility in New England remained fairly low, especially as far as migration to the frontier is concerned.[2]

To some extent the inhabitants of the early Hampshire towns were able to regulate the size of their communities by encouraging a limited degree of out-migration to other areas close by. Around 1677, for instance, a number of families from Northampton led in the settlement of the town of Northfield further up the Connecticut River; likewise, most of the original settlers of Belchertown came from Northampton, Hadley, and Hatfield. This pattern of intracounty migration and settlement of course had its practical limits. The hilly lands on the northern frontier or away from the river seemed remote, difficult to farm, and considering the recurring threat of war and Indian attack, dangerous. More often the people in the county towns dealt with their growing populations simply by dividing more land and opening new areas to settlement. Even Northampton, the second oldest town in the county, did not have its last division of land until 1749. In the cases of Springfield and Hadley, the spread of population to the outlying areas of town was great enough by the 1730s to warrant the creation of separate precincts capable of supporting their own churches and ministers.[3] But even these precincts were relatively close to the original towns, and their inhabitants, like the residents of the other county towns, lived a fairly uncrowded existence within the fertile lowlands of the Connecticut River Valley.

Even for those few goaded by desire or necessity to move to the frontier, there was one other significant factor holding them back: the military situation in Hampshire County seemed dangerously uncertain. Both prospective newcomers and the inhabitants of the older Hampshire towns had before them the often violent history of the county to make them think twice about moving too far into the frontier. In the late part of the seventeenth century the danger was so great in the northern part of the county that the original inhabitants of Northfield had to give up their homes less than a decade after they had settled; the town was abandoned in 1685 and not resettled on a permanent basis for almost thirty years. Moreover, the celebrated sack of Deerfield in 1704 achieved widespread notoriety throughout New England, and the legend of captivity and death served as a grim warning to everyone. Even inhabitants of the well-established towns had to be wary of occasional attack, and every town had its own tales of local farmers who ventured out into the distant fields and did not come back alive.[4] Though Hampshire County never became a major battleground in the eighteenth century, the threat of warfare remained more than just an abstract possibility in the minds of westerners. The thin string of undermanned forts along the western frontier did less to provide a sure means of defense than to underline how isolated and vulnerable the region actually was.

With the end of the Seven Years' War in 1763, however, the situation changed dramatically. By settling once and for all the long-standing competition with the French for control of North America, the English victory removed the last barrier to settling the New England frontier. As one popular farmers' almanac put it,

America will reap the happy Fruits of a bloody war. A vast extent of Territory will be added to the British Empire in America . . . so that the war which at first seemed like to break up our new Settlements will in the Conclusion greatly promote and increase the Settlement and Peopling of America . . . But now behold! the Farmer may have Land for nothing . . . Land enough for himself and all his Sons, be they ever so many.[5]

The writer's emphasis on property and progeny could hardly have been lost on New England farmers. As a number of recent studies of Connecticut and eastern Massachusetts towns have suggested, the older and more densely settled parts of New England were beginning to experience a general economic and demographic crisis: towns were becoming more crowded, and not everyone in the growing population could hope to obtain an adequate holding to support a family. Land was unequally divided to begin with, there was seldom any more common land to divide, and what there was for sale was scarce and expensive. In a society where most people still took their living from the soil, the difficulty of acquiring land proved to be an especially critical problem for many families.[6]

One concerned father, Nathan Birdsey of Stratford, Connecticut, seemingly spoke for a whole generation of eighteenth-century parents when he described his family's predicament in a letter to Joseph Hawley of Northampton:

> As God has blest me with a numerous off-Spring, and it Suiting my Affairs much better to bring my Boys up to Husbandry than to put em out to Trades; but not having Land Sufficient for Farms for em all; I purpose if God shall please to Spare mine & their lives, to Sell Some out-Pieces of Land, & purchase Some of em Settlements in Some new Towns where Land is good & cheap, & ye Title uncontroverted, & Shall be glad of your advice where it wou'd be best to purchase.[7]

On the one hand, Birdsey reflected the standard assumptions of most fathers in agrarian society, a preference for "Husbandry" over "Trades," a desire to see his sons become independent yeomen like himself. But like many other fathers, he could no longer hope to divide his lands equitably among his sons, and the sons in turn could not really hope to make a living on whatever land they did inherit. Other young farmers throughout New England were in similar straits and faced an often unhappy choice: either to take up a different trade or to take up a different residence. Some of them headed for the larger towns and commercial centers to look for work as laborers or tradesmen, but many others began to look to the uncrowded spaces of the western counties "where Land is good & cheap" to find land and a living.

Perhaps the most revealing index of the widespread economic dislocation and migration within New England during the middle of the century was the rise in the number of transients, especially in western Massachusetts. Almost every town in the county had to deal somehow with impoverished newcomers who threatened to be a burden on the town's tolerance and taxes, and local officials increasingly began to exercise their authority to encourage the migrants to keep moving: during the 1760s almost six hundred individuals and families were issued formal warnings, some by more than one town. Following the main highways from the east and the south, and also following their hopeful expectations of relief, many transients eventually came to the larger, wealthier towns in the southern half of the county. Springfield alone issued eighty-seven warnings between 1760 and 1769, and together

111

with Westfield and Northampton accounted for well over a third of all warnings in the county in the 1760s.[8]

The Reverend John Ballantine of Westfield began to worry about the many transients who were flooding into his town. They came to beg or steal, he thought, and in the end they quite often wound up at the town's whipping post before being sent on their way. A few arrived at Ballantine's door. "It is difficult to know one's duty to such persons," he wrote; "there are so many imposters. Kindness encourages them, some of them get more and fare better than many laborious men, which may tempt some to neglect labor and betake themselves to such mean practices." Surely nothing in Ballantine's Harvard eduction had prepared him for dealing with such a sensitive and vexing social problem, but he decided finally that some kind of standard must be enforced. "Every town should maintain their own poor," he concluded, "and if in any case it should be necessary to go abroad, they should be well recommended." Apparently he put his opinion into practice. When he found a strange woman trying to hide herself in his kitchen one night, he asked her to give a good account of herself, and when she failed to do so he turned her out.[9] Unfortunately for Ballantine, very few transients came well recommended by their former towns, but they came nevertheless.

In the end, though, the wandering poor represented only a part of the total, the unwanted underside of a larger movement of humanity that filled Hampshire County in the middle of the century. Other migrants brought the money to buy land and settle more or less permanently, and these permanent settlers were the ones who had the greater impact on the county. In the years following the Seven Years' War, between the provincial censuses of 1765 and 1776, the population of Hampshire County rose from 17,298 to 34,947, a growth of over 100% in a decade, far in excess of both the rate of natural increase and the rate of population growth in Massachusetts as a whole.[10] Yet even more important than the sheer size of the population in Hampshire County was its pattern. Rather than remain concentrated in the established towns of the Connecticut River valley, the population of the county increasingly became widely dispersed over the landscape. People moved into the previously unsettled lands of the frontier or into the sparsely settled outlying areas of the older towns, and as they did so they created dozens of new communities, most of which eventually became independent towns.[11] Indeed, it is the history of the settlers' collective experience, their attempt to establish and maintain themselves in these new towns, that provides the most useful focus for assessing their emerging role in the county as a whole.

To be sure, the process of recreating the familiar patterns of town life seldom came easily. For one thing, people who migrated to Hampshire County in the middle of the eighteenth century did not for the most part come west in groups, inspired by the same ideals of utopian harmony and purpose that had apparently motivated some of New England's first settlers a century or more before. They came together in their new settlements by necessity and chance and therefore had little reason to feel immediately neighborly toward one another. Moreover, the work of establishing a town often provided a better opportunity for contention than for cohesion. Rather than embrace their new neighbors in a spirit of cooperation and communal harmony, some settlers seemed inclined to take issue with them over local grievances. Certainly the experience of the early inhabitants at Ashfield, as we have seen, should counter any overblown notions about the universal prevalence of peace in the new frontier towns. As the Congregationalist proprietors sought to burden the Baptist settlers with increasing taxation and vexation, they made it clear that they were not only unwilling to tolerate a Baptist church, but even unwilling to tolerate the Baptists themselves. If there was any sense of unity in the town, it was defined only by the desire of one faction to have nothing to do with the other.[12]

In other towns the terms of conflict were usually not quite so distinct or divisive. A few towns had ecclesiastical disputes of one sort or another, ranging from doubts about the character of the minister to disagreements about the location of the meetinghouse; at Murrayfield, for instance, the inhabitants had barely been settled before they fell into a dispute over the meetinghouse site that eventually ended with a decision to divide the town into two separate parts.[13] Elsewhere the early settlers often engaged in controversies over somewhat more prosaic issues, like the location of roads, the construction of fences, or the division of land. In a new settlement in which there was much to do, there could understandably be several opinions about what ought to be done, how, and by whom. Such initial disagreements seemed an almost predictable and even necessary part of establishing a new town. Moreover, especially in the wake of the Great Awakening, when the tendency to proclaim the correctness of one's position became common in religious affairs, the insistence upon having one's own way might spill over into secular matters. In general, implicit in the settlement process was the inhabitants' need to define exactly what their town would look like and what it would be like. In the early years, while such fundamental issues remained unresolved, there were many occasions for people to express not just their differences but sometimes even their mutual intolerance of those differences as well.

Still, in order to understand the eventual significance of these new towns in the broader political context of Hampshire County, it is necessary to appreciate the extent to which they represented important sources of political independence and collective identity for their inhabitants. As much as new settlers might bicker among themselves as they tried to sort out their local affairs, as much as they might insist upon shaping the town to fit their own particular needs, they could not long remain unaware of the common needs they shared with their neighbors. Each new settlement eventually became a collective enterprise that engaged the interests and energies of its inhabitants.[14]

On one level there was simply the organization of human resources, the business of assigning people to perform certain necessary tasks in the community. In new towns as well as in old ones, the familiar institutions of town politics provided the formal means by which people defined their collective interests and acted together to pursue them. Moreover, in most new towns the residents had both the opportunity and the need to share the responsibilities widely. When the settlers at Chesterfield held their first town meeting in 1762, they immediately set about creating the major offices of selectman, moderator, treasurer, clerk, and assessor, as well as a few of the lesser offices like fence viewer, surveyor, field driver, and hog reeve. A year later they added even more of these functionary positions, choosing tithingmen, wardens, a sealer of weights and measures, even a sealer of clapboards and roofs. For some men, geographic mobility could lead to upward political mobility. Joseph Burnal, one of the original settlers of Chesterfield, had served his former town of Dudley as tithingman, surveyor of highways, and constable between 1755 and

114

1762, the year he left for the west. In Chesterfield he became selectman in 1762 and later town clerk, a position he continued to hold for years. Almost every man, in fact, got something: in a town of only thirty families, twenty-one of the adult males held some kind of town office.[15]

Such a proliferation of offices was not merely a case of featherbedding or an unnecessary division of labor. It ensured that a large number of men would take responsibility for the various things that needed doing, and that each of those men would have some formal recognition of his service to the town. It goes almost without saying that some jobs were more respected and even more enjoyable than others. And it should also be clear that such a high proportion of the number of jobs to the number of eligible residents could not really continue as the town grew: there were simply not enough town jobs to keep up with the expanding population. But even so, most adult males in the new settlements could expect a generally freer access to town offices than they were likely to have had in the older and larger towns. Where everyone was essentially a newcomer, where no one had any extraordinary claim to wealth, family ties, or tradition, where the number of eligible office holders remained comparatively small, the opportunity for political equality and active involvement could be an important part of binding the people of the community together.[16]

The mutual responsibilities inherent in town politics reflected an even more fundamental aspect of life shared by new settlers, the challenge of making a farm village out of the frontier. An early migrant to one of the unsettled tracts of land in the hills above the river would encounter essentially a wilderness landscape, or at best a settlement struggling through the first stages of clearing and building. The physical obstacles alone could seem frightfully intimidating. Young Joseph Burnal, the six-year-old son of the Joseph Burnal just mentioned, formed vivid memories of the contrasts facing many migrants to Hampshire County. When the Burnals and their cartload of belongings arrived in Northampton, he recalled seventy years later, his main impression was that everything there looked very old. Indeed, Northampton was old – old enough and prosperous enough to have seen its share of unwanted transients. The town constable warned the Burnals not to linger too long in town, and after a very short stay the family moved on a few miles west along the road until they reached a small clearing called Fairfield's Camp, at which point the road more or less ended. Beyond lay only a crooked path through the woods marked occasionally on the larger trees; some of the smaller trees had been cut away and a few logs rolled out, but it was still fairly hard going for people with a cart. When the Burnals arrived at their new home in Chesterfield they found nothing like Northampton; they were only the sixth family in the settlement.[17]

Another migrant, Peter Gibbon of Granville, had an even stronger reaction to his new home. Gibbon had been an apprentice tanner in his former town of Hardwick, and by his mid-twenties he thought he was doing rather well, "gaining property so as to be forehanded and . . . going to set up tanning the next spring." But in 1756 or 1757 a Sergeant Church interrupted Gibbon's serenity and offered to sell him land out in Granville. Gibbon refused the offer, but his wife, apparently somewhat more inclined to be a pioneer – or less inclined to spend the rest of her life in Hardwick – fell prey to Church's sales talk. "And then both of them worried me out," Gibbon lamented,

> and got me to yield to come and settle on this rocky mountain and that just undid me and when I got here, I was as poor as poverty itself, I was deceived by the old man. He told me that he knew to be faults in recommending the land to be better than it was. However, I had got into the woods and a howling wilderness it was. No roads in any direction to lead anywhere but by marked trees. The first summer I had to hire my team work when I could get it and sometimes it came to nothing, and when it did well the vermin of the woods destroyed half of it . . . But I kept clearing my land yearly and I gained slowly and in about eleven years I built a 26 foot barn and I cut hay and grain enough to fill it and had stock enough to eat it, and in fifteen years I built me a house so that I lived in it and kept up a finishing it and adding to it as I was able and I got to live tallerable comfortable.[18]

Such accounts, although no doubt embellished and exaggerated by time, nevertheless contain a basic truth about the unsettled regions of Hampshire County: they were wild and remote, a challenging prospect to a New England farmer. After a trip through some of the Hampshire hilltowns around the beginning of the nineteenth century, Timothy Dwight, one of New England's best-known and most perceptive observers, would point to an enduring

116

problem of the hilltowns, the generally inferior quality of the soil. In the northeastern part of the county, for instance, the town of Montague contained areas of both "tolerably good land" and "lean, miserable soil." Moving south, Dwight found similar conditions in other hilltowns: Shutesbury with soil "encumbered with rocks and stones . . . moist and of an indifferent quality," Belchertown likewise with soil of "loam, mixed with gravel, replenished with stones, and of difficult and expensive cultivation." At Ware the land could best be described by a joke: the land, so the story went, was like self-righteousness – "the more a man had of it, the poorer he must be." It was with good reason, of course, that the first few settlers of the county in the seventeenth century had planted their towns along the Connecticut River. The river itself provided the obvious advantages of easy travel and communications, but more important, the rich alluvial soils of the valley offered farmers an agricultural opportunity unsurpassed in New England. In some of the valley towns – Hadley, Amherst, Northampton, Deerfield, and Hatfield, for instance – Dwight found "eminently pleasant" townships with "fertile and delightful" land, "no more productive grounds in New England."[19]

There seemed, in short, almost a world of difference between the valley and the hills. Certainly young Joseph Burnal's image of "old" Northampton suggests a striking contrast to the unmarked, undeveloped newness of the lands in the hills above the Connecticut River Valley. Almost everything the settlers had they would have to build themselves, not only their own homes, but a meetinghouse, roads, and every other convenience they had been able to take for granted in their former towns. It should hardly be surprising that the very new towns boasted almost none of the shops, mills, and other commercial enterprises that existed in the older towns. But even in the case of the farmer's main source of production, cleared land under cultivation, the residents of the new towns faced a struggle to provide an adequate standard of living. Unlike the inhabitants of the older towns, who enjoyed the fruits of several generations' labor on the land, migrants had before them the onerous, time-consuming task of making farms out of the frontier. Clearing the rocky and wooded land, as Peter Gibbon pointed out, invariably took years, and if the settlers were lucky, the land would give them enough to live on, but not a great deal more.

117

The case of Pelham, one of the hilltowns in the eastern part of Hampshire County, provides a useful insight into the progress of agricultural development. Originally part of a large tract of land owned by John Stoddard and a few others, Pelham was purchased in 1739 by Robert Peebles and James Thornton, leaders of a group of Scotch-Irish inhabitants of Worcester County.[20] As one might well expect, the early years of settlement proved to be a time of slow and almost certainly difficult growth for the farmers of Pelham. By 1745, five years after the first group of migrants arrived, the average farm family had just over ten acres of land cleared for production. Of the seventy heads of household listed in the tax records, only ten appear to have been landless, a fairly low percentage for most New England towns. Only six men, however, had over twenty acres of what was described as improved land, and of those only one had over thirty acres. Most of the inhabitants remained in the middling range, the vast majority with under fifteen acres.[21]

Tolstoy's question—"How much land does a man need?"—has no easy answer, of course. In early New England much depended on the terrain, the quality of the soil, and the use the farmer chose to make of the land: producing grain, perhaps, or raising fruit trees, or grazing cattle and sheep. Recent work by historians has provided rough estimates of the amount of improved land needed to provide a reasonably comfortable and secure existence in eighteenth-century New England. Charles Grant's figures for Kent, Connecticut, for instance, suggest that with about five acres of tillage land and another thirty-five or so acres of other land a farm family could probably get by, "if not burdened with too many mouths to feed." It would take about fourteen acres of plowed land and another seventy-five acres of pasture, meadow, and the like to provide them a living safely above the level of subsistence. More recently Robert Gross has figured that about eight to ten acres of tillage land and fourteen to sixteen acres of pasture and meadow—a total of around twenty-five acres of improved land—would give a family of six a "middle class standard of living." By either standard it seems evident that most Pelham farmers fell well below the line of middle-class comfort in the 1740s.[22]

It would be only reasonable to argue, of course, that the first few years are always the hardest, that conditions would improve steadily over time. Certainly such was the case in Pelham, but

118

only to a degree. Almost twenty years after the initial settlement, most of the inhabitants of the town were able to scratch out barely more than a subsistence living from the soil. The average Pelham farmer of the 1760s had around four to seven acres of land cleared for tilling, another ten or so for mowing, and a few set aside for pasture and orchard. Because it took about an acre of land to support a cow, he could not have too big a herd, and most farmers had fewer than five or six cows if they had any at all; most were more likely to have a dozen or so sheep. Most of the plowed fields were given over to corn and rye, with some perhaps set aside for oats; only a very few farmers grew any wheat, the crop most valued for commercial exchange.[23] Provincial valuation figures for 1771 indicate that by the standards Gross and Grant have suggested for New England agriculture, about two-thirds of the farmers of Pelham still got by on a little less than the average amount of land needed for a comfortably prosperous existence. Although a few families had worked to expand their farms to moderate size, most Pelham residents continued to live on the small plots that had been the norm in previous decades.[24] Because there is no evidence to suggest that their land was especially productive – if anything, it was probably a little below average in quality – we can assume that the Pelham people lived a generally modest life, producing enough for their own consumption but hardly a marketable surplus.

The situation in Pelham was to a large degree the situation in most of the new settlements in Hampshire County: compared to the older towns in the valley, the hilltowns were underdeveloped, and they showed little promise of developing at a very rapid pace. Local officials at Murrayfield took care to add a note to the town's valuation sheet in 1771, pointing out that "Thirty of the above Number of Houses [sixty-five] are Round Log Huts," not the more substantial clapboard houses typical of established New England communities. And at Bernardston the residents based their 1764 appeal for tax relief squarely on the issue of undeveloped land: among the thirty-one families in the town, there were only four hundred acres of improved land – tillage, pasture, meadow, and orchard – barely enough to keep the people going. In a sense the people in the frontier hilltowns lived an almost paradoxical existence of scarcity amidst plenty: their townships contained vast amounts of land for comparatively few people, but only a fraction of it had been put to use.[25] To some extent, of course, the lack of rapid economic development may well have reflected a lack of rising economic desire. That is, rather than push themselves to produce surplus goods for exchange, most farmers may have been generally content to adhere to the standards of family-centered, noncommercial agriculture – to be "tallerable comfortable," as Peter Gibbon had put it, clearing and maintaining just enough land to feed themselves and their livestock.[26] The evidence for the early years of settlement still suggests, however, that achieving even this level of modest comfort was not altogether assured. Most families continued to live on the margin of uncertainty between sufficiency and need. In the years before the Revolution, in short, theirs was a world of possibility rather than prosperity.

For many it could also be a world of debt. No family could be completely self-sufficient, of course; at the very least families usually relied on a system of reciprocal exchanges of goods and labor with their immediate neighbors.[27] But for some finished products – tools, farm implements, household utensils, and the like – hilltown settlers often had to turn to merchants in the larger and more economically developed towns of the county, and with merchants the nature of exchange was not always quite so intimate and informal. The accounts of one such merchant, Elisha Alvord of Northampton, describe a fairly wide commercial network that extended well beyond his own town to nearby Southampton and on up into some of the surrounding hilltowns: Chesterfield, Belchertown, Ashfield, Montague, and Murrayfield. Indeed, between 1762 and 1776 slightly over half of Alvord's accounts involved people outside Northampton, and the pattern of his dealings with hilltown inhabitants provides an interesting indication of the nature of their indebtedness. Like most merchants doing business in the agrarian economy of rural New England, Alvord could not always expect to receive an immediate cash payment for his goods, so he entered into a variety of arrangements with his customers, usually extending credit for long periods of time and often accepting farm produce, homemade goods, or labor in exchange for shop goods. Alvord apparently had slightly different ways of dealing with his local and his out-of-town customers, however, because his willingness to engage in noncash exchanges seemed to depend in large measure on a person's proximity to Northampton. Of some seventy-nine accounts Alvord had with people from the newer towns in the area, only a dozen were paid off solely with goods and labor, and all but four of those twelve were debts owed by residents of Southampton, the village lying next to Northampton. Although in a handful of cases Alvord accepted a combination of cash and noncash payment, for the most part – in forty-four of the seventy-nine accounts – he recorded that the debts were to be paid only "by cash in full" or by the customer's "note of hand" for cash.[28]

Other merchants and creditors might have offered hilltown residents slightly different and even more flexible terms of repayment, but in general both account books and court records suggest that the farmers in these newer settlements increasingly found themselves burdened with notes of indebtedness to men outside their own towns.[29] However patient the creditor might be, those notes would eventually come due, and if the debt were still not paid, the creditor would eventually bring his case to court.

The Hampshire County Inferior Court of Common Pleas heard several hundred debt cases each year – indeed, that was its main function – and an examination of the identities of creditors and debtors reveals quite clearly the position residents of the newer towns most commonly held in the regional network of indebtedness. Not surprisingly, perhaps, around three-fourths of the creditors in debt cases came from the older, more commercially developed towns, and almost half of these plaintiffs identified themselves in the court records as gentlemen, merchants, or traders, or gave some other indication of occupation or status than that of yeoman or artisan. By comparison, inhabitants of the newer towns, most of whom were identified as yeomen, accounted for only around a fifth to a quarter of the plaintiffs, but over a third of the defendants in the early 1760s and almost half ten years later. Hilltown farmers, in general, appeared in court as defendants about twice as often as they appeared as plaintiffs.[30] Many defendants, of course, chose not to appear at all. Given the fairly straightforward nature of the evidence in debt cases and the fairly predictable prospect of a creditor's winning a judgment (the note of indebtedness would usually suffice to prove his case against the debtor) defendants understandably defaulted in their cases to save themselves the time and expense of a trip to court. But whether they appeared in person or not, a growing number of the hilltown inhabitants came to feel personally the weight of legal judgment adding to the general pressure of an already tenuous economic situation.

In one respect, of course, such economic difficulties were individual problems, personal crises that befell particular farmers and their immediate families. At the same time, however, a farmer in a small village struggling to clear his fields and stay clear of debt knew that he was by no means alone in his situation; most likely a good number of his neighbors faced much the same predicament at one time or another, and they too were probably not unfamiliar with creditors and the court. The prevalence of poverty could provide the basis for shared attitudes and even collective activity. People in the hilltowns repeatedly joined together to express in a variety of ways their common antipathy toward the external economic powers that seemed so often to threaten them. The people of Pelham, for instance, gave a very forceful demonstration of their feelings to Solomon Boltwood, a prominent man in neighboring Amherst and a deputy to Sheriff Oliver Partridge. One day in February 1762, Boltwood came up the hill to Pelham on some sort of official business – the exact nature is unclear, but probably to take action in a debt proceeding – and found himself confronted by a group of men and women who greeted him "with Axes, Clubs, sticks, hot water and hot soap in a riotous and tumultuous manner." As Boltwood later complained to his superiors in the county judiciary, the Pelhamites "uttered menace and threatenings of bodily hurt and death . . . and with force of arms obstructed, opposed, hindered and wholly prevented" him from doing what he had gone there to do.[31]

Boltwood's experience may have been extreme, but it nevertheless provides an indication of the vehement nature of the popular response to economic problems. Other economically and politically powerful groups of men, not just judicial officials but sometimes the nonresident speculators who owned undeveloped land in the new towns and sometimes the local elites who ran the military apparatus in Hampshire County, likewise became the focus of intense local hostility, convenient targets to be tagged with the blame for local difficulties. However shortsighted or unfair the attacks on outsiders may have been – and occasionally they were indeed both – the projection of animosity onto unseen if not necessarily unknown adversaries helped forge or perhaps reinforce a sense of common identity and political cohesion among disparate migrants lately arrived on the frontier.

To some extent the very terms of settlement had created the potential for conflict between settlers and outsiders. Land in Massachusetts had never been intended for squatters; it was granted generally in large tracts to individuals or groups of proprietors with the assumption that they would in turn sell smaller parcels of land to actual settlers. In 1735, for instance, the General Court granted three tracts of western lands to the selectmen of Boston for the support of the town's poor and the town's schools, and four more tracts to the survivors and descendants of the 1690 military expedition to Canada. In both cases the land grants were intended to provide financial relief for the grantees, but at the same time the General Court tied important restrictions on the sale and disposition of the lands. Each tract formed a township six miles square, encompassing a total of around twenty-three thousand acres; each township was to contain sixty-three parcels of land of a hundred acres each, one lot to go to the first settled minister, one to go to the support of the ministry, one to go to the support of a school, and the others to go to actual settlers. Though no one necessarily assumed that the grantees would occupy the frontier townships themselves, the landowners were still expected to pay for building a meetinghouse in each settlement, laying out roads, and perhaps even providing a gristmill. In short, the General Court hoped to encourage the original proprietors to help establish stable New England towns. In 1762, when the General Court sold another ten tracts of western land, the same conditions applied.[32]

As long as the proprietors carried out their responsibilities to sell the land promptly and provide a few basic structures, the system worked reasonably well. The proprietors of Roxbury Canada even took the extreme step of offering bounties of ten pounds to actual settlers. John Worthington and the other proprietors of Township Number Three joined the thirty or so inhabitants of the town in petitioning for full incorporation in 1765, arguing that "the Settlement thereof (if duly encouraged) will hopefully be Soon compleated – and they humbly conceive the Incorporation of the Said Township will encourage & forward the Settlement to the advantage of the Inhabitants & the Publick."[33] The interests of settlers and proprietors coincided when both groups were anxious to attract additional settlers to the townships.

But when the western townships failed to fill up quickly enough, when the proprietors appeared to be holding onto the land and waiting too patiently for the right price, the people who had already settled began to feel cheated, and they began to speak out. In a sense they saw themselves engaged in an almost moral struggle in which the yeoman farmer, who made an honest and productive use of the land, had to contend with the parasitic speculator, who took his wealth from the land without even touching it. Such, at least, was the common sentiment that reached the General Court in petitions from a number of the western townships. In 1752 the handful of inhabitants at Charlemont wrote that the township had been "sold and conveyed, chiefly in large parcels, to persons who have not made any settlements or improvements on the same." Those who had gone ahead and settled, thinking that the rest of the town would soon fill up, found themselves "brought under great and unsupportable difficulties and hardships, not being able to support the ministry, build mills, or even mend the roads and make suitable bridges." So too petitioned the twenty families living at Belchertown:

> Three quarters of the township is in the hands of five or six
> or a few more proprietors, who have drawn us into difficul-
> ties; and now seem to cut us off. Some of us who own 150
> acres of land only, have been rated in a single rate *over twenty
> pounds*. Some proprietors (non-resident) own thousands of
> acres around us, and pay not a penny.

Faced with such a heavy and unfair tax burden, the settlers concluded that the only solution lay in their being able to tax the nonresidents, forcing them to contribute something to the maintenance of the community. And from a number of other Hampshire towns—Shutesbury, Chesterfield, New Salem, Bernardston, and Blandford—came similar pleas and petitions, all groaning about the difficult straits of the inhabitants' existence, all asking for at least the power to tax nonresidents. At Chesterfield the people went beyond mere complaining and took final action against the non-resident proprietors. Disgruntled by the refusal of the non-residents to occupy their lands or to pay taxes on them, the settlers posted a "Notification Set upon ye Pine Tree . . . to Let those Proprietors belonging to Chesterfield know that their lands will be Exposed to Sale if their tax be not paid." Whether the nonresidents ever got to town to read the notice on the pine tree is unclear, but in 1765 the Chesterfield residents went ahead and confiscated the land, auctioning it off among themselves.[34]

The general significance of these petitions may be as much political as economic. The point is not necessarily that the settlers presented an altogether accurate assessment of the reasons for their economic problems, or that the nonresident proprietors always deserved the blame heaped upon them. Certainly, before 1763, the indefinite military situation in western Massachusetts caused by the recurring colonial wars did as much to inhibit rapid settlement of the frontier townships as did the speculative practices of allegedly greedy proprietors; some landowners may actually have been hard pressed to find an abundance of willing settlers. But such extenuating circumstances did little to mollify the townships' residents. The more important point is that the settlers' perception of a shared disadvantage almost invariably tended to draw them more firmly together, to give them a sense of their common attitudes and common identity. Moreover, whatever their disagreements among themselves, they began to realize that they had a common enemy in those outsiders who not only lived far away, but also lived in a different way, making profits from the settlers' privations. The act of joining together in some collective political effort to deal with the outsiders – whether drafting a petition or taking more forceful action, like confiscating unsold land – gave a kind of concrete expression to the sense of political unity that was beginning to emerge among the inhabitants of each particular new town.

Beyond the immediate significance it had for the inhabitants themselves, this growing self-consciousness in the newer towns became a factor in the political world of some of the region's more established inhabitants, most notably the members of the Williams clan and their allies in the county elite. Many of these men owned substantial chunks of undeveloped land in the hills above the Connecticut Valley, and for years the frontier had been their special domain, subject in large part to their economic and political control.[35] Though they were themselves nonresident owners of land in some of the frontier townships, they had other roles to play as well. Especially during the long period of intermittent Indian warfare in the middle of the century, their positions as military leaders tended to underline their importance and influence: they were not only protecting their own lands but providing a number of vital services to the few frontier inhabitants as well. But as the forests increasingly gave way to human settlement, and as war eventually gave way to peace, gratitude occasionally gave way to grievance. The new settlers of the county began more often to perceive that their own local interests did not always coincide with the regional interests of the county leaders, and the inhabitants of the new towns repeatedly came to express their disfavor and some-times even disdain for the role the old leadership played in their lives. As a result, the position of the county elite in the frontier regions became much less certain and secure.

The history of the Seven Years' War provides the clearest con-text for understanding the nature of this transformation. When fighting between the British colonists and the French first broke out in 1754, the people of Hampshire County were dangerously unprepared, vulnerable, and exposed. Those few who dared to inhabit the isolated lands up in the northern hills found that life could be almost too risky to endure. The first settlers at Colrain wrote in 1755 that Indian troubles had almost brought them to the point of breaking up and moving away: it was simply too difficult and too dangerous to plant and harvest crops, "for fear of the Sword of the Wilderness." They could sell neither their land nor their cattle, "nor our selves for Bondsmen & Bondswomen." Isolated on the frontier, beset by enemies, hard put even to pro-vide food for themselves, they claimed there was no possibility "of making language of our present State & Circumstances."[36]

With crumbling fortifications manned by a bare handful of sol-diers on active duty, the military defense of the county would have seemed laughable had it not been for the alarming gravity of the situation. Almost immediately, then, the role of the county militia—and especially that of its chief commander, Colonel Israel Williams—became a matter of critical importance in the county. As it turned out, Williams did about as well as could be expected, at least during the early part of the war. Although he received little support from detachments of British regulars or from militia regiments in Connecticut and New Hampshire, he nevertheless managed to compensate for the critical manpower shortage in the Hampshire regiment and put his troops in a firm defensive stance; in order to guard the northern frontier against sudden attack,

Williams developed a "constant scout" plan to patrol the territory, and he sent militiamen from the valley towns to reinforce the line of forts in the upper part of the county. Though some of his military decisions caused friction among one or two fellow officers – most notably Joseph Hawley, who felt injured by too little consultation or consideration – Williams's first attempts to shore up the county's defenses seemed a timely response to a tense situation.[37]

But as Colonel Williams reinforced the military defenses of Hampshire County in the early years of the war, he also reinforced the economic position of his own kinsmen and colleagues. It took very little imagination for inhabitants of the region, whether those few in the upper realm of the county elite or the majority below, to grasp one simple truth of war: military power led to monetary gain. The sudden pressure to rebuild fortifications and to recruit soldiers brought a substantial flow of government money into Hampshire County, most of which passed at least once through the hands of the leading officers of the militia. The case of Israel Williams's cousin, Ephraim Williams, for instance, offers a good example of an officer's ability to make the most of his post. Ephraim had command of one of the northern outposts, Fort Massachusetts, and needing timber for fortifying the garrison, he sent his soldiers to cut wood on one of his own plots of land nearby. He then billed the province for the logs taken from his land and thereby gained, all in the name of service to the government, both a cleared piece of land and a clear profit. Other favored members of the officer corps, similarly blessed with access to free labor and public funds, engaged in a number of other schemes that were founded less on patriotism and scruple than on assertive self-interest and, when needed, creative bookkeeping. Some of the benefits of these schemes would invariably trickle down to a few chosen locals – artisans, small merchants, and so forth – in the form of low-level patronage jobs, but the real wealth remained within a small circle of friends.[38] Quite simply, no one in the chain of command found it difficult to fulfill both his economic desires and his military duty without raising too many eyebrows in Boston.

Most local inhabitants, especially those living in the isolated hilltowns in the north, could also let such practices go by without too much criticism as long as the militia officers did a decent job of their primary task, protecting the frontier. In a few cases, however, hilltown residents began to feel that they were being served poorly while the county leaders were serving themselves quite well. A group of settlers at Ashfield, for instance, complained to the General Court about Israel Williams's failure to provide them with adequate protection, and the people at Greenfield, reminding the officials in Boston that "we are a frontier & have had our Brethren & Friends kill'd & captivated from among us by the Salvages this war," begged for greater military protection from British regulars.[39]

Moreover, as the British-American troops moved on the offensive outside New England into Canada and New York, recruits from Hampshire County often became reluctant to fight so far away from home and for so long a time. Their uneasiness may have been reasonably well-founded. The Hampshire troops who took part in one venture early in the war, the Crown Point expedition of 1755, suffered heavy casualties, especially at the battle of Lake George. Israel Williams had cause to grieve along with other county residents, for he lost his cousin Ephraim and several other relatives, but he still had to take responsibility for drafting more troops for other offensives. By the second or third year of the war, Williams found some Hampshire farmers actively resisting impressment into the expeditionary forces, and many others at least had reason to feel divided in their loyalties to the Crown and to the county. It was one thing to respond to an immediate threat to their own neighborhood, as indeed most did when the French and Indians overran Fort Henry in eastern New York in 1757 or, even worse, when Indians raided the hilltown of Colrain in northern Hampshire County in 1760. It was quite another matter to march off to Canada to serve for an indefinite period under Lord Jeffrey Amherst in 1759. For the men of the Hampshire hilltowns, on whom Colonel Williams drew rather heavily, the sacrifices of soldiering seemed especially severe. At a time when they might better have spent their time defending their own towns and developing their own farms, many had to face the prospect of departing for distant service and seriously depleting the already scarce manpower in their new hometowns.[40]

The point is not to argue that Israel Williams and the other leaders in the county militia were widely perceived as rapacious warlords callously sacrificing the lives and fortunes of their countrymen in distant battles for their own glory and gain. As county commander, Williams often expressed frustration with the government's demands that he deplete the local defenses by sending troops outside the county, and most people no doubt recognized that he and his fellow officers were merely doing their assigned duty – while doing a little unassigned business on the side, of course.[41] The point, rather, is that whatever credit the county leaders might have gained in the eyes of county residents in the early years of the war eventually gave way to disenchantment and, in some places, at least, to criticism. Though the Hampshire officers could not be held ultimately responsible for the conduct of the war, neither did they find themselves held in absolute esteem for their role in it. Local farmers were too reluctant to be pressed into service to be too impressed with the men who would then lead them.

In a sense the military situation suggests a more general way of looking at the relationship between the established leaders in Hampshire County and the newcomers moving to the new towns on the frontier. For the most part these settlers remained outside the mainstream of the Hampshire elite's political affairs, geographically isolated and necessarily involved in the more pressing work of settlement and survival. The newer settlers seemed more detached and less dependent than the inhabitants of the older Hampshire towns, who had occasion for much more direct contact with the county leaders on a variety of personal and political matters. Yet settlers in the new towns could never consider themselves altogether beyond the reach of the county political authorities, and the nature of the dealings they did have was likely to lead, at best, to somewhat mixed attitudes. On the one hand the prominent men who were large landowners in the frontier townships, officers of the county militia, or, in more peaceful times, justices of the county court could at times be helpful to new settlers, providing various services and benefits ranging from financial assistance to protection to resolution of disputes. More often, though, the men who played those roles could just as easily seem burdensome or even oppressive in the eyes of some settlers, retarding settlement and even driving up land prices, calling upon young farmers for distant military service, or bringing judgment against struggling farmers who could not stay ahead of their debts. Even newcomers with no immediate fears or complaints quickly became aware of the kind of power, both actual and potential, the county elite could wield over their lives. Perhaps the most reasonable assessment would be that a few people came to look upon the members of the county elite with gratitude and admiration, many others looked upon them with hostility and contempt, and probably most looked upon them with anything from wariness to indifference, but generally with a desire to be left alone. New settlers had enough to do in their own communities without having to deal with the powers who governed the whole region.

It was not until the first months of the Revolutionary crisis, in fact, that the hilltown inhabitants would become seriously involved in broader political activity on the regional level. At that time, however, their role in pushing for political change and especially in unseating the established county leaders proved to be quite significant, even decisive.[42] Expressing openly and forcefully their independence from the "Great men" of Hampshire County, hilltown residents rose up quickly to be among the very first to challenge the men in the county elite and ultimately to take the most emphatic action against them. And yet the apparent suddenness of this political transformation may be misleading. Though it came in response to immediate issues, it also had roots in the recent past. Again, some of the frontier farmers had years before developed particular grievances against the military and judicial authorities, and their defiance of the "Great men" at the time of the Revolution was no doubt fueled by their earlier disapproval and disdain. More generally, though, the settlers in the frontier communities had over the years begun to develop a growing awareness of their local interests and independence, and they had on occasion had to take action to defend themselves against external threats. By the mid-1770s, when the policies of the British government and its allies in the Hampshire leadership seemed to pose an extremely serious threat, the inhabitants of the frontier hilltowns were quite prepared to respond. Indeed, when the Revolution offered hilltown residents both a reason and an opportunity to challenge the role of the county elite, it was largely their well-developed sensitivity to their own local interests that led them to take such an active part in that challenge.

Not everyone moved to the frontier, of course. In order to appreciate more fully the significance of population change for political

life in the pre-Revolutionary era, it is necessary to look more closely at events in the older towns that had traditionally been at the center of county politics. During the middle of the eighteenth century those older and well-established towns also received an influx of newcomers to add to their already growing populations. In most cases the greatest degree of population growth and new settlement occurred in the outlying areas of the town, and new inhabitants soon transformed what had been only sparsely settled or even unsettled regions into a nascent community distinct from the original town. More important, they began to develop a sense of their own local independence. During the years before the Revolution, the attempt to transform these outlying areas into independent towns provided a significant challenge to the political order and stability of Hampshire County, and for that reason it merits a closer consideration.

Chapter 6

THE POLITICS OF PAROCHIALISM

In the many histories of New England towns, the story of growth and division has become a very familiar one. Throughout the seventeenth and eighteenth centuries the process occurred so often as to seem an almost natural part of development, perhaps even a predictable event in the overall demographic history of any town. The patterns of land use and family size common in colonial American society led unavoidably to the dispersal of a town's population, and somewhat like amoebas, many towns divided as they grew larger and more spread out. Without defining any rigid standards of maximum population size or distance, early New Englanders nevertheless followed the practice of town division repeatedly and arranged themselves across the landscape in a pattern of regularly spaced small towns.[1]

And yet the orderly appearance is deceptive. However commonplace or predictable, the division of a town was still a political as well as a demographic phenomenon. It was determined not just by some function of population, time, and geography, but by human consciousness, choice, and action. In a sense there emerged two differing ideas of community, one defined by identification with the original town as a whole, the other based on identification with a particular section within that town. Shared lands and shared disadvantages helped create shared interests, and outlying residents began to recognize those interests and to act together as a group. Like maturing children, they began to agitate for greater independence, perhaps first seeking to form their own church, then almost inevitably seeking complete political separation later. And like many New England parents, the central residents of the original towns proved reluctant to let them go. For every push for separation there usually followed an opposing pull to keep things

132

intact, and as often as not the townspeople fell into a period of convulsive dispute over their competing desires.[2]

What was striking about Hampshire County was not that such a familiar pattern of division occurred at all, but that when it did occur, it occurred so rapidly and on such a wide scale. For years most of the divisions of towns had taken place in the eastern part of the province, and for the first century of settlement the towns of Hampshire County had been relatively free of internal disputes over separation. After an early uproar over the separation of Hatfield from Hadley in 1671, the towns of the county remained unified and intact if not altogether harmonious. Beginning in the 1740s, however, as the population of the county began to climb steadily, the number of town divisions in Hampshire County increased dramatically. During the middle of the century almost every one of the older towns divided into two, and sometimes even three or four, parts; in some cases the newly created parts would themselves divide. By the time of the Revolution, Hampshire County had seen the creation of nineteen new towns through separation – these in addition to the towns recently settled on the frontier.[3]

More important, as a result of the internal discord that usually shook a town undergoing division, the county had also experienced a rising level of political unrest, a recurring conflict between new local interests and the older established order. By gaining independent status for their own towns, not only did outlying residents break free from the immediate authority of the individual older towns, but they also put themselves somewhat outside the traditional network of county authority that had linked those older towns together. By the early 1770s, in short, Hampshire County had acquired a new set of political actors who had proven themselves to be quite unwilling to remain tied to the old.

People living on the outskirts of an established town could find themselves in a paradoxical situation: they were in the town, but not really of it. That is, they were bound by a technical and legal obligation to the town by the fact of being inside its boundaries, and they were governed by its secular and ecclesiastical institutions. But they remained beyond easy reach of the center and the daily exchanges that took place around the meetinghouse, shops, and taverns; they were rather more likely to share those kinds of exchanges with each other at the crossroads and meeting places of their own area of town. Moreover, living several miles distant from the center meant that participating in the secular and religious affairs of the community became a chore as much as an accepted and welcome duty. The people in the Chicopee section of Springfield adopted a fairly standard line of argument, writing to the General Court about being "under very great and distressing Difficulties with respect to their attendance upon publick Worship of God" because they were on the far side of the Chicopee River from the Springfield meetinghouse; distance and bad weather might force them to stay home from church services, and they feared that their children might be "brot up in Heathenism and Ignorance."[4] Faced with such difficulties, then, a group of people on the fringe areas might with good reason try to establish their own institutions in a closer and more convenient location.

But underlying such complaints about distance was most often a more serious problem, a growing sense of political disadvantage with regard to participation and representation. What the Chicopee petitioners did not explicitly point out, for instance, was that the meetinghouse itself had recently been a sore spot for reasons other than location alone. In the late 1740s the people of the Springfield church were discussing the construction of a new meetinghouse, and although most center residents favored a brick building, people in Chicopee argued for a wooden one. Perhaps their advocacy of wood was simply an honest attempt to hold down costs for everyone, but more likely it represented their particular reluctance to pay for an expensive structure they would have to trouble themselves to use. When the final vote came, they lost. But they had made their opposition clear, even to the point of listing their names on a wood-versus-brick tally sheet in the parish records, and they stood out as a distinct sectional faction in the town.[5] They would remain, however, a minority faction, too small to balance the power of the center residents, too small to make the political decisions of the town as a whole accommodate their particular local interests.

Likewise, the inhabitants of another outlying section, West Springfield, began to complain in the 1750s that the problem of crossing the river made it difficult for them to go to the center for business or town meetings; they were thus "debarred the Privilege of acting for Themselves in Publick Meetings & affairs of the

Town," and forced to "trust to the honesty of the Inhabitants of the east side to do us justice." As if to erase any doubt about their estimation of the justice provided them, the West Springfield people noted that they "groan under the Burden & pray to be delivered from it." Deliverance, of course, lay in the direction of separation. The initial appeal might ask only for the right to build a new meetinghouse and establish a new parish, but as people in Springfield and throughout the county would increasingly come to learn, seeking parish status was only a short step away from demanding more complete political independence. The people of Chicopee and West Springfield were beginning to take the first moves toward separating from the town.[6]

Fearing the loss of tax revenue, the loss of land, or even the loss of valuable citizens, the older towns generally did what they could to prevent or postpone separation and keep their distant neighbors under town control, at least for the time being. In response to the growing unrest in the outlying sections, inhabitants of the center might initially adopt an air of almost paternal protection. As the people of Springfield pointed out, their refusal to accede to the desires of the outlying residents came "not from an Insensibility of the Difficulties of the Petitioners or want of Compassion and good Will to Them, but from hearty Friendship & a full Conviction that the Effect thereof (if any it had) towards their being set off, would be very unhappy." In short, they only wanted to do what they thought best for their neighbors and for the interests of the town as a whole. Certainly the sudden sense of urgency with which those neighbors pushed for separation struck center residents as "a little too Chimerical and Extravagant," if not downright disingenuous. West Springfield people had crossed the river to town meeting for over a century without having suffered severe political oppression; so presumably had the Chicopee inhabitants made their way to church in Springfield center often enough to avoid falling into the "Heathenism and ignorance" they claimed was about to befall their children. Rather than yield to the demands of the parts, then, the center residents continued to uphold the idea of town unity.[7]

But however much the center residents might proclaim their benign concern, they could not convince the inhabitants of the outlying areas. People throughout Hampshire County continued to grow restless as minority groups in the politics of the estab-

135

lished towns, and they were not willing to let the people of the center protect them from the supposedly unhappy effects of separation. The more they felt themselves able to support their own institutions, the more they insisted on gaining the necessary independence to do so. To that end they continued to badger their local town meetings and the provincial government with petitions for separation, with complaints, arguments, accusations, and pleas for action. From all parts of the county it seemed to happen at once, and it kept up throughout the 1750s and 1760s, creating a rising level of disharmony in the region, turning the political life of town after town into an enervating war of sectional nerves.

The growing intensity of sectional politics in Hampshire towns can perhaps best be described by events in South Hadley in the middle of the century. South Hadley was by no means one of the oldest towns in the county, nor was it one of the largest or wealthiest. First settled in 1727, it had been set off as a precinct of the parent town of Hadley. After two decades of steady growth—from around twenty-one families in the beginning to almost a hundred by 1750—the precinct was granted district status in 1753, apparently without any strong opposition from the people of Hadley. In that sense the early history of South Hadley provided an almost perfect case of gradual and peaceful transition from outlying area to separate and independent entity. The inhabitants' unanimous decision in 1751 "to do something this year in preparation for building a meeting house" not only testified to the precinct's growth; it also coincided nicely with the change from precinct to district and could have served as a symbol of their new status in the eyes of the General Court and Hampshire County. As it happened, however, the decision to build the new meetinghouse signaled the beginning of over a decade of conflict, animosity, and bitterness that wrenched the new district and ultimately tore it apart. Years after the initial vote to build there still was no new meetinghouse, and the apparent harmony of the original decision had become a hollow, almost ironic memory.[8]

The main problem was location. The first vote in 1751 had suggested merely that the new building be constructed "as near the place where the present m.h. stands as may conveniently be." But a month later the voters decided to place the meetinghouse "where the center of travel is."[9] By 1755 the town clerk could only record that the people of South Hadley "Voted to go on in building a meeting house if we can agree to a place to set it." And three years later the townspeople seemed no closer to a solution, but only voted to set the meetinghouse "where it will best suit the present inhabitants."[10]

The "present inhabitants" proved to be a changing group. Since its early settlement, South Hadley had been a community of two parts, an east side and a west, separated by a rise called Cold Hill. The western part had long been the more populous part, as people chose most often to settle in the lands closest to the parent town of Hadley. Even by 1750, the year before the meetinghouse controversy began, the west side had well over twice as many households as the east. And consequently, since the early years, the old meetinghouse had stood on the west side, centered more by the pattern of population and settlement than by the geographical bounds of the precinct. But throughout the 1750s the sparsely settled lands on the east side were filling up, gaining population much more quickly than the west. Between 1750 and 1763 the two dozen or so families of the east were joined by forty-eight new families, almost trebling the population of their area. During the same period the west side had its new residents too, some thirty-five new families; but neither the absolute number nor the percentage of increase was anywhere near that experienced by the east-side residents.[11]

The west-siders still maintained a numerical superiority, but the east side was expanding in ways that changed its situation within the town of South Hadley. During the course of a decade it had come to be populated, even dominated, by a swell of new landowners who, unlike their counterparts in the west, quickly became the majority in their part of town. To a great extent, then, the collective experience of the people of the east was this rapid growth that had brought them together as new neighbors almost overnight. And to a great extent it was that collective experience which in turn helped the men of the east become a strong and cohesive political unit and helped shape the turbulent politics of South Hadley in the 1750s and 1760s.

During the 1750s, as the east-siders took part in the debate on the meetinghouse site, they may have reflected on the overall state of politics in the town. In doing so they could find great cause for worry. Town politics had repeatedly been dominated by men from the west side, and when men from the east side did manage to get themselves elected to office they always found themselves outnumbered by west-siders. The east-siders could usually elect two men to the board of selectmen during good years, but never enough to constitute a majority. Only three east-side men — William Eastman, Samuel Moody, and John Moody — had served more than two terms apiece, whereas thirteen west-side men had held office three terms or longer.[12]

At the same time, as voters from the east side became a greater part of the whole, they became more active and contentious in town meeting, more determined and assertive in pressing for their particular interests. They seized upon the meetinghouse issue as their single main goal in town politics and tried to block the west-siders from building. It was not a matter of relative piety or religious devotion.[13] It was a way, rather, of using a religious symbol to give meaning to a more openly political conflict. The people themselves saw the meetinghouse as an important element in the structure of the town. Where it stood came to be as important as what it stood for. More to the point, where it stood and what it stood for came to be essentially the same thing. It was the one cultural symbol that more than anything else defined the heart of the town and gave people a sense of where they were in that town — an important economic as well as psychological consideration. When the population swelled beyond the capacity of the old meetinghouse, the decision to build a new one gave implicit recognition to the increasing significance of new residents in town; moving the site of the meetinghouse closer to the growing east side would give even more explicit recognition, redefining the center of things and making the main public meetingplace more accessible to them. But trying to accommodate the newcomers merely by building a bigger meetinghouse on the site of the old one did not accommodate them at all. Indeed, it seemed only to make them resentful.

The people of the east side occasionally mobilized themselves enough to win a particular point or even to control a particular meeting, but in general the meetinghouse question teetered back and forth from meeting to meeting through many adjournments and overturned votes, and neither side could do much. Town meetings began with "Long Debating about the Legalitie of the meeting," votes began to be recorded by tally or by the notation of a "bare majority," and decisions lasted only so long as the opposition took to get itself organized to overturn them.[14]

After frustrating deadlocks in 1755 and again in 1758, the people decided to let a committee choose a meetinghouse site, but each time they refused to accept the committee's decision. By the beginning of 1759 the town had progressed to the point of voting "that the votes that have been tacken this Winter Respecting Building a Meeting House Shall not be put upon Record." By the end of the year the situation had become even more chaotic, and a vote on December 5 to let another committee decide on the site was overturned twelve days later by a vote not to let the committee decide anything. By early March 1760 the people appeared to be willing to choose by lot from six proposed sites, but later that month they voted again to leave the matter to a committee. In August of 1761 the east-side voters managed after a "demur or Dispute" to gain control of the meeting, and they happily pushed through a number of measures favorable to their cause. But in December of that year the west-siders gained control and declared that "sd Votes & orders are Disagreeable to the Mind of the District therefore it is now Voted and ordered that all the Votes and Orders made & passed in sd Meeting and at the Several Adjournments thereof are Revoked Repealed Superseded and Utterly made Voide." As Sylvester Judd, the nineteenth-century historian of the town, put it, "Thus they voted and unvoted."[15]

Clearly, voting and unvoting was doing little to erect a meetinghouse. Quite the contrary: the inability to decide on a site threatened to make future construction altogether impossible. While the people were involved in debating sites, committees, and so forth, some partisans tried to influence the outcome by hauling the cut timber over to their favored site; their opponents hauled it back, and after a few such moves one side complained that the wood "hath been hued one year already, and drawn from place to place that it is in danger of being ruined."[16]

Equally in danger of ruin was the town meeting itself. After ten years of disagreement and indecision, the whole process of local town democracy seemed to be failing the residents of South Hadley. Certainly there was no sense of harmony and unanimity to help determine a commonly acceptable site, no consensus invoked for the good of the whole. Opposing groups shifted votes back and forth just as they apparently shifted the lumber back and forth. No position remained dominant or even durable. The democratic process became a vehicle for expressing disagreement rather than one for assuring harmony, and the decade of conflict left the people in a state of confusion and exasperation with no clear end in sight. If one thing became evident, it was that the traditional means of dealing with local disputes at the local level had failed them over a period of time, and had failed quite miserably.

This failure eventually became apparent, at least to some of the people, and in 1760 a group of them petitioned the governor for help. Most of them – forty-three of the forty-six signers – were east-side residents, and of those forty-three well over half were the younger, more recent settlers, the men who had taken up land after 1750.[17] In a way the list of signers represented a capsule summary of east-side development over the past decade; a group of younger men joined with older residents of the east, including the men who had served as selectmen from the east side, to form a group that could speak plainly and clearly about the interests of their area. They had identified themselves in town meetings, and now they began to act on another level, going beyond the town to the officers of the province.

Their petition seemed, above all, circumspect. They pointed out that "the Said Inhabitants are So Scituated at the Various parts of the Town, & are So unhappily divided in their Sentiments as to the Conveniency of the place & Scituation for erecting the Same, as not to be able to Agree." The continuing debate over "place & Scituation" threatened to divide the district into two separate parishes, and that was a result the petitioners claimed to want to avoid.[18] At this point the east-siders were careful to phrase their appeal for the governor's intervention as an appeal for the maintenance of unity, even if unanimity no longer seemed possible. In doing so they were dutifully adhering to the prescribed terms of political discourse. Rather than appear as the agents of separation and division, they cast themselves as supporters of the good order of society, the advocates of unity. By raising the specter of a possible division in the town, the east-side petitioners sought to encourage the governor to act quickly, and to act in their favor.

But when Governor Bernard sent a committee to look into the situation in 1760, the east-siders came out on the short end. The governor's committee made its inspection and then recommended

that the people leave things as they were and build the new meetinghouse where the old one stood. Perhaps astonished and certainly dismayed, the east-side men sent off another petition to the
governor in January 1761. They politely but emphatically told
him that his committee had made a poor choice, that the chosen
site was "vastly less convenient (as we apprehend) for that purpose than some other place nearer the easterly part of said
District."[19] But the east siders were not content to leave it at that,
and they added another point. If the governor did not reconsider
and see the error of his committee's ways, if he allowed the meetinghouse to be built on the west side, "then it will necessitate A
Division of said District, which will be altogether against our
Interest and Inclinations if it can be avoided." Still using the
language of reluctance, the east-siders nevertheless made it clear
that they would not tolerate an unfavorable ruling. As much as
they might want to avoid separation, they argued, "we humbly
apprehend the Inconveniences of such a Separation will not be so
great, even to Ourselves, as being obliged constantly to attend the
public worship [on the west side]."[20] What in 1760 had seemed
an unwanted or destructive possibility had by 1761 become an
apparent necessity. Despite their claims to the contrary, their "Interest and Inclinations" had begun to point toward separation. If
they could not have the meetinghouse in their part of town – and
that increasingly looked to be the case – they wanted out of the
town altogether. It was a point they wished to make clear, both to
their opponents in South Hadley and to the officials in Boston.

But in the end the appeal to Boston for help proved no more
satisfactory than the endless wranglings of town meeting. No
one – not the governor, the council, or the General Court –
seemed either willing or able to make a final decision for the
people of South Hadley. After sending several committees to view
the situation, the officials in Boston could only agree to dismiss
the petitions, close the case, and let the inhabitants of the town
reach their own solutions. Having to give up any notions of getting outside assistance, each side went to work in its own way.
Sometime in the early summer of 1761, while the town meeting
was still in a snarl, the west-siders decided to go ahead and begin
building a new meetinghouse without approval from anyone.[21]

A few months later the east-siders took an equally direct approach: they tore the new meetinghouse down. First they drew

away some of the cut timber and left it in a swamp, but when the west-side people completed one end of the meetinghouse frame, the east-siders came and pushed it over.[22] There is no record of violence against persons, only against the building itself. Still, the meaning of the action was clear: the people of the east side were willing to take forceful, even illegal, measures to keep their neighbors from achieving a de facto victory. Unless or until the east side could become a separate entity, its people would not tolerate such a strong visual symbol of west-side dominance as that of a new meetinghouse on the old site.

For their own part, the west-side people were quite unwilling to tolerate such an affront to their collective pride and property. They voted to have the men who attacked their meetinghouse arrested and prosecuted before the Hampshire County Court of General Sessions. But the county officials, who had apparently not been involved in the whole controversy, did no more than the provincial officials to provide a suitable resolution. They summoned some thirty South Hadley residents before the bench, no doubt gave them a stern warning about proper behavior in town disputes, and then discharged them without further legal action.[23] If the accused had cause to feel harassed by being made to appear in court, their accusers had equal reason to feel unhappy with the result of their prosecution. The justices of the court had perhaps provided a temporary restraint against further acts of violence, but they had failed to reduce the general level of frustration, and they had certainly failed to win themselves any significant amount of gratitude on either side.

With the destruction of the meetinghouse and the subsequent arrest of the men who carried out the act, it became evident that the relationships among the people would be harder to repair than the meetinghouse itself. In fact, they were beyond repair. For a decade the people of the eastern part of South Hadley had disagreed strongly but had still observed the accepted forms of conflict. They had resorted to votes, committees, petitions, lotteries, and probably at some point prayer. In short, they had done everything they could do to arrive at a decision through peaceful and legal means. But in the end their willingness to take the grievance through the established channels gave way to their willingness to take action. Their effort to change the location of the meetinghouse eventually became an effort to change the very definition of the town, and they demonstrated quite forcefully that their political sensibilities lay not in accommodation and submission but finally in separation. Rather than continue fighting a divisive battle with the other residents of the town, they chose simply to make division real. One meetinghouse, however large, could no longer hold the people of South Hadley together.

In 1762, several months after the destruction of the meetinghouse, the General Court took the necessary if somewhat belated action of dividing South Hadley into two parishes, leaving the people of the west and east sides to settle the costs of building two meetinghouses, as well as the costs of damages already incurred. For six years the two parishes remained partially separated and unhappily joined, frequently bickering over the costs of righting past wrongs, until finally in 1768 the people of the east side got what they had wanted years earlier. The General Court set them off as the independent town of Granby.[24]

South Hadley's experience did not define the exact pattern of events in other towns, for in a way there was no one specific pattern that could fit all the towns. To be sure, no other town in the county had to undergo the destruction of its meetinghouse before the necessity of a sectional division became clear. But the process of division that took place in South Hadley did suggest the general outlines that became evident elsewhere: the rapid growth of population in the outlying areas, the growing cohesiveness and identity among the residents of those areas, the challenge to the established order of the original town, the frustration with the failure to work out a solution at the local level, the lingering political hostilities, and almost inevitably the eventual separation of the outlying section as a separate town. By the middle of the eighteenth century the desire for local autonomy seemed generally to be much more compelling, and people became increasingly vocal in challenging the political status quo and increasingly active in struggling to achieve political independence.[25] From Springfield, Westfield, and Brimfield in the south on up the river to Northampton, Hatfield, Deerfield, and Sunderland in the north, most of the main towns in the Connecticut Valley found themselves dealing with groups of people who wanted out. And all those towns eventually had to divide. Likewise some of the newer towns – not just South Hadley, but South Brimfield, Amherst, and even the infant settlement at Murrayfield – had to deal with demands for division. Coping with these demands was a serious and frequently difficult matter, whether it happened only once or several times in a town's history.

The timing of this sudden upsurge is rather difficult to explain with certainty. On the one hand there was simply the general population increase throughout Hampshire County in mid-century that brought newcomers to the region at a time when the older towns were already expanding as a result of natural increase. The concurrent arrival of newcomers and movement of center residents outward gave these outlying areas the sheer number of inhabitants – the critical human mass – that made local autonomy seem more politically and economically feasible.

Other reasons, however, had less to do with population growth than with a general rise of popular unrest, a widespread change in political behavior and attitudes that, if somewhat less quantifiable than demographic change, was no less important. The people themselves never spoke directly of their perceptions of such political attitudes, of course, and they certainly never attempted to explain themselves in terms of a broader historical context. They were too involved in making change to reflect or speculate upon the fundamental historical significance of their actions. Still, given the nature of the rising level of political as well as religious dissent that marked the history of Hampshire County in the years between the Great Awakening and the Revolution, one must begin at least to appreciate the connections, however indirect, between isolated incidents in one town or church and the changing tenor of political life throughout Hampshire County. Although there was no formal political network or movement, there did seem to be a general political mood or spirit, even a political consciousness, growing among many people at the time.

In some respects the growing separatist spirit in secular affairs reflected the sentiment that emerged in religious disputes during and after the Great Awakening. Just as dissenters and Separates had begun to insist on proclaiming their own notions of ecclesiastical purity, and eventually on creating their own churches, so did outlying residents begin to insist on defining their own notion of local identity – a kind of parochial purity, perhaps – and creating their own communities. The religious groups, motivated by their uncompromising spiritual imperatives, refused to support the established churches and rejected the idea of living peacefully and tolerantly as saints among sinners; they wanted their own churches in which people of shared belief and beatitude could share fellowship with each other. Similarly, the people in the outlying sections seemed unwilling to remain tied to established communities where they felt somewhat isolated and unrepresented. They refused, that is, to accept their place in the increasingly complex economic and political arrangements of the older towns as inhabitants of suburbs around a central core. In political terms, they refused to accept their status as minority factions or geographically defined interest groups in a larger, pluralistic political system that relied on compromise and concession for the good of the whole.

At Springfield, for instance, the almost constant agitation for separation among people in four outlying precincts long kept the town meeting, as the Reverend Stephen Williams put it, "in a russle." Himself a resident of the Longmeadow precinct, Williams noted that with the growth of the outlying sections, Springfield had become "too large and too much disunited to manage ye publick affairs to advantage and comfort." At the March meeting of 1773 the voters were faced with an agenda item calling for them "To Consider the State of the Town Respecting Divitions of the Same into Seperate and Distinct Towns or Districts and pass any Acts or Votes Relitive Thereto." As Williams described it, they went through a "Great ado" in choosing their officers and then adjourned with "nothing ferther done." When the meeting reconvened two days later, the people seemed to Williams to be "yet in confusion": "I pceive ye Spirits of people are rais[ed] & [they] are hot – & in danger of running into Extremities – ye Lord mercifully interpose – & Give [them] all to consider they are *men* Brethren – ye Lord – Bless ye Town."[26] But the Lord apparently chose not to get involved in these secular affairs, and in the end the controversy did not subside until two of the precincts – West Springfield and Ludlow – were set off as separate towns. People in Williams's own Longmeadow precinct and nearby Chicopee would still have to press for independent status in the years to come.

Clearly this heightened spirit of parochial independence – some might even call it intolerance – flew in the face of the traditional standards of town unity and harmony. Ironically enough, one of the clearest statements of those standards came in the midst of

Springfield's division controversy, when a committee of prominent men from several towns in the county came to Springfield to serve as a kind of external review board to help resolve the dispute. Though the members of the committee quickly realized that the situation in Springfield was far beyond reconciliation, they apparently could not resist making a more general statement about the nature of towns and the central place they held in society. The resulting report offered a reflection on the events of the past years, not just in Springfield, but in the other towns of the county as well. It was not a philosophical tract, but it did focus a brief discussion on what it meant to be part of a town, and why it became such a serious matter to separate from one. It seemed a "great unhappiness," they noted, that the town had to be divided, because for so many years the public affairs of the town had "done much Honour to the Inhabitants and established a just Veneration for their leading men." A town represented not just a place to live, but a source of identity and pride to its people. Its people could experience the "General Benefit and Advantages accruing to the Community from that Constant and Unavoidable Intercourse occasioned by the Public Business of every town," not the least of which were the "greater Sociability and more generous Sentiments among the Inhabitants" created by their shared participation in the life of the town, and especially in its political affairs. In that sense a town provided an important source of order and cohesion in people's lives, and therefore its integrity should be defended and almost revered, certainly never given up too easily: "Nothing but Absolute Necessity Can ever Justify the lessening or Dividing a town," they argued; "nothing but oppression or Injustice or the evident want of Harmony and peace in the joint Management of the common Concerns of a town Consisting of Divers parts or parishes Can create that Necessity."[27] The town should encompass all its people and parts, and they in turn should remain steadfastly loyal to the continued existence of the town.

It was a noble sentiment, but too late for Springfield, and indeed, too late for most of the older towns in the county. After all, those fine words about the importance of town unity and identity came in the written prescription for dividing the town; the committee's report seemed almost to be an epitaph for eighteenth-century Springfield. The town apparently no longer provided "greater Sociability and more generous Sentiments among the Inhabitants," but seemed instead to produce feelings of distance and separateness among the residents of its outlying parts. People in these areas had come to adopt a much more parochial notion of community, pitting their local identity against the more encompassing identity represented by the corporate whole. Their various frustrations with the center, their sense of isolation and political inequality, only made that sectional identity stronger and pushed the inhabitants closer to an understanding that their desire for unity with Springfield had reached an end.

Some historians, in fact, have seen in these separation controversies a fundamental rejection of communal values, an assertion of individual interests over the collective requirements of town life. Richard Bushman, for instance, in writing about the divisions of towns in late seventeenth- and early eighteenth-century Connecticut, depicted outlivers as people who "were to a degree at variance with the community and with the ideal of social order, for they chose to promote their economic interests at the expense of their spiritual welfare." That is, they moved away from the communal regulation of the town in the first place to live closer to their distant landholdings in the far parts of town. And when they began to agitate to have a meetinghouse in their neighborhood, it was not so much for the sake of religious values as for the sake of property values: if they could not own land near the center and the old meetinghouse, they would create for themselves a new center and a new meetinghouse, thus gaining both prestige and profit. Moreover, so the argument goes, by moving away from the center and petitioning for separate status, outlivers could likewise gain "social and psychological independence." They escaped the restrictive authority of the old town and did not create the same kinds of controls in their new communities: in the process of living "out of sight of the leaders and only vaguely connected to one society or another . . . a person's total attachment to any community whatsoever diminished." In general, then, this line of explanation has emphasized the decline, even the destruction, of the sense of community in eighteenth-century society. Residents of the separating sections tend to be portrayed as being economically motivated and politically disaffected people who chafed under the controls of Puritan society and broke away to discover "enlarged freedom and the possibility of new ways of life"–in a word, the more "modern" habits of acquisitive autonomy that would define the world of the nineteenth-century "Yankee."[28]

There is, of course, an element of truth in that analysis. Like migrants to the frontier communities, people in the outlying sections could reasonably hope for some degree of individual advancement they might not have been able to gain in one of the older and more established towns. Many of these newcomers to the county had no strong familial, economic, or political attachments to the old towns; indeed, they may have had some feeling of disadvantage after moving west to a new location only to find themselves, almost by definition, marginal members of their communities. In that sense separation from the established town offered them a substantial chance for personal gain without any great threat of loss.

At the same time, though, this emphasis on nascent individualism tends to overlook and obscure a different kind of social vision, one that reflected not so much the ideology of self-interest that would emerge in the future as the standards of common interest derived from the past. Quite simply, the process of town separation was not an individual act, but a collective one. The end of separation was not the release of a number of families to live an altogether independent existence on isolated plots of private property; on the contrary, separation gave people a new communal identity with the creation–indeed, the re-creation–of a town. Certainly the commonly expressed desire to build a separate meetinghouse bespoke something more than a cynical attempt to inflate the value of land. A meetinghouse was, after all, a place where people repeatedly came together as a group, where they joined with each other to deal with the spiritual and secular concerns that affected them all; it was, in short, both an instrument and a symbol of their common purpose.[29]

Admittedly, people in the newly separated towns, like settlers in the frontier townships, did not establish the tightly gathered, nucleated, covenanted utopias of the early seventeenth century; for that matter, that particular pattern of settlement had survived hardly anywhere in New England beyond the first generation of Puritan settlers. But even though the old forms of strict communalism had proved unworkable and had died out, some of the basic assumptions about the value of town life still remained. In that respect the words of the Springfield committee did not ring altogether hollow. By establishing their own independent towns, people in the newer outlying sections not only could create for themselves the more formal communal institutions and arrangements of the New England town; they could perhaps also recapture the sense of closeness, participation, involvement, and face-to-face familiarity – what the Springfield committee had called "greater Sociability and more generous Sentiments" – that had so long been associated with town life. In a period of increasing demographic expansion, economic instability, and geographic mobility, the old standards of social unity and cohesion could provide an important source of certainty in an otherwise uncertain world. No less than the post- Awakening religious dissidents, who looked back to the fading vision of an earlier Puritanism, these secular dissidents could also draw on the familiar notions of town life in order to confront the changing conditions in their lives.[30]

It was, however, a conservative impulse that had a very unsettling effect on the political position of the county elite. In Northampton, for instance, Gideon Lyman, a resident of the Southampton precinct, campaigned for office by attacking some of the leading figures in the local political hierarchy. As Israel Williams complained some years later,

> This person . . . gave himself great liberty . . . in diverse places, in publick houses, more especially in his own Town . . . declaiming against the Conduct of the Great men (as he called 'em) at the General Court, representing them as destroyers of their Country with Lucrative views to their own Emolument . . . and the only way to remedy these inconveniences was for the Towns to send honest Plowmen to represent them at Court.

To further his case among his fellow Southamptonites, Lyman also promised to "get them made a District, and obtain for 'em a Grant of [a] large Tract of unappropriated land."[31] Williams and some of the other county leaders no doubt dismissed Lyman's performance as sheer demagoguery. But to Lyman's listeners in Southampton, an attack on established leaders and an attempt to secure independent political status no doubt seemed an altogether just and sensible platform. Anyone who had been around even briefly could understand how the traditional order of the county was reflected by both the established towns and the established leaders. In helping to send Lyman to the General Court, the Southampton people were posing a direct, and apparently conscious, challenge to both.

The prospect of future division controversies and the proliferation of even more new towns provided reason enough for Williams and his allies to be uneasy, but at the same time they had cause to realize that in some instances they would have to yield to an increasingly apparent necessity. In Williams's own town of Hatfield a group of people living at a part of town called the Straits of Canterbury first appealed for separation in 1768, and after "a Considerable debate" in town meeting, the voters of Hatfield, like the people of Springfield, decided to turn the matter over to a committee for further consideration. At the same time they made the equally wise if somewhat uncommon decision to "Consider the Circumstances of the town of Hatfield with relation to Setting off Districts or Parishes in sd Hatfield in time to come."[32]

No other town in the county had yet acted with the clear foresight to anticipate what was likely to happen "in time to come," but by 1768 the people of Hatfield must have been aware of the experience of other towns as well as of their own. They had only to reflect on the events of the past thirty years or so to see how the issue of division had affected their peer towns along the river. Moreover, Hatfield's leading citizen, Israel Williams, had only to talk to his colleagues and kinsmen in other valley towns to find out how division crises were creating unsettled conditions even at that moment. Springfield's John Worthington could well attest to the unhappy state of politics in his town, with people from all sections of town still tying up the town meeting with repeated petitions for separation. Williams likewise knew from his relatives in Deerfield about the tensions that continued to exist between their town and the neighboring district of Greenfield, which had been set off back in 1753. An initial disagreement over the rights to a tract of land called Cheapside had lain dormant for fifteen years until 1768, when Deerfield men marched over to Cheapside intent on mowing their hay, and a group of men from Greenfield, equally intent on stopping this supposedly legal outrage, opposed them. According to local legend, "clubs and pitchforks were freely resorted to." When the brief battle was over, the Greenfield men had carried the day and won the hay. The Deerfield men took the case to court.[33]

Israel Williams needed none of that. Though he no doubt still had the political influence at the town, county, or provincial level to block a division of Hatfield if he chose to make a fight, he also had the politician's good sense to avoid a fight. A powerful man like Williams could be pragmatic and conciliatory when the situation so demanded, and there is nothing in the town records to suggest that he acted otherwise in the case at hand. The question of dividing Hatfield called forth from the residents a careful examination of the tax lists to see how money should be divided, an appeal to "Judicious Disinterested persons out of the Neighboring Towns" to see how land should be divided, and always more debate to see how sentiment was divided. But in the end Hatfield set off two new districts in 1771 – Whately to the north and Williamsburg, named for (and perhaps even by) Israel himself, to the west – and did so without the sharp acrimony and disorder that had plagued many other towns. To be sure, within a few years the people of these newer towns would prove themselves to be less than grateful children of their parent town, and the people of Williamsburg would turn with intense hostility on the man for whom their town was named. But for the moment they seemed content with their independence, and Williams and the other residents of Hatfield seemed equally willing to let them have it.[34]

Across the river in Amherst, however, the struggle over division would have a much more disruptive, even disastrous, effect on the political stability of the town. Like so many outlivers elsewhere, residents of the north and south ends of the town, many of them relative newcomers, began to push for a division of the town, and when the residents of the older part of town resisted, the outlivers managed to take control of town politics and unseat a number of men prominent in both town and county affairs. As had been the case earlier at neighboring South Hadley, the catalyst for political action came with discussion about building a new meetinghouse for the town's growing population. Rather than accept the construction of a new building on the old site, a group of outlying residents put before the town meeting in March 1772 a plan to build not one but two new meetinghouses. Basically the idea was to divide the district horizontally in half, destroy the old meetinghouse, and build a meetinghouse in the center of each half. The effect would be to create two new parishes, one northern and one southern, making the old center of town the extreme end of either parish. Such a radical proposal for change could not help but disturb many people in the town, and when the vote was tallied at the district meeting it "paist in the Negative by a tie of votes." The people were so evenly divided that no action could be taken, and for the rest of the year the issue was put aside. By the time of the next town meeting in April 1773, however, the balance had shifted slightly in favor of the faction calling for division. First they swept all five selectmen's seats, and then they carried a vote to "Build two Meetinghouses in the District of Amherst."[35]

Suddenly faced with political ouster and the real prospect that their old meetinghouse would be replaced by two new ones, the center residents petitioned Governor Hutchinson for aid. Led by Isaac Chauncy, one of Israel Williams's allies in county and provincial politics, the people of central Amherst took care to point out that they were the more stable members of the community: they had lived longest in Amherst, they claimed, and they had more than half the estate in town. In general they represented themselves as "oppressed and likely still to be oppressed . . . *an injured and innocent Party*." They went on to warn Hutchinson that if Amherst were allowed to be split, "the same must hold and hold much stronger in almost every town and District and produce Divisions and sub-divisions throughout the whole."[36] The petitioners knew, just as Hutchinson must have known, that what was happening in their town had happened before and was almost certain to happen again.

In Amherst the division never took place, at least not until after the Revolution. In early 1774 Governor Hutchinson ordered the people of Amherst not to build any more new meetinghouses anywhere.[37] A few months later, agitation over the meetinghouse question died down as the people of Amherst, like Hutchinson, began to turn their attention to the larger political problems of the province; with such a great struggle brewing to the east, it was hard to spend too much more time worrying about where to put the meetinghouse in Amherst. But still, the brief victory of the residents of the north and south ends underlined the increasing political power they, like their counterparts in other towns, were coming to have. After gaining control of the board of selectmen in 1773, they held onto all five seats for the next three years; throughout the early years of the Revolutionary period, in fact, they managed to keep the leaders of the center faction almost completely out of the major town offices, allowing them at best only a slight minority status. Some of Amherst's most prominent men – including Isaac Chauncy, like Israel Williams not just a town official but a man with influence at the provincial level as well – never held political office again. In the end the outlying residents in Amherst may not have been able to tear down the old meetinghouse, but they certainly succeeded in redefining the nature of politics in the town for the time being.[38]

On a larger scale the same situation held true throughout Hampshire County as a whole: the creation of new towns changed the very nature of the county in both population and politics. Indeed, by the early 1770s, it was becoming quite clear in Hampshire County that the political desires and demands of people in the outlying sections of towns could hardly be thwarted. The warning of the Amherst center residents about the spread of "Divisions and sub-divisions throughout the whole" seemed hardly a warning at all; it was more a reflection of what had already taken place. In town after town the push for independence by people on the fringes had become such a common political goal that it must have seemed almost like a contagion. By the time of the Revolution almost three-fourths of the county's inhabitants lived in towns incorporated since 1740. No other Massachusetts county gained more new towns in the pre-Revolutionary era, and in no other county, with the exception of newly established Berkshire County on the western frontier, did new towns constitute such a large part of the whole.[39]

In political terms this widespread pattern of settlement and separation had an extremely significant effect on the traditional order of the county. Most important, the growth of new towns eroded the importance of the old ones. Each new town became an autonomous political entity, and more and more people came to live outside the limited universe defined by the original Hampshire towns and dominated by the established network of county leaders. The "Great men," as Gideon Lyman had called them, still held considerable power in the affairs of the county, but people living in the newer towns were not quite so directly subject to their influence and control. In some cases the challenge had been direct: as people sought to separate from the older towns they often disrupted the internal harmony of those towns and defied the authority of the local leaders. In other cases the political implica-

153

tions were less obvious but not really less significant: in the process of establishing their towns, many of the new inhabitants shared the experience of a common struggle – sometimes economic, sometimes political, sometimes both – and in the end their struggle helped them forge a sense of collective identity and independence. Throughout the pre-Revolutionary era this growth of local political autonomy, like the earlier spread of religious dissent, proved to be a critical factor in the gradual political transformation of Hampshire County. It was only with the coming of the Revolutionary crisis, however, that the full extent of that transformation would be most strikingly revealed.

Chapter 7

REVOLUTION IN THE NEIGHBORHOOD

The people of Hampshire County were hardly in the forefront of the Revolutionary movement. For almost a generation they had been too embroiled in their own local affairs—too worried, for instance, about the state of their religion, the boundaries of their towns, the location of their meetinghouses—to pay much attention to the growing crisis in Boston. It was only through the repeated efforts of the urban radicals on the Boston Committee of Correspondence that the majority of people in Hampshire County were awakened to the larger colonial issues. Even so, that awakening came relatively late, generally not until 1774.

But when the westerners did enter the Revolution, their political attitudes were not simply the creation of the Boston Whigs. The parochial disputes that had so engrossed the inhabitants of Hampshire County during the previous thirty years had their own political meaning and importance. On one level many people had gained experience as political actors, organizing and mobilizing themselves into groups to pursue a particular local issue. Moreover, in defining those issues, many people had gained a clearer and more immediate sense of the fundamental political values, independence and self-government, for instance, that underlay the Revolutionary movement. In that sense local politics helped create the basis for a popular response to the politics of the larger colonial struggle.

At the same time the larger struggle had its effect on local politics. The recent events in the county had begun a political transformation in Hampshire County, giving new groups of people a greater degree of political autonomy and undermining the influence and authority of the traditional county leaders. In the first years of the Revolution many of these people pushed that

155

transformation even further, not just by taking a generally more forceful role in county politics but also by taking the lead in deposing the old county leaders. In that respect the sword of the Revolution cut two ways. Just as the political change in the county helped prepare the way for the Revolution, the Revolution in turn provided an opportunity for emphasizing and accelerating many of those local changes. Put differently, the Revolution both followed and furthered a widespread local revolution in Hampshire County that had been growing for years.

A year or two before the outbreak of the American Revolution, a man with the remarkable name of Silent Wilde began work as an express rider between Boston and the Connecticut Valley. Every two weeks he would ride into Northampton and then on up the river to Deerfield carrying the latest Boston newspapers for his regular customers, each of whom paid him a dollar for six months' service. Wilde's problem was that he had too few customers, only about eight or ten in Northampton, probably no more in Deerfield. As any modern-day news carrier could quickly attest, this was not a terribly profitable route.[1]

Silent Wilde's problem as news carrier was only part of a larger problem that existed in Hampshire County even into the early 1770s: communications between Boston and the west remained sporadic, sparse, and fairly limited. News traveled slowly and was often stale by the time it reached everyone in the far parts of the province. Moreover, Wilde's circulation figures suggest that the demand for such news in western Massachusetts was relatively slight. People did not seem to be clamoring for stacks of newspapers and broadsides; they appeared content to keep to themselves, just as they had done for years.

At the time of the Stamp Act crisis, for instance, the political life of Boston was punctuated regularly by protest and riot, violence and tumult, while Hampshire County remained comparatively quiet on the whole issue. Politics in the city was not confined to the council chambers or House of Representatives but spilled out into the street. The popular anger over the Stamp Act reached a climax as mobs tore through Thomas Hutchinson's house, smashing furniture and household goods, taking vengeance on his belongings when they could not find the man himself.

From 1765 on, relations between the people of Boston and the royal government were marked by violence of both word and deed, and the heat of the Stamp Act crisis subsided only temporarily before rising repeatedly during the decade before the Revolution.[2]

In Hampshire County, by comparison, response to the changes in British policy seemed mild and almost nonexistent. Certainly nothing matched the vigor or violence of the Boston crowds. People in the west were aware of the Stamp Act, of course, and there was some scattered reaction. Josiah Pierce, a farmer in Hadley, did record in his diary that "The Repeal of the Burdensome Stamp Act laid upon the American Colonies by the British Parliament . . . was past and assented to by the King 18th March 1766 to take place 2nd May 1766." But then, without any further comment or reflection, Pierce turned his attention to other passing matters and noted in the next entry that "This year Worms prevail in orchards in the Beginning of June."[3] Though radical pamphleteers in Boston might rail against the "parasites" in the British government who seemed to be threatening American liberties, a farmer like Pierce had to be more immediately concerned with the real parasites threatening his fruit crop. Throughout Hampshire County, in fact, the Stamp Act crisis passed without any great burst of protest. A group of men at Westfield, thinking that the unavailability of stamped paper would make it difficult for them to sell land or make bail, banded together to protect each other from debt proceedings. Their minister, John Ballantine, dismissed the matter as a "Jubilee for debtors," since court proceedings were generally rendered ineffective. When Ballantine made further note of the response to the crisis, though, he wrote mostly of the "great tumult in Boston" or even of an ill-fated celebration in Hartford, where a bonfire spread to the local gunpowder supply and exploded. Nothing on the local scene really caught his eye. Indeed, during the 1760s the only serious instance of popular defiance of Crown policies took place in Northampton when a number of men stole over three hundred pine logs marked as royal property under the Pine Laws. Resistance to the Pine Laws, however, was a fairly old and fairly common reaction among New England woodsmen, not necessarily connected to the other problems or protests of the 1760s. In general, people in Hampshire County spent most of the decade before the Revolution still living in a state of relative isolation from Boston, giving only the slightest attention to the wider controversy developing in the east.[4]

Probably the surest sign of Hampshire County's remoteness from the imperial debate was the general failure of county towns to send representatives to the Convention of Towns in 1768. Keeping a man in Boston had never been a common habit, of course, as it was too expensive for most of the small western towns; throughout the 1760s only a few of the larger, wealthier towns of Hampshire County were represented in Boston.[5] But even in this time of crisis the involvement of western towns did not increase; some towns actually drew back from the controversy. Joseph Hawley, for instance, had generally served his town as representative in Boston, and during the 1750s and 1760s he had gradually broken with Israel Williams and the other Hampshire representatives and had risen to some prominence among the radical leadership in the General Court. In 1768 he joined Sam Adams, Thomas Cushing, James Otis, and John Hancock in drafting the Circular Letter in protest of the Townshend Acts. But his radical activity in Boston was essentially a matter of his own doing, not the express wishes of his town. When Governor Bernard dissolved the assembly because of its refusal to rescind the Circular Letter, and when the town of Boston subsequently called for the Convention of Towns in defiance of the governor's action, Hawley's neighbors and constituents at Northampton voted almost unanimously not to send him or anyone else as a representative to the convention.[6]

An even chillier response came from Hatfield, one of Northampton's neighboring towns. There the members of the town meeting, still under the influence of Israel Williams, wrote that

in our opinion the measures the town of Boston are pursuing and proposing unto us and the people of this province to unite in, are unconstitutional, illegal, and wholly unjustifiable, and what will give the enemies of our Constitution the greatest joy, subversive of government and destructive of the peace and good order which is the cement of society.[7]

In the end only three Hampshire County towns – Brimfield, Montague, and Colrain – chose to send delegates to the 1768 convention. Especially for the people of Montague and Colrain, such an act must have been an important undertaking, for both were newer towns that had never sent a representative to Boston before. But other county towns simply failed to send a delegate and let the matter pass without comment; if they, too, worried about possible cracks in the cement of society, they never said so.[8] For Hampshire County as a whole it seems likely that the extraordinary political situation of 1768 failed to alter the political habits of ordinary times: the people of the west made no great effort to participate in shaping either provincial policy or protest.

From 1768 almost until the beginning of the Revolutionary War their reticence continued. While people in Boston denounced the tyranny of each successive British move, their fellow provincials in the west seldom communicated with them or sent their support. Even by late 1772 and early 1773, when the Boston Committee of Correspondence sent out its first pamphlet and circular letter warning each town of the growing danger, there seemed to be little evidence of interest or urgency in Hampshire County. Over half the towns throughout Massachusetts responded, and most offered their hearty support of the efforts of the Boston leaders. In Hampshire County, however, the response was again fairly paltry, as only seven of the forty-one towns and districts bothered to write back.[9]

To be sure, those few that did respond—for the most part smaller, newer towns that had not been active in provincial politics before—were no less supportive than other towns to the east, expressing a sensitivity to the questions of natural rights and British oppression. As the people of Pelham put it in a long and emphatic letter, "We have considered your Circular letter and are Not a little Shoked at the attempts upon the liberty of America." Yet rather than commit themselves to following the possibly precipitous actions of urban radicals, the Pelhamites noted that "we Study to be Quiet and do nothing rashly" in order to avoid the charge of mutiny and sedition. They further urged all others in Massachusetts to "have Patience alonger in our humble Suits for Justice to the British throne." But if patience should prove fruitless, they concluded,

> and our Humble Petitions for our own Natural and Promised Rights Shall be baffled & Refuge on Earth and Hope of Redress Shall fail us we trust We shall be Wanting in nothing in our power . . . to Unite With our Dear Countrymen for our Mutual Good and Shall Venture our Properties &

Lives in Executing any Plan Pointed out by the Supreme Ruler and as the innate . . . Principles of Self Preservation & love to our Posterity may oblige us.

Their words of caution gave over to a declaration of resolution, and the Pelham people placed themselves apart from the general isolationism of their neighboring towns; they closed their letter pledging themselves to "Remain united with our breathren in the Common Cause of American Liberty."[10] Such a firm sentiment, though, was exceptional: more often the first appeals of the Boston Committee brought back nothing from Hampshire County towns but the uncertain meaning of silence.

It was not really until the middle of 1774 that most Hampshire towns took it upon themselves to write. In May of that year Parliament, angered specifically by the Boston Tea Party and generally by the rising level of radicalism and resistance in Boston and the surrounding towns, passed what were collectively known as the Coercive Acts, by far the most stringent regulations Boston and the rest of Massachusetts had seen. Almost immediately the political crisis that had hitherto been largely confined to eastern Massachusetts became a much more compelling issue for the province as a whole. With no thought of exaggeration, people throughout Massachusetts – and indeed, throughout the American colonies in general – began to talk seriously of their own enslavement at the hands of the British ministry. Hardly anyone could mistake the harshly punitive effect the Boston Port Act was intended to have on the people of Boston, nor could anyone doubt that such measures might soon be in store for other Americans in other places.[11]

The British officials in London seemed determined to act with a heavy hand; the radical leaders in Boston reacted swiftly by taking pen in hand. Once again the Boston Committee of Correspondence took the initiative in proposing a popular response to such tyranny, and on June 8 it sent out another circular letter to all the towns in the province, this time calling for concrete and concerted action. It drafted a Solemn League and Covenant whereby the towns of Massachusetts would agree to cut off all commercial dealings with the mother country by August 31, 1774, thus establishing a specific timetable for joint action. It was not the kind of demand to be easily ignored, and Hampshire towns could no longer remain aloof from the urgent situation facing Boston and the colonies at large. Throughout the summer of 1774 they responded in numbers far greater than before, and by September half the towns in the county had communicated at some point with the Boston Committee. This upsurge in letter writing created a new and weighty responsibility for Silent Wilde, "our News Carier," who, as the main communications link between Boston and the western region, found himself much more in demand than he had been even a year earlier.[12]

The people of the western Massachusetts countryside, however, did not react just to show their sympathy and support for their fellow provincials in the city. They faced an immediate problem of their own with the Coercive Acts. In order to curtail the growing political activity and unrest that seemed to be emerging in Boston and other towns, the British Government had imposed the Massachusetts Government Act, restricting the townspeople to no more than one town meeting a year without special permission from the governor; in addition, to offset further the political independence of all regions of the province, the new regulations placed county judicial officials – judges, sheriffs, and by extension jurors – under direct control of the governor, who alone would have the power of appointment. Much as it had done in the revolutionary times of the early 1690s, in short, the British government sought to consolidate its authority in Massachusetts by increasing its hold on the county political machinery, strengthening it at the expense of the individual towns.[13]

In that respect the Massachusetts Government Act seemed to run counter to the recent movement of events in Hampshire County. For the past quarter-century the history of the county had been marked in large part by the rapid growth of new towns and by the concurrent if somewhat more gradual decline of the county elite. The two trends were by no means unrelated. As the county became more crowded and complex, many people – most notably many of those whose recent arrival had added so greatly to the swell of population – came to seek a kind of smaller-scale simplicity. Rather than try to accommodate themselves to the expansion of the older and larger towns, they struggled to establish their own separate communities, each one an independent entity with its own political institutions and political leaders. In a sense their actions bespoke a fundamentally conservative impulse to recreate for themselves the traditions of localism and communal autonomy that were deeply rooted in the past of early New England. At the same time this parochial conservatism posed a growing challenge to an equally well-rooted (albeit rather more English) form of regional conservatism, the system of county-wide authority defined in Hampshire County by the Williams family's kinship ties and enhanced greatly by the government's generous patronage over the years. That is, as people created new and independent towns, they began to place themselves outside – and in some cases in opposition to – the traditional network of the established county leaders; by the early 1770s the power of Williams and his regional allies had not been destroyed, but it had at least been significantly diluted.

The new Crown regulations seemed clearly destined to reverse that trend. Scarcely had the inhabitants of some of the new towns begun to hold town meetings than they found themselves facing new restrictions on their right to do so. Moreover, as if their own loss of local political authority were not bad enough in itself, they also had to consider the prospect that the authority of the Williams organization would be reinvigorated and reinforced to the point at which it would overshadow the independence of the individual towns and once again stand as a pervasive source of political order for the county as a whole. In short, though the people of Hampshire County did not feel the full weight of repression that fell on Boston in 1774, many of them still had good reason to fear for their own rights in their own neighborhood.

It should hardly be surprising, then, that the people of some of the newer, smaller towns took the lead in communicating with the urban radicals. Indeed, the growing exchange of correspondence seemed to underscore their political emergence. As the Boston Committee recognized even the smallest frontier towns as autonomous, politically independent bodies, the towns had a compelling opportunity to recognize that autonomy and independence for themselves. Faced with framing a collective reply to Boston, the people of these towns necessarily had to assess local feeling and put that feeling clearly into words – in some cases for the first time in the town's history.[14] They might be on the one hand understandably deferential toward the Boston leadership, hesitant about the limits of their own abilities as "infant settlements." It was not for them, as the committee from Williamsburg noted, to

> Be so Arrogant as to undertake to direct you as to any Particular conduct in Such an important Critical Day But leave

that to your Juditious Judgment together with Those that
are better Quallified to give you advice than we.

But even as they drew this self-effacing distinction between themselves and the Boston Whigs, the people of Williamsburg seemed
to warm to the task of expressing clearly their own political
stance. "The principal aim of our wrighting," they went on,

> was to let you know That we are almost unanimously of the
> opinion by all mean to Resist Great briton in their unconsti-
> tutional measures By which they usurp upon our character
> priveledges even to blood. Also if you (being in the front
> rank) need our assistance in Aposing them we stand ready to
> grant it according to the Utmost of our Small capacity.

In closing they offered a forceful, almost militant, declaration of
their collective will; both their duty and their interest compelled
them, they asserted, "and when duty and interest agree We esteem
him a poor Souldier indeed that will not exart Himself to his very
utmost."[15] For the people of Williamsburg as for people elsewhere,
confronting the issues raised by the Boston Committee caused them
to confront the reality of their own political identity. The more they
wrote to Boston, the more they wrote about themselves.

To some degree, of course, the language of most Hampshire
County letters tended to be circumspect, full of both hesitation and
resolution, not too different in general tone from that of letters from
other towns in Massachusetts. Quite simply, no one wanted to act
recklessly or alone. Only a few towns declared themselves to be as
militant as Williamsburg or, like the small frontier town of Murrayfield, "Willing and Ready to Assist the Town of Boston together
with the Rest of the Province in all prudent and proper measures . . . and likewise . . . ready (if we are called to it) to Defend
our Rights and Priviledges even with the point of the Sword."
Most other towns were quite a bit more guarded. The overall hope
expressed by people throughout Hampshire County – and indeed,
throughout the American colonies – was for the "Recovery and Establishment of their just rights and Liberties Civil and Religious
and the restoration of that union and harmony between Great Brit-
tain and her Collinies Most Ardently Desired by all good Men."
Good Englishmen all, these rural westerners shared the common
ability to distinguish between George III as their rightful sovereign
and Parliament as a corrupt body whose acts were "callculated to
perplex and enslave his Majesty's free and Loyal Province." With

absolutely no sense of irony or contradiction they could "Sympathize with their Suffering Brethren of Boston and Charlestown" and yet still see themselves as part of the "Mother Country . . . with Just Rights, Priviledges, and Honour of the English Nation in General." Although British oppression appeared to be real enough, people urged "Prudence, Moderation, and Firmness." To many the exact terms of the Boston proposal, the formal signing of a covenant with a rigid deadline of August 31, seemed "rather Premature and too precipitate." The basic sentiment toward some sort of nonimportation agreement was mostly favorable, and as the people of Granby made clear, they had "generally agreed to enter into the Measures therein proposed." There was, however, "a Question Arising in the Minds of Some whether the Form of that Covenant should be Literally adopted." Given this almost universal hesitancy, perhaps the radical leaders in Boston had to content themselves with the simple fact of the response itself: more people were writing, and mere communication was an important first step.[16]

Still, some letters went beyond the normal language of response and proved to be especially revealing, providing a fresh look at the parochial political world of Hampshire County. Not surprisingly, these western farmers did not deal simply in abstract political principles or even in terms defined solely by the Boston Committee of Correspondence. They wrote sympathetically about the problems of Boston, but they also took the occasion to discuss a few problems of their own. Many of these letters – again, most notably those from some of the newer towns – clearly drew a connection between the general colonial crisis and the political situation that existed in Hampshire County. However uncertain people might have been about their role in the former, they had emphatic opinions about the latter.

Above all, they made it quite clear that the current situation only heightened their suspicion of the local political elite. As the people of Colrain put it, Hampshire County was a dangerous region where "some of the Great men" were devious enough to spread false rumors and undermine patriotic zeal. From a number of towns came the disturbing message that "It is generally Reported in these parts that Very few Towns fall in with the proposals" of the Boston Whigs, and that

> by false Insinuations, some of our people are led to think the
> Covenants are a plan laid by the Merchants, in Boston, tye

the hands of the people, to vend of the goods they have on hand, and at Extravagant price. We therefore desire, something may be made publick, relative to the affair (which may have a Tendency to open the eyes of a great Number in the County of Hampshire) and if you think best in your wisdom to send to this Town in particular, it will Give Satisfaction to us.[17]

The Boston Committee was quick to counter such rumors and sent back reassuring replies. The "Art of the Tories in your part of the Province" had to be acknowledged, the Committee admitted; someone, it seemed, had been clever enough to take advantage of the backwoods settlers' fears of big city merchants. For that reason the people of the towns had to be especially vigilant and independent, refusing to let themselves be misled by designing men in positions of power.[18]

Some people scarcely had to be warned. At Wilbraham the local Committee of Correspondence noted that anyone not following the lead of the Continental Congress in adopting its "Salutary Measures" could not be a friend to the county, and "We Shall not think our Selves obliged to Show any Special Regards to them." As the writers added with pointed emphasis, "If they be Judges in Law, or Attorneys at the Bar, we will neglect them as much as possible."[19] For the people of Wilbraham, who counted no judges or attorneys among their neighbors, the specific reference could hardly have been an automatic or unthinking turn of phrase. Their letter reflected a sensitivity to the political loyalties of a whole class of local leaders beyond the bounds of their small town. By no means did they express the toleration of and desire for reconciliation with their errant countrymen that they had declared for their mother country and king. In general, in some of the towns outside the traditional seats of power, people were showing themselves to be increasingly unwilling to take their political cues from the established leaders of Hampshire County. With such "Enemies to American Liberty" in positions of authority, it became important for many towns to communicate directly with Boston; doing so had "opened the eyes of some" and might further "have a Tendency to open the eyes of a great number in the County of Hampshire." Armed with information from the Boston Committee, people could discount the rumors, leaving the perpetrators of falsehood to "tell that to some body else."[20]

165

Even as the people of Hampshire County embraced the wider provincial and national movement, then, one very important focus of their radicalism remained primarily local. Many westerners may have come to look to Boston for political guidance, but they had to look no further than their own county for political targets. The several unflattering references to the "Great men" of Hampshire County that crop up in the letters to Boston serve as only a small indication of the ill will many people already felt toward the traditional county leadership, a reflection of an antipathy that had been growing for years. That earlier hostility had never been so clearly articulated by so many people at once, of course, but had tended to emerge somewhat sporadically in particular towns over particular grievances. With the heightening of the general colonial crisis, however, the political antagonisms in Hampshire County also became more sharply defined. The established county leaders suddenly seemed not just unpopular but potentially oppressive, their local authority dangerously augmented by a distant and devious group of ministers in the British government. In that sense the actions of the British government focused attention on the position of the county elite and forced people throughout Hampshire to confront the prospects for the future of the county. Unless they were willing to accept a new local political arrangement imposed from outside their neighborhood, they would have to take immediate action within. And for that reason the first burst of revolutionary activity in the county turned out to be an almost entirely local affair. No matter what the people of Wilbraham had said about their desire to ignore their unpatriotic county leaders and "neglect them as much as possible," these leaders quickly became the victims of close and sometimes quite painful attention.

The whole process of local upheaval began on a rather grand scale. On the morning of August 30, 1774, people from towns all over Hampshire County, a mob between one and three or four thousand strong, converged on Springfield, where the county court was scheduled to sit that day. The ringing of the bell across the river in West Springfield provided the signal for the final march, and the crowd moved into the center of Springfield and surrounded the courthouse. There they called out the justices. One by one the members of the court were questioned about their loyalty to the Crown and to their country, each one being asked to sign a declaration renouncing all authority derived from royal commissions. Faced with such a menacing throng before them, most of the justices submitted to the will of the crowd quietly if not altogether sincerely. The two most powerful figures, John Worthington and Israel Williams, tried to defend themselves before the mob, but in the end they merely succeeded in increasing the anger and passion of the people. Especially Worthington, who was being humiliated in his hometown by outsiders, attempted to maintain some sense of his authority before the crowd. But according to one witness to the scene,

> The sight of him flashed lightning from their eyes. Their spirits were already raised and the sight of this object gave them additional force. He had not refused his new office of counsellor. For that reason especially he was very obnoxious. But the people kept their tempers. He attempted to harangue them in mittagation of his conduct, but he was soon obliged to desist. The people were not to be dallied with. Nothing would satisfy them but a renunciation.

Likewise, Israel Williams tried to argue that even though he had disagreed with the people before, he would henceforth "join them in the common cause." Few people believed him, of course, and he was forced to renounce his commission along with the rest.[21] His troubles were only beginning.

Such a massive event was something hardly anyone in Hampshire County had ever experienced. To some it offered quite a frightening prospect. As the Reverend Jonathan Judd of Southampton wrote in distress, "Every Body submitted to our Sovereign Lord the Mob – Now we are reduced to a State of Anarchy, have neither Law nor any other Rule except the Law of Nature . . . to go by." Judd's fear of anarchy, however, may have been a bit overblown. As a number of historians have convincingly argued, one must not assume too readily that mob action – or crowd action, to use a less emotive term – necessarily involved excessive violence, injustice, or anarchy. More often the actions of mobs in preindustrial Europe and America represented a means of defending traditional rights or of dispensing justice when local magistrates seemed unable or unwilling to do so. This European heritage of crowd behavior crossed the Atlantic with the migrants to British North America, and during the colonial period there were recorded numerous instances of mob action throughout the American colonies, even in pre-Revolutionary Hampshire County. Far from being something altogether foreign and fearful, extralegal activity had its place within the cultural traditions of early American society, and however much some people may have thought it an unwelcome inheritance, others clearly saw it as a legitimate form of political behavior.[22]

Some reports of local mob activity, in fact, emphasized not so much the fear of chaos and disorder as an appreciation of the careful self-restraint of the people involved. At the time of the closing of the Hampshire County court, the Reverend Judd's visions of chaos were countered by a somewhat more sympathetic observation by Joseph Clarke of Northampton, who noted that "the strictest order of justice [was] observed" by the assembled thousands at Springfield. "The people to their honor behaved with the greatest order & regularity, a few individuals excepted, and avoided, as much as possible, confusion." Perhaps nothing could suggest this sense of self-conscious discipline better than the final action of the mob after its work was done for the day. Having come together as a single body to exert mass pressure on the county justices, the people of the various towns ended the day by drawing themselves up into individual town companies and marching around Springfield carrying staves and playing martial music.[23]

The action of the mob at Springfield represented an important break with the political patterns of the past and provided a massive foreshadowing of the changes that were to come over the course of the next few months. The people of the towns, acting together as a coherent group, became a regulating force to challenge and discipline the county's ruling men. Implicit in their final parade was the notion that the large crowd gathered that day was in reality a collection of smaller groups, each one representing a particular town: even in a large collective effort localism still provided a form of order and political identity for the participants. Yet in closing the court the several mobs acted together for a goal of county-wide importance. It became immediately apparent that the established political leaders, especially those whose influence extended into the government of the county, could no longer expect to exercise the power and authority they had long known, nor could they expect to have to deal only with their own townspeople on political matters. People were beginning to express their concerns for the political situation of the county as a whole, and they were therefore beginning to take action on a county level.

In the months following the events at Springfield there erupted a number of other smaller incidents of isolated mob activity in Hampshire County, and in this early period of unrest the crowd actions shared a common pattern that revealed even more clearly the significant changes in the particular political situation of the county. In most cases people of one town moved on another neighboring town to attack the leading citizens there, generally before there had been any real attempt by the local townspeople to take direct action against their own leaders. More to the point, the inhabitants of the newer towns tended to be the first to undertake such actions, just as they had been among the first to respond to the call of the radicals in Boston. Compressed into a fairly brief period in late 1774 and early 1775, these outbreaks of external regulation by outsiders helped bring about a kind of regional revolution within the larger political context of the national revolution. Once the large mob at Springfield had made the first overt challenge to the county leadership, these local mobs pushed that challenge even further.

Some of the older, more comfortable towns quickly became uncomfortable havens for many of their leaders, and as one inhabitant of Deerfield wrote to a friend, "It is a Bisy time with us, mobbing." Just a week or so after the Springfield incident, for instance, a mob from Williamsburg marched on Hatfield to seek out Israel Williams, Oliver Partridge, and some of the other town officials. A crowd from Montague repeatedly threatened to move on Deerfield, and the people of Pelham and Shutesbury were reportedly "ready to act in a mob way" against the suspected Tories in Amherst. In February of 1775 a mob from Pelham descended on Hatfield, once again aiming to get Israel Williams. The Pelham people took Williams and his son, carried them to Hadley, and in one of the most locally famous acts of ritual retribution, smoked them overnight in a house with a clogged chimney. Upon their release the next morning both Israel and his son were encouraged to sign yet another confession and declaration of loyalty. The next day the same mob moved on to Northampton to seek out Solomon Stoddard, son of John Stoddard and grandson of the Reverend Solomon Stoddard – certainly one of Northampton's finest pedigrees. Not only was Stoddard generally suspected of being a Tory, but he was also an important creditor for many of the Pelham men and therefore a doubly attractive target. He was in poor health, however, and the Pelhamites spared him the smoking they gave Williams, asking only that he sign a confession and repent. Once again, one of the most succinct observations on the mob's behavior in its dealing with Williams and Stoddard came from Southampton's Reverend Judd, still no friend to extralegal activity. "They act like mad people," he complained, "tho well for a Mob."[24]

Judd was by no means alone in his uneasiness; he could report with grim satisfaction that "People condemn the Mob very freely to Day and I fancy that something will be done by the Committee about it." Even Joseph Hawley, Northampton's leading Whig, reacted with alarm when the Pelhamites came after his kinsman Stoddard, declaring himself opposed to "Such private disturbances and restraining people of yr liberty." Hawley himself had been perhaps too soft on Stoddard, but there were also others in the town who "were engaged . . . to endeavor to stop the Mob from any further abuse to those they have." Throughout Northampton and elsewhere the fear spread among other leading Whigs that people acting on their own accord might too easily go out of control. Indeed, at the very first outbreak of mob activity in the fall of 1774, a group of local leaders meeting in a county convention passed a pointed resolution that "we would heartily recommend to all the inhabitants of this county, not to engage in any riots, or licentious attacks upon the person or property of any one, as being subversive of all order and government." If there was to be a political upheaval in Hampshire County, some men clearly hoped to keep it within certain bounds.[25]

As the local mobs continued their actions, however, others saw them in a much more favorable light and were not so quick to condemn their actions. There may have been people in Northampton, for instance, who "were engaged . . . to endeavor to stop the Mob," but according to the town's historian, the Pelham crowd did its work in Northampton "aided and abetted . . . by men residing here."[26] The point is not that a substantial number of people in Northampton or any of the other county towns actually looked forward to a future of permanent mob rule, but, rather, that extralegal activity represented an extraordinary way of dealing with extraordinary circumstances, and some people accepted mob activity because they appreciated its political possibilities. Outsiders could sometimes do what insiders themselves could not do: they could act without the traditional restraints of neighborliness and local deference and thus take more direct and extreme action against their selected targets. In that sense the outsiders provided a useful service by being the first to disrupt the order within the town, saving the locals from having to take full responsibility later for their own actions or desires.

The most detailed account of one such crowd action in Hampshire County survives in a series of depositions written by members of a mob from the "infant settlement" of Williamsburg. On September 6, 1774, less than two weeks after they had drafted their first reply to the Boston Committee of Correspondence, a crowd of Williamsburg people gathered around the Liberty Pole in the center of their town and made ready to set off for neighboring Hatfield, their parent town and still the home of Israel Williams. From their descriptions of their march we get a sense not only of their own goals and desires, but of the reaction of the Hatfield people as well.[27] On one level, then, the incident serves to reveal something of the changing relationship between the people of the old towns and those of the new and, in even more general terms, to highlight some of the critical issues and tensions underlying the rapidly changing political context of Hampshire County on the eve of the Revolution.

Perhaps buoyed and somewhat emboldened by the force of their own words to the Boston Committee, the Williamsburg people were still uneasy as they milled around the Liberty Pole, and some fell into a nervous discussion about what exactly they were going to do. Fearing resistance in Hatfield, a few men had brought their guns. Most of the members of the crowd seemed unwilling to risk such a potentially dangerous confrontation, and they urged a general agreement that everyone leave his weapon at home. Their hope was that strength lay in numbers, and they sent a representative, James Hunt, to the neighboring village of Cummington to round up a few more people. They also sent another man, Benjamin Read, into Hatfield to get a better idea of the situation there.[28]

When Read arrived at Hatfield he was met by Israel Chapin, one of the Hatfield constables. Chapin asked Read what business the Williamsburg people had in mind, "whether we were comeing to rectifi privet Damages Especly to punish Coll. Williams Reletive to an old Difuculty." As Read later described the incident, the Hatfield constable at first

> Labour'd to Discourage us But after he understood that we had no desire to Rectifi privet Damages he Did not Disapprove of our comeing But incoraged it and said to this purpos that their was a corupt vicious . . . crew in Hatfield and that they ought to be Delt with he said I told Clark Williams last night that he Deserved Stripes he said that the two Colonels Williams and . . . Leut partridg David Biling Obediah Dickenson Asa White Trobridg and Left Biling deserved to be Delt with in Severity.

No doubt startled by such a sudden and vitriolic outburst against Hatfield's leading citizens, Benjamin Read hastened to assure Constable Chapin that "we was comeing in Regular order and that we Do not Desire to damage any person [or] property with whom our Busness might Lead us to have to Do." In response, Chapin assured Read that if the mob acted with the discipline and purpose described, virtually everyone in Hatfield would join them and help take action against "those toryes." Exactly what happened after that remains unclear, lost in conflicting stories and incomplete evidence. There is no record that the Williamsburg people actually found Israel Williams or the other Hatfield leaders that day, or even that they got all the way to Hatfield in one body.[29]

Yet even if the Williamsburg people never did actually lay hands on Israel Williams, the exchange between Benjamin Read and Israel Chapin still had an important meaning of its own. Above all, both men had no trouble agreeing that Williams and his local allies deserved, as constable Chapin put it, "to be Delt with in Severity." Moreover, both seemed likewise to agree that it was not inappropriate that a mob from outside Hatfield come into town to take action against Williams and the others. Indeed, Constable Chapin seems to have put aside his normal task of maintaining order in Hatfield in favor of giving strong encouragement to the outsiders and in the end even becoming especially vehement in his denunciation of his townsmen. If there was any hesitation or confusion in his mind, it arose only with regard to the actual motives of the people from Williamsburg, a suspicion that somehow they were "comeing to rectifi privet Damages . . .

Reletive to an old Difuculty" and not to deal with the Hatfield leaders for being "toryes."

However much Chapin might have been convinced by Read's response, he had raised an important question that defied an easy answer. For insiders as well as outsiders, the issue of motive may have been much more complex than either party was willing to admit. Neither Read nor Chapin said, of course, what private grievances the people of Williamsburg might hold against Israel Williams. Perhaps everyone knew what the problem was, and no one had to say; it may have had to do with the terms of the recent separation of Williamsburg from Hatfield, or it may have stemmed from even earlier problems that may not have been related to or resolved by the separation. Unfortunately, there is nothing in the records of either town to make it possible to identify the issue with any certainty. The point is simply that there apparently was some local grievance recognized fairly readily by people in both towns, and at least one person thought it plausible that the "old Difuculty" might still be the motive for mob action even at a time when newer, more menacing difficulties seemed to be emerging all around. Although Chapin and Read both implicitly agreed that a commingling of past and present complaints should not occur, they both implicitly admitted that it could happen.

Even so, such an admission would not necessarily imply a conscious and cynical attempt by the Williamsburg people to use the broader political context as a convenient cover for pursuing their own parochial ends. In all fairness, one must suspect that they would have been unable to separate one set of issues completely from the other. How could they actually say, for instance, that their animosity toward Williams was simply a product of his stance in the current national crisis and not at least partly related to the position he had held for so long in their community and their county? Certainly Williams was a Tory, and since he had not renounced his allegiance to the Crown he stood as an obvious target. At the same time, however, Williams was a consistent symbol of the conservative social and political order within Hampshire County itself. He was the single most important source of authority in the whole region, and everyone – especially every dissident, whether religious or secular – knew that Williams was not far removed from any issue that affected the towns or people of the county. How could they deny that their desire to take abusive action against him did not indeed grow from a desire to settle old scores? Just as it would be impossible to estimate the variety of private debts people owed him, so would it be impossible to calculate the number of "privet Damages" people held against him. How, in short, could they essentially give Israel Williams a clean slate and then, suddenly in the summer of 1774, start making altogether new marks against him? Try as they might to stress the immediacy of their motives, they could hardly have forgotten all they had known, felt, or feared in the past.

In a somewhat different manner, the past figured equally heavily in the actions of the Hatfield people. If, as Chapin asserted, the townspeople were so hostile toward Williams and the "corupt vicious . . . crew" in Hatfield, why did they not take some action themselves without waiting for the instigation of outsiders? The question had in fact been raised just a few days before the mob appeared. Some Hatfield men had been talking with men from other nearby towns about Israel Williams and some of the other local Tories, and though the Hatfielders expressed the sentiment that someone should deal with Williams and the others, these men declined to take action themselves; explained one Hatfield resident, "It would Brake Neighborhood and therefore would Not Do so well as for . . . Strangers."[30]

It was an important request the Hatfield men made, and an interesting way of expressing it. Their desire for outside action was not simply a sign of cowardice or even hypocrisy among people unwilling to take direct action themselves. It suggested, rather, a conflict between their immediate political desires and their long-term political background. On the one hand, some Hatfielders, like the people of Williamsburg, had their own grudges and grievances from the past. They had challenged Williams and a few other town leaders before, occasionally denying them election to town office in recent years.[31] Now they wanted to go beyond the bounds of normal political procedures, to subject some of their leading townspeople not just to the will of the electorate but to the hands of a mob; implicit in this desire was the notion that mere electoral processes were not strong or forceful enough, and that the designated victims should undergo the personal, visible experience of public humiliation and perhaps even physical harm. On the other hand, though, the traditions of town life had a tempering effect. The inherited standards of communal unity and proper deference toward local leaders made it difficult for the Hatfield men themselves to inflict such exceptional treatment on their fellow townsmen.[32] As they explicitly pointed out to the outsiders, it was a serious matter to "Brake Neighborhood" and be the ones responsible for disrupting the order and integrity of the town. Only if someone from outside could come in and disrupt that order first would Hatfielders feel comfortable about joining in. Their sense of neighborhood, in short, did not keep them from wanting to attack certain neighbors, but it did make them maintain certain appearances.

To some extent, of course, the mob from Williamsburg could likewise have been accused of violating the neighborhood. Until the time of their separation from Hatfield in 1771, the Williamsburg people were themselves part of the Hatfield neighborhood, neighbors also of Williams and the other suspected Tories in the town.[33] Even after they formed their own separate town they could not escape all the old ties. But their political independence ultimately gave them a certain freedom of action their Hatfield neighbors did not have. At the very least they were no longer so directly under Williams's influence and control, no longer expected to deal with him as a fellow townsman or town leader. Despite his unquestioned prominence in the political affairs of the county, Williams could not participate directly in the political affairs of Williamsburg or impose his awesome presence on the town meeting. Indeed, the very fact that the people of Williamsburg had a Liberty Pole around which to gather was a visible indication of their newfound independence from Williams and the other Hatfield leaders. No one had dared raise a Liberty Pole in Hatfield, and as long as Williams and his sympathizers were still powerful in the town, no one was likely to do so. Anyone needing an example had to look no further than Deerfield, where local radicals had raised a Liberty Pole only to have it torn down by the town's strong conservative faction – among them several of Williams's kinsmen.[34]

But the people of Williamsburg did not have to worry about so direct a confrontation, either on the issue of a Liberty Pole or on any other issue. The Williamsburg people acted as an external force somewhat less hindered than Williams's townspeople by the inherited norms of town politics and communal harmony. In a

sense they could "Brake Neighborhood" on the county level precisely because they did not have to do so on the town level. It was
a subtle and almost artificial distinction, but not an unimportant
one. On the eve of a local as well as a national revolution, the old
standards of duty, deference, and obligation did not pass easily
away. It became the task of outsiders like the Williamsburg mob
to help accelerate the change.

In time, of course, the locals became a bit more forthright. After
the brief period of mob actions in late 1774 and early 1775, and
especially after the outbreak of hostilities at Lexington and Concord in April of 1775, there no longer seemed any reason to be
overly delicate in dealing with people suspected of political deviance. In towns throughout Hampshire County, 1775 marked the
beginning of open attacks by townspeople on their own leaders,
both secular and ecclesiastical. In some cases the action taken was
relatively gentle; in other cases it was exceedingly harsh. But
within the space of about a year important men in a number of
towns found themselves humbled, harassed, or even expelled,
never again to enjoy power in quite the ways they had known it
before. Throughout the county the old figures of authority fell
with surprising speed and even more surprising ease. Once the
first real challenge had been successfully made at Springfield in
August of 1774, the pattern of change had begun. It may have
been altered in style and intensity in a few instances, but it was
never really reversed.

Once again, the case of Israel Williams best suggests the conti-
nuities between external and internal regulation. After his vocal
encounter with the mob at Springfield, his near encounter with
the smaller mob from Williamsburg, and his smoky encounter
with the mob from Pelham, he eventually found even more severe
trials facing him at the hands of the people of Hatfield. At first
with some remnants of deference, but later with a stronger atti-
tude of defiance, his townspeople turned against him and stripped
him of his authority and his freedom. He lived the last years of his
life among his fellow citizens as an outcast among them, increasingly a symbol of their rejection of all that he had once stood for.

In May of 1775 the town's Committee of Correspondence openly broached the subject of support for the American cause in a
letter to Williams and several other suspected Tories in Hatfield,
asking that those "whom the Comtee may suspect as being inimi-

cal to their Country be requested to sign a declaration" professing their commitment to the defense of American liberties. Even so, the terms of the letter remained temperate if not necessarily deferential. The Hatfield Committee requested that Williams "walk over to Deacon Mortons and Satisfy the Committee of his Readiness to Join his Countrymen." They did nothing to intimidate him, and Williams remained at large, no longer a town leader but not yet a town prisoner. The longer he remained free, though, the more he came to be suspected of actual treason. The Hatfield Committee of Correspondence joined with other committees in the county and with officers of the county militia in writing Williams a blistering letter late in 1775 accusing him of "acting a part & executing a plan perfectly inconsistent with the Sense of this Province and all British America."

> Your Conduct has been from first to last one continued Series of Treason and Rebellion at your County and you have been and are Still an open avowed Enemy to your Country . . . You with your little Banditti of Sons and Tools made it their Business to collect Names in Order for Prosecutions—your Plans and Designs of betraying and ruining your Country are all laid open . . . you can make no movement to execute your cursed detestable Plans but you are discovered—the People throughout the Province know you and all your Machinations and movements and think Death too mild a Punishment for you.

The letter closed with the suggestion that Williams depart for Boston and stay out of the county until the war should end.[35]

The fear of Williams's sedition was only compounded in late 1776 when some papers addressed from him to Thomas Hutchinson were intercepted. In his letter to Hutchinson Williams allegedly expressed "his certain Hope & expectation that our Enemies would very soon entirely defeat & fully Subdue the Americans," and according to the Hatfield Committee, such sentiments were enough to settle the question.[36] Williams and his son were arrested and locked up despite their protests of innocence.

The concern over so powerful and imposing a man as Israel Williams could hardly be exaggerated in the minds of his fellow citizens. As the Hatfield Committee explained to the Provincial Council after the arrest, "He has been & still is a Man of Considerable Influence with the People, & consequently has perswaded a

Considerable number of Persons not only in this Town but we apprehend more or less in every Town in the County to adopt his Sentiments."[37] The charges against him served to indicate the kind of respect his townspeople still accorded him: they no longer recognized him as their own leader, but they still recognized him as a powerful and therefore dangerous man.

Israel Williams remained a prisoner in his own town for over three years, disgraced politically and disdained socially. The church even voted to deny him communion. Throughout the period of his incarceration Williams complained bitterly of "the hard Measures he has met with . . . owing to the People of Hatfield." His former neighbors would not deal with him honestly or openly, he argued, and he called upon them to submit all their accusations to public hearing "That He may vindicate himself if able – For there is no fencing against Daggers and Darts thrown in the dark." In a way, of course, the people of Hatfield may not have been able to express all their true feelings against Williams. Once they had him in jail for what appeared to be legitimate political reasons they could no doubt take some secret satisfaction in punishing him for his pride and power of former years. Those "Daggers and Darts" may have been thrown from the darkness of the past, sharpened long before the distinctions between Whig and Tory ever became clear. When he was finally let out of jail in 1780 and given the relative freedom of staying under house arrest, he remained in Hatfield until his death eight years later, a fallen if not forgotten man.[38] Abused first by the people of his county and then by the people of his own town, he had experienced perhaps more extensively than anyone else the full impact of political change in the region he had long governed. Once the initial break had been made in the neighborhood, he had nowhere to turn for refuge. In the end his own closest neighbors in Hatfield gave him the worst treatment of all.

In a number of other towns local leaders suffered some form of the same treatment, ranging from outright political opposition to imprisonment. Most notably in some of the older towns in the county, where ruling elites had governed for years without any serious disruption in their authority, did the political changes in the early years of the Revolution seem sudden and striking. At Springfield, for instance, the once-powerful John Worthington found himself no longer able to direct the political affairs of his people, but instead was subject to their direction himself. After having to defend himself before the huge crowd of outsiders at the courthouse in August of 1774, Worthington had to make a similar declaration of his patriotism before the people of Springfield. His patriotism was already highly suspect, for he had maintained clear allegiance to the Crown throughout the early stirrings of revolt; he had even considered at one point emigrating to Canada to avoid the hostile sentiments of his neighbors. Worthington eventually managed to clear himself in his public declaration and to remain in Springfield, but he was stripped of his power and influence for a few years. He and a number of other Springfield leaders were turned out of office in 1774 and 1775 and replaced with men who had begun to emerge as leaders in the local Revolutionary movement. As a later historian of the town described the political situation of the early Revolutionary period, "The names prominent in the doings at that time were not the best-known Springfield names." Faced with the growing hostility of their fellow townspeople, some of the old leaders decided to leave town for good; others stayed, and some of these, after altering their political views to fit the dominant popular opinion, even made it back into elected office during the middle years of the Revolution. But for a brief period at least, from 1775 until 1778, Springfield was the scene of a minor political upheaval. The old town leaders had been made victims of popular attack and had been deposed according to a new political standard defined by the people of the town.[39]

Similar changes took place in other towns as well, as the first months of the Revolutionary period brought an important break with the politics of the past. Formerly entrenched rulers were finally rooted out and replaced. Israel Williams's kinsmen at Deerfield, for instance, fell at about the same time he did. The Deerfield Williamses and their Ashley cousins had long been dominant both in local and in county offices, variously holding positions as selectman, town clerk, county judge, and justice of the peace; throughout the 1750s the family's power was at its peak. During the next decade that power began to wane somewhat, but even so, the clan continued to play a significant role in the politics of the town: Jonathan Ashley, Esq., repeatedly represented the family on the Board of Selectmen, and Thomas Williams served as town clerk until 1774. Moreover, several members of the family still held on to the appointive offices acquired through the good graces

179

and patronage of their Hatfield relative. In 1774, however, they were cleaned out of office entirely.[40] The Deerfield voters were no longer willing to keep them in positions of power, and Israel Williams was no longer able. Indeed, their connection to Israel Williams, along with their own political attitudes, clearly marked them in the new political context of the county. Whatever degree of indulgence or respect had kept them politically active in the early 1770s vanished. The severe and sharp political distinctions of the Revolution brought on the immediate demise of the family in the town, forcing some into political exile, the others into political limbo. Their only allies were the core of local Loyalists, a sizable but surely suspect lot.

Likewise, in Amherst, as we have seen in the dispute over the meetinghouse, the events of the Revolution provided the final setting for resolving internal antagonisms that had been brewing for years. By 1774 the power of newcomers in the town could hardly be taken for granted, and by combining both national and local issues they gained the political impetus to push most of the old leaders out. A few of those leaders made themselves agreeable to the new majority, but a few others wound up in jail. Those latter victims of the political shift in the town complained indignantly of their fall from dignity. From the new jail in Northampton Isaac Chauncy and several other Amherst men incarcerated there wrote bitterly of their fellow citizens, calling their actions "irregular" and "Not Reasonable."[41] Being locked up and exposed to such obvious humiliation was a hard blow for some former leaders to accept, for jail represented the severest form of public expulsion and repudiation. Simply being turned out of office probably seemed mild by comparison. If there remained any consolation for Chauncy and his allies, it might only have been that the walls of the jail offered a gentler form of punishment than the hands of a mob.

It was not only the secular leaders who suffered, but the clergy as well. Ministers, in fact, seemed to be singled out for especially severe abuse and correction by their townspeople, made to declare openly their sentiments toward the Revolutionary struggle and pressured to make those sentiments reflect the will of the community. Townspeople could not well leave their spiritual fates to a man they would not entrust with their political fortunes. Moreover, the symbolic value of the minister's position, more than his actual political function, made this collective pressure necessary and strong, for he was the most visible figure representing the town's communal identity. It was no longer enough that he speak to his parishioners; he also had to speak for them. His role as local leader was far too important for his political opinions to remain his alone.

The nature of the relationship between pastor and people became very clear to Longmeadow's minister, Stephen Williams. Throughout the first months of the Revolutionary crisis he remained torn in his loyalties and unsure of his duty, praying for the safety of the Longmeadow militia company as it went off to fight in 1775, but also praying that God keep him "from doing anything displeasing to His Majesty." His ambivalence apparently became a question among some of his people, for in June of 1775 he wrote Eleazar Wheelock that he was disconcerted by

Reproaches cast upon me because I have prayed that the King might do that which is right in the Eyes of the Lord and not be Led astray by . . . corrupt counsellors (the very expressions I made use of in a public prayer, the very day a warm man reproached me for praying for the King & told me, I ought to have prayed he might have his Head cutt off).

"Such reproaches dont much disquiet me," Williams claimed. "I can & do pray for them, that Abuse me & would represent me as inimical to ye Country."[42] But whatever his disclaimers, such reproaches could hardly leave him unmoved. For almost sixty years he had held his pulpit and led his people, and now in the midst of a confusing political situation some of them were turning on him, threatening to deny the dignity of the office he had maintained for so long. He was, after all, a relative of Israel Williams and somewhat tainted merely by family association. In the end the Reverend Williams's age and long service to the community no doubt tempered the abusive action of the most radical local Whigs, but he had clearly been warned.

So too had the Reverend Jonathan Ashley at Deerfield. Like Stephen Williams, Ashley was part of the kinship network that united most members of the county elite, but unlike Williams, Ashley had no uncertainty about where his loyalty lay. He identified himself clearly with his kinsmen in the Tory faction in Deerfield and in the county at large, and he made no secret of his support for the Crown. As Deerfield became increasingly divided during the early months of the Revolution, Ashley still managed

181

to hold onto his pulpit, just as he had done during the height of the Great Awakening. In the Revolution as in the Awakening, in fact, most of those opposed to Ashley withdrew from the church and left him to his supporters. But he did not escape harsh treatment altogether. Although he was never jailed or removed from office, he was occasionally insulted and treated rudely; throughout the Revolution he also had trouble getting his full pay or allotment of firewood – always a clear sign that people could choose to punish their minister in the town meeting if not in church. By the time of his death in 1780 he had lived with both political and financial uncertainty for over five years. It was with some feeling of bitterness that his heirs brought a substantial claim against the town in 1782 to try to recover some of the money owed the late pastor. By then the harmony between pastor and people had long been broken and was in a state of decay. The posthumous legal action served only as a final indication of just how far the decay had gone.[43]

Some of Ashley's Old Light colleagues suffered even greater personal abuse for their political Loyalism, and their people resorted to much more direct and immediate punishment. Like Ashley, Abraham Hill of Shutesbury tried to douse the inflamed spirits of his people by spreading fear and urging caution. He once warned three would-be volunteers – one of whom was Daniel Shays, soon to be the most famous radical of western Massachusetts – about the danger of enlisting in the colonial army: "I understand you think of taking up arms against your King. The king can send a company of horse through the country and take off every head; and in less than six weeks you will be glad to labor a week for sheep's head and pluck." But Hill's estimation of the Crown's military capabilities proved a little overdone, and he instead found his own head in danger. After a few such incidents of open hostility to the patriot cause, Hill was confined to the town pound and, according to popular accounts, fed only on herring thrown over the wall. After a subsequent confinement under house arrest he was dismissed from his ministerial office in 1778. His thirty-six years of service in the town could not save him from a couple of years of open political disfavor.[44]

Similarly, Jedediah Smith at Granville and Jonathan Leavitt at Charlemont were dismissed during the first years of the Revolution. Smith, it will be recalled, had been involved in a growing dispute with a group of Separates and eventually with most of the people in his town; his continued support for the Crown after 1775 became the final source of antagonism that sent him on his way to the Mississippi and to death. Leavitt, too, had fallen into disfavor with his people because of his supposed Arminianism and "suspected lukewarmness towards the Revolution." He lost first his salary and eventually his job. David Parsons at Amherst, though never suspected of Arminianism, was suspected of Toryism, and he too had trouble collecting his salary; at one point the people of Amherst even wrote to get help from Northampton "in the important trial of the Rev. Mr. David Parsons upon a Complaint of his being unfriendly to the interests of the Continent." But the people in Northampton had their own minister to think about. Early in the Revolution one of the more vociferous Northampton Whigs felt compelled to offer the Reverend Hooker a pointed reminder that he had better make his opinions about the American cause a little clearer; Hooker understood the suggestion well enough and thereafter added his voice to the cause of liberty. After similar prodding and implied threats, John Hubbard at Northfield and Roger Newton at Greenfield also made themselves more agreeable to the sentiments of their people. At New Salem Samuel Kendal simply despaired of the whole situation and resigned.[45]

In many ways the early days of the Revolution confronted both ministers and secular leaders with many of the problems they had had to face during the Great Awakening. Like the Great Awakening, the Revolution was not just a matter of belief, but also a pattern of behavior. Both the Awakening and the Revolution began as widespread popular movements that swept the American colonies, combining intense emotionalism with sometimes extreme and disruptive activity. The Reverend Stephen Williams, for instance, expressed many of the same fears about the Revolutionary period he had had about the Awakening over thirty years before. Already one of the old ministers in Hampshire County by the time the Awakening reached its peak, Williams had looked out from his Longmeadow parish in the early 1740s and noted his concern at the phenomenon he witnessed. "I find ye country in a tumult," he wrote of the Awakening; "I am in great concern & pray God to help & relieve in this dark day—I fear ye interest of religion is like to Suffer on all hands—& I pray God to Show himself gracious."[46]

By 1774 Williams had still not grown accustomed to displays of violent or extreme behavior among his people. Once again he worried: "I hear uneasiness & *tumults* – & frettings – in one place & another – some uneasy with civill rules – Some with ministers – oh yt God would have mercy upon us – & Give to thy people to consider – & realize it yt an house divided against it Self *cant Stand*." At other times he complained about "ye mobbish disposition" and the "danger of going to Extreams," and generally he continued to be dismayed and confused by the excess of popular sentiment he saw brewing around him.[47] Williams supported liberty as much as he supported piety. He did not feel happy, however, about the effect those goals seemed to have on his people: a new sense of purpose led a suddenly awakened populace to develop very clear distinctions between good and evil, between right and wrong, and those distinctions were quickly turned on the leaders of society as strict standards of judgment. Especially when he sensed "some uneasy with civill rules – Some with ministers" in the early days of the Revolution, he began to become uneasy himself. He once again saw a danger posed to his society and to his very position.

And yet, however much Williams and others in his situation may have found the sudden intensity of such challenges disturbing, they could hardly have found the general upsurge of local unrest altogether surprising. It must have been obvious to everyone by the summer of 1774 that the recent actions of the Crown represented an immediate crisis that needed an immediate response. Certainly many people in the rural regions of Massachusetts recognized the very real threats inherent in the new imperial policies, and they moved quickly to take action against anyone who seemed in any way sympathetic or even insufficently hostile to those policies. And in that sense it may have seemed equally obvious that the leading members of the Hampshire elite, like many other local leaders in other parts of the colonies, would be likely targets for attack primarily or even solely because of their apparent continued loyalty to the Crown. Whatever a man's actions or attitudes in the past, his present position – and that alone – would be enough to condemn him.[48]

At the same time, however, such a narrow focus simply on the immediate context of the crisis would tend to obscure the significance of other events, at least for twentieth-century observers.

Taking a somewhat broader view than that available to the Reverend Williams, one must try to appreciate the way the Revolution also represented a moment of historical intensity that reflected a subtler historical transformation that had taken place gradually over the previous decades. That is, the Revolution, like the Great Awakening a generation earlier, provided both the context and the terms, an immediate reason and a new standard, for a sharply articulated critique of the state of society, or at least the state of the county. But that critique had been developing for years, emerging from scattered conflicts over local issues to become a more general spirit of discontent.

Throughout most parts of the American colonies, in fact, expressions of extreme dissatisfaction with local conditions had become commonplace if not altogether constant in the period between the Awakening and the Revolution. Looking eastward from Hampshire County, Stephen Williams could hardly have been unaware of the social turmoil and political turbulence that dominated public life in mid-century Boston. But turning his attention in the other direction, he would find numerous other examples of widespread, even massive, unrest. Across the border in New York, for instance, the Hudson Valley had been scarred by land riots in the 1750s and 1760s, as tenants rose up against the landlords who owned so much land and held so much power over them. Tenants also took violent action in New Jersey, and in Pennsylvania a band of over a thousand western frontiersmen, the "Paxton Boys," marched on Philadelphia in 1764 to protest the government's failure to provide them with adequate protection during Pontiac's Rebellion. Backcountry settlers in the western counties of North Carolina engaged in armed resistance against local officials throughout the 1760s, and the provincial government eventually had to send several thousand armed troops west to defeat the "Regulator" movement in 1771. In many cases the people who undertook these violent uprisings against established authorities were, like the newer settlers on the frontier of Hampshire County, fairly recent migrants to their respective regions, struggling to survive in a world of increasing social dislocation and recurring economic uncertainty. They did not for the most part share some millenial or revolutionary vision of a radically restructured society, nor did they articulate a coherent theory of class conflict. They did, however, attempt to challenge the power

185

of the political and economic elites who governed their regions and, in doing so, to gain a degree of control over their own lives. In the end, of course, their attempts failed; provincial officials usually chose to deal with their protests with arms rather than arguments. Yet however short-lived or unsuccessful, these movements represent the most visible and violent manifestations of a growing tension between authority and autonomy that pervaded much of pre-Revolutionary America and provided part of the context for the Revolution itself.

To be sure, the people of Hampshire County did not engage in huge mass mobilizations in the years before the Revolution. They carried out their struggles at the community level, and in town after town and in church after church the old standards of stability and order – and the men who upheld them – came under frequent attack. The strength of the challenge proved to be cumulative rather than cataclysmic. By the time of the Revolution the established county leaders had suffered a gradual erosion of their power as their domain had come to be populated largely by people who wanted to define their own political and religious standards and who therefore seemed more resentful than respectful of the power those leaders had traditionally held. After some thirty years of recurring unrest in the towns and churches of the county, the Revolutionary crisis of 1774 brought the widespread disorder into a sharper and more immediate focus. For the people of Hampshire County, who were apparently so late in being awakened to the crisis by the Boston radicals, the impending break with the traditions of British authority caused a more rapid and forceful break with the traditions of local authority. Certainly at no other time in the county's past had so many men of high status and position been unseated, punished, and replaced so quickly. With good reason did many of these old leaders feel vulnerable and fearful as they looked out and saw the "tumults" and "danger of going to Extreams" in the people around them. The antagonisms of past and present seemed to merge quite easily, making it much simpler than before for people to oppose their former leaders with proper patriotic zeal, helping them finally to reject men they were no longer willing to follow.

The early months of the Revolutionary period were extreme times for people throughout Massachusetts and the rest of the

186

colonies, but in Hampshire County as elsewhere, the habits of peace had long been disrupted. When the minutemen of Hampshire County marched off to war in April of 1775, many of them had already been embattled farmers for quite some time, veterans of significant (if somewhat less violent) engagements within their own neighborhood.

APPENDIX

Table I. *Patterns of office holding for selectmen in early Hampshire County towns*

Town	Total no. of selectmen	Distribution by No. of terms			Average no. of terms per selectman
		1 term	2-4 terms	5+ terms	
Springfield	88	20	31	37	5.0
(1644-1734)		(22.7%)	(35.2%)	(42.0%)	
Northampton	92	32	24	36	5.0
(1655-1750)		(34.8%)	(26.1%)	(29.1%)	
Hadley	126	56	36	34	3.6
(1660-1750)		(44.4%)	(28.6%)	(27.0%)	
Westfield	66	27	21	18	3.5
(1669-1750)		(40.9%)	(31.8%)	(27.3%)	
Hatfield	62	14	21	27	6.0
(1678-1750)		(22.6%)	(33.9%)	(43.5%)	
Deerfield	64	28	18	18	3.8
(1686-1750)		(43.8%)	(28.1%)	(28.1%)	
Northfield	30	7	16	7	3.3
(1718-50)		(23.3%)	(53.3%)	(23.3%)	
Brimfield	33	13	14	6	3.0
(1731-50)		(39.4%)	(42.4%)	(18.2%)	

189

Table 2. *Office holding among leading families in selected Hampshire County towns to 1750*

Town	No. of leading families[a]	No. of selectmen	% of total selectmen	No. of terms served	% of total terms
Northampton	10	49	53.2	307	67.9
Springfield	9	37	42.0	225	50.2
Hatfield	3	9	14.5	90	24.6
Westfield	7	39	59.1	147	62.5
Hadley	6	57	45.2	269	60.0

[a]I have defined a "leading family" as one in which either three or more men of the same surname served as selectmen or two men of the same surname served five or more terms each.

Table 3. *Hampshire County ministers, 1743-5*

Name[a]	Town	Year settled as minister	Identification with publication		
			T&A[b]	ST[c]	TNA[d]
Robert Abercrombie (Presbyterian)	Pelham	1742			
Samuel Allis	Somers	1727	x		
Jonathan Ashley	Deerfield	1732		x	x
John Ballantine	Westfield	1741		x	x
Edward Billing	Cold Spring (Belchertown)	1740	x		
Robert Breck	Springfield	1736		x	x
James Bridgham	Brimfield	1736		x	x
Benjamin Doolittle	Northfield	1718			x
Jonathan Edwards	Northampton	1727	x		
Ebenezer Gay	Suffield	1743		x	x
John Harvey (Presbyterian)	Palmer	1734			
Abraham Hill	Road Town (Shutesbury)	1742		x	x
Samuel Hopkins	Springfield (West Springfield)	1720		x	x
Jonathan Hubbard	Sheffield	1736			x
Samuel Kendal	New Salem	1742		x	x
Jonathan Judd	Southampton	1743			

Table 3 *(cont.)*

Name[a]	Town	Year settled as minister	$T\&A$[b]	ST[c]	TNA[d]
William McClenathan	Blandford	1744			x
Noah Merrick	Springfield (Wilbraham)	1741		x	x
John Norton	Bernardston	1741			x
David Parsons	Amherst	1739	x		
William Rand	Sunderland	1724		x	x
Peter Reynolds	Enfield	1725	x		
John Sergeant	Stockbridge	1737		x	x
Edward Upham (Baptist)	Springfield	1740		x	x
Chester Williams	Hadley	1740	x	x	
Stephen Williams	Springfield (Longmeadow)	1716	x		
John Woodbridge	South Hadley	1742	x		
Timothy Woodbridge	Hatfield	1740	x		

[a]Unless otherwise noted, these ministers were Congregational.

[b]*T&A = The Testimony and Advice of an Assembly of Pastors of Churches in New-England, At a Meeting in Boston, July 7, 1743, Occasion'd By the late happy Revival of Religion in many Parts of the Land* (Boston, 1743).

[c]*ST = Seasonable Thoughts on the State of Religion in New England* (Boston, 1743).

[d]*TNA = The Testimony of the North Association in the County of Hartford, in the Colony of Connecticut, convened at Windsor, Feb. 5, 1744-5, Against the Rev. Mr. George Whitefield and his Conduct. And an Address From some of the Ministers in the County of Hampshire, to the Rev. Mr. George Whitefield* (Boston, 1745).

Appendix

Table 4. *Congregational ministers ordained in Hampshire County, 1750-9*

Name	College and class	Town	Year ordained
John Hubbard	Yale, 1747	Northfield	1750
Grindall Rawson	Harvard, 1741	Ware	1751
Judah Nash[a]	Yale, 1751	Colrain	1753
John Hooker[a]	Yale, 1751	Northampton	1753
Edward Billing	Harvard, 1731	Greenfield	1754
Samuel Hopkins[a]	Yale, 1749	Hadley	1755
Joseph Lathrop[a]	Yale, 1754	West Springfield	1756
Justus Forward[a]	Yale, 1754	Cold Spring	1756
Jedediah Smith[a]	Yale, 1750	Granville	1756
Robert Cutler[a]	Harvard, 1741	Greenwich	1759
Ezra Thayer[a]	Harvard, 1754	Ware	1759

[a]These ministers were probably opposed to Edwards in theology. See Clifford K. Shipton, *Sibley's Harvard Graduates: Biographical Sketches of Those Who Attended Harvard College*, 17 vols. (Boston, 1942), IX, XI, XII; and Franklin B. Dexter, *Biographical Sketches of the Graduates of Yale College*, 6 vols. (New York, 1903), I, II.

Table 5. *Ministers dismissed from Hampshire County pulpits for reasons other than health, 1745–76*

Name	Town	Year Dismissed
William McClenathan	Blandford	1747
John Harvey	Palmer	1748
Jonathan Edwards	Northampton	1750
Edward Billing	Cold Spring	1752
Moses Tuttle	Granville	1754
Grindall Rawson	Ware	1754
Pelatiah Webster	Quabbin (Greenwich)	1755
Alexander McDowell	Colrain	1761
James Morton	Blandford	1767
Joseph Patrick	Blandford	1772
Jacob Sherwin	Ashfield	1774
Robert Burns	Palmer	1775
Jedediah Smith	Granville	1776
Samuel Kendal	New Salem	1776

Note: One other minister, James Bridgham of Brimfield, died in office in 1776 before his troubles with the town brought about a dismissal.

Table 6. *Population densities of Massachusetts counties, 1765*

County	Area (sq. miles)	Pop. per sq. mile
Suffolk	410	82.1
Essex	442	97
Middlesex	770	45
Bristol	514	41.5
Plymouth	570	45
Barnstable	324	38
Dukes	9.27	23
Nantucket	23.7	140
Worcester	1462	23.3
Hampshire	1711	12.53
Berkshire	892	12.6

Source: Albert Bushnell Hart, ed., *Commonwealth History of Massachusetts*, 4 vols. (New York, 1928), II, 386.

Appendix

Table 7. *Population of Hampshire County towns, 1765-76*

Town	Year incorporated	Population 1765	Population 1776	% increase (decrease)
Group I (incorporated before 1740)[a]				
Springfield	1646	2,755	1,974	(28.3)
Northampton	1654	1,289	1,790	38.8
Hadley	1661	473	681	18.8
Westfield	1669	1,324	1,488	12.3
Hatfield	1670	815	582	(28.5)
Deerfield	1673	737	836	13.4
Northfield	1714	415	580	39.7
Sunderland	1714	—	409	—
Brimfield	1731	773	1,064	37.6
Group II (incorporated after 1740)				
Blandford	1741	406	772	90.1
Pelham	1743	371	729	94.4
Palmer	1752	508	727	43.7
Greenfield	1753	368	735	99.7
Montague	1753	392	575	46.7
New Salem	1753	375	910	142.6
Southampton	1753	375	740	69.3
South Hadley	1753	817	584	(28.5)
Granville	1754	682	1,126	65.1
Greenwich	1754	—	890	—
Amherst	1759	645	915	41.8
Monson	1760	389	813	109.0
Belchertown	1761	418	972	132.5
Colrain	1761	295	566	90.5
Shutesbury	1761	330	598	81.2
Ware	1761	485	[420][b]	(15.5)
Bernardston	1762	230	607	163.9
Chesterfield	1762	161	1092	578.2
South Brimfield	1762	624	850	36.2
Warwick	1763	191	766	301.0
Wilbraham	1763	491	1057	115.3
Ashfield	1765	—	628	—
Charlemont	1765	—	[380]	—
Murrayfield	1765	—	405	—
Conway	1767	—	897	—
Granby	1768	—	491	—
Shelburne	1768	—	575	—
Worthington	1768	—	639	—
Whately	1770	—	410	—

195

Table 7 (*cont.*)

Town	Year incorporated	Population 1765	Population 1776	% increase (decrease)
Southwick	1770	—	[680]	—
Williamsburg	1771	—	534	—
Norwich	1773	—	[766]	—
Leverett	1774	—	293	—
Ludlow	1774	—	413	—
W. Springfield	1774	—	1744	—
No. 7	unincorporated	—	244	—
Subtotals				
Group I (9)		8,681 (50.2%)	9,404 (26.9%)	
Group II (35, plus one unincorporated)		8,617 (49.8%)	25,543 (73.1%)	
Total		17,298 (100%)	34,947 (100%)	

[a]Group I does not include five former Hamphire towns: Sheffield and Stockbridge, which were set off with Berkshire County in 1761; and Enfield, Somers, and Suffield, which became part of Connecticut in 1747.

[b]Population figures shown in brackets were not included in Greene and Harrington; I have taken them from a manuscript census list for 1776 in Massachusetts Archives, CCCXXII, 99, State House Boston, and have included them in the totals.

Source: Evarts B. Greene and Virginia D. Harrington, *American Population before the Federal Census of 1790* (New York, 1932), pp. 26-7, 33-4.

Table 8. *Patterns of office holding for selectmen in selected Hampshire County hilltowns*

Town	Total no. of selectmen	Distribution by no. of terms			Average no. of terms per selectman
		1 term	2-4 terms	5+ terms	
Blandford (1742-75)	39	11 (28.2%)	16 (41.0%)	12 (30.8%)	4.3
Palmer (1752-75)	25	5 (20.0%)	11 (44.7%)	9 (36.0%)	4.7
Pelham (1743-75)	54	11 (20.4%)	33 (61.1%)	10 (18.5%)	3.0
Granville (1754-75)	14	6 (42.8%)	4 (28.6%)	4 (28.6%)	4.7
Colrain (1761-75)	29	15 (51.7%)	10 (34.5%)	4 (13.8%)	2.5
Worthington (1768-75)	11	6 (54.5%)	4 (36.4%)	1 (9.1%)	2.2
Chesterfield (1762-75)	15	7 (45.7%)	5 (33.3%)	3 (20.0%)	2.8

APPENDIX

Table 9. *Distribution of acres of improved land per Pelham household*

	Number of households	
Acres improved land[a]	1745	1771
0–10	37 (52.9%)	50 (38.2%)
11–15	18 (25.7%)	22 (16.8%)
16–20	9 (12.9%)	14 (10.7%)
21–30	5 (7.2%)	29 (22.1%)
30+	1 (1.4%)	16 (12.2%)
Total	70 (100%)	131 (100%)
Mean acreage per household[b]	10.5	15.2

[a]Improved land includes tillage, pasture, upland meadow, and fresh meadow.

[b]Both town and provincial records recognize some landless individuals as heads of households, and their inclusion in the totals obviously skews the average to the low side. It could be argued, of course, that these landless people probably lived in joint households with their kin, and therefore should not be considered independently in determining household averages. If one excludes the landless, the adjusted averages for 1745 and 1771 are 12.1 and 19.4, respectively–still somewhat below the "middle-class" standard suggested by Gross.

Sources: 1745 Pelham Tax List, in Pelham Town Record, 1743–1779, University of Massachusetts Library, Amherst (microfilm); 1771 valuation, Massachusetts Archives, CXXXIII, 255, State House, Boston.

Table 10. *Individual assessment returns for Pelham, 1760*

	Number of returns listed	Average per return	Median
Land			
Tillage	37	5.5 (acres)	6
Mowing	38	10.5	9
Pasture	20	6.6	4
Orchard	21	1.8	1.5
Grain			
Oats	23	20 (bushels)	14
Indian corn	32	27	25
Rye	28	14	12
Wheat	14	9.5	10

Source: Based on C. O. Parmenter, *History of Pelham from 1738 to 1898* (Amherst, Mass., 1898), pp. 102–10.

APPENDIX

Table 11. *Acres of tillage land in selected Hampshire County towns, 1771*

Town	Acres of tillage	Acres per household
Group I[a]		
Springfield	6,228	9.4
Northampton	1,130	7.6
Hadley	1,421.5	10.0
Westfield	2,338	10.9
Deerfield	1,634	12.7
Northfield	1,269	13.8
Group II[b]		
Blandford	229	2.5
Pelham	502	3.8
New Salem	318	2.4
Greenwich	792	6.0
Ware	495	5.0
Shutesbury	241	2.5
Chesterfield	224	1.6
Ashfield	361	4.4
Murrayfield	503	2.2
Charlemont	385	6.9

[a]Group I consists of towns settled before 1700, mostly along the Connecticut River Valley.
[b]Group II consists of towns settled after 1740, mostly in hills above the Connecticut River Valley.
Source: 1771 valuation, Massachusetts Archives, CXXXII, CXXXIII, CXXXIV, State House, Boston.

Table 12. *Debt cases heard by Hampshire County inferior court for selected sessions*

	1762–3 ($N = 677$)		1772–3 ($N = 696$)	
	Plaintiff	Defendant	Plaintiff	Defendant
Resident of new town[a]				
Yeoman/artisan	94	221	122	314
Gentleman/merchant	28	23	69	27
Other	0	0	0	0
Total	122 (18%)	244 (36%)	191 (27.5%)	341 (49%)
Resident of other town[b]				
Yeoman/artisan	274	364	276	312
Gentleman/merchant	272	67	221	42
Other	9	2	8	1
Total	555 (82%)	433 (64%)	505 (72.5%)	355 (51%)

Note: The Inferior Court of Common Pleas usually sat four times each year – in February/March, May, August, and November – primarily to hear debt cases. The February/March and August sessions were by far the busiest, and I have recorded all cases from those sessions for the two-year periods indicated. The table shows the number of cases, not the actual number of persons involved. On a few occasions two or more persons were named as either plaintiffs or defendants; in such circumstances I have assigned the case to a particular category according to the residence of the person with the highest status.

[a]"New towns" include all Hampshire towns incorporated after 1740, both frontier settlements and towns subdivided from older towns.

[b]"Other towns" include all Hampshire towns incorporated before 1740 and all towns outside the county.

Table 13. *Incorporation of Hampshire County frontier townships*

Town	Year granted or sold to proprietors	Year incorporated
New Salem	1729, 1734[a]	1753
Belchertown	1731/2	1761
Shutesbury	1734	1762
Bernardston	1734	1762
Ashfield	1735	1765
Colrain	1735	1761
Charlemont	1735	1765
Warwick	1735/6	1763
Chesterfield	1737	1762
Greenwich	1737	1754
Pelham	1738	1743
Blandford	1739	1741
Granville	1718, 1739[b]	1754
Ware	1742	1761
Worthington	1762	1768
Murrayfield	1762	1765
Cummington	1762	1779

[a]Originally granted in 1729, regranted in 1734.
[b]Sold as early as 1686, again in 1713, and finally in 1718 to proprietors; sale confirmed in 1739.
Source: Joseph B. Felt, *Collections of the American Statistical Association* (Boston, 1847), pt. I, pp. 36–7, 54–5, 56–7.

Table 14. *Town divisions in Hampshire County to 1775*

Town	Year incorporated	Towns or districts set off	Year incorporated
Springfield	1636	Wilbraham	1763
		West Springfield	1774
		Ludlow	1774
		Longmeadow[a]	1783
		Chicopee[a]	1854
Westfield	1669	Southwick	1770
Brimfield	1731	Monson	1760
		South Brimfield[b]	1762
Northampton	1654	Southampton	1753
Hadley	1661	Hatfield	1671
		South Hadley	1753
		Granby (from S. Hadley)	1768
		Amherst[c]	1759
Hatfield	1670	Whately	1771
		Williamsburg	1771
Sunderland	1714	Montague	1753
		Leverett	1774
Deerfield	1682	Greenfield	1753
		Conway	1767
		Shelburne	1768
		South Deerfield[a]	1808
Murrayfield	1765	Norwich	1773

[a]Dispute over separation started as early as 1750s.
[b]Had its own division controversy starting in 1762.
[c]Had its own division controversy starting in 1772.

Table 15. *Towns incorporated in Massachusetts, 1740–76*

County	Total no. towns incorporated by 1776	No. towns incorporated, 1740–76	% of total
Barnstable	11	2	18.2
Berkshire[a]	19	17	89.5
Bristol	12	1	8.3
Dukes	3	0	0
Essex	21	2	9.5
Hampshire	44	35	79.5
Middlesex	37	5	13.5
Nantucket	1	0	0
Plymouth	16	0	0
Suffolk	18	2	11.1
Worcester	42	22	52.4

[a]Before 1761 the towns of Berkshire County were part of Hampshire County. For the purposes of showing regional consistency, however, the two counties are considered separately here.

Source: John Hayward, *A Gazetteer of Massachusetts* (Boston, 1846), "Population Table," pp. 321–9.

NOTES

INTRODUCTION

1 Amherst Town Records, March 1774, in Carpenter and Morehouse, *The History of the Town of Amherst, Massachusetts* (Amherst, 1896), pt. II, pp. 68-9.
2 On the exchange of letters between the Boston Committee of Correspondence and the rural towns, see Richard D. Brown, *Revolutionary Politics in Massachusetts: The Boston Committee of Correspondence and the Towns, 1772-1774* (Cambridge, Mass., 1970), esp. chaps. 5-8; and L. Kinvin Wroth, ed., *Province in Rebellion: A Documentary History of the Founding of the Commonwealth of Massachusetts, 1774-1775* (Cambridge, Mass., 1975).
3 Adams to Hezekiah Niles, 1818, quoted in Bernard Bailyn, *The Ideological Origins of the American Revolution* (Cambridge, Mass., 1967), p. 160.
4 See, for instance, Robert Zemsky's 1971 note of warning in *Merchants, Farmers, and River Gods: An Essay on Eighteenth-Century American Politics* (Boston, 1971), pp. ii-xiii.
5 Bailyn, *Ideological Origins*, p. vi; for examples of this ideological emphasis in the study of non-elite groups, see the work of two of Bailyn's students: Pauline Maier, *From Resistance to Revolution: Colonial Radicals and the Development of American Opposition to Britain, 1765-1776* (New York, 1972); and Brown, *Revolutionary Politics*.
6 The recent secondary work on the Revolution is far too extensive to list here, but a few notable examples will suffice at this point. Probably the first substantial attempt to revise Bailyn's analysis was Gordon Wood's "Rhetoric and Reality in the American Revolution," *William and Mary Quarterly*, third series, 23 (1966): 3-32. Though hardly a harsh critic of Bailyn, Wood sought to place the colonists' use of Whig ideology within a context of "social strain . . . that sought mitigation through revolution and republicanism" (p. 30). Following Wood's

205

lead have been Kenneth A. Lockridge in "Social Change and the Meaning of the American Revolution," *Journal of Social History* 7 (1973): 403-39; and Robert A. Gross, *The Minutemen and Their World* (New York, 1976), esp. chap. 4. Gross, for instance, argues that the inhabitants of pre-Revolutionary Concord experienced "a deepening of social and economic malaise . . . The disturbing social and economic changes did not 'cause' the townspeople's rebellion against the new British moves . . . But the continuing decay in their fortunes added special poignancy to their fears." Still, he continues, the men of Concord "shared the same whiggish values and goals" (pp. 105-8).

A more direct challenge to Bailyn has come from those historians who have questioned the degree of ideological consensus Bailyn and his followers found between elite radical leaders and colonial non-elites, especially rural and urban crowds. Rather than accept the notion that the political action of Revolutionary crowds simply reflected the assumptions and desires of Whig elites – or was in some cases even directed by the Whigs – these historians have argued that popular risings in the cities and countryside were movements of largely lower-class people acting on their own, for their own goals, and with their own political values, or "popular ideology." The best short statement of this position is Jesse Lemisch's "Bailyn Besieged in his Bunker," *Radical History Review* 3 (1976): 72-83. See also the essays in Alfred F. Young, ed., *The American Revolution: Explorations in the History of American Radicalism* (DeKalb, Ill., 1976); and two recent monographs, Gary B. Nash, *The Urban Crucible: Social Change, Political Consciousness, and the Origins of the American Revolution* (Cambridge, Mass., 1979); and Edward Countryman, *A People in Revolution: The American Revolution and Political Society in New York, 1760-1790* (Baltimore, 1981).

7 Carl L. Becker, *The History of Political Parties in the Province of New York* (Madison, Wis., 1909).

8 Bernard Bailyn, "The Central Themes of the American Revolution: An Interpretation," in Stephen G. Kurtz and James H. Hutson, eds., *Essays on the American Revolution* (New York, 1973), p. 12.

9 Kenneth A. Lockridge, *A New England Town: The First Hundred Years, Dedham, Massachusetts, 1636-1736* (New York, 1970), p. xiii.

10 Among the most useful recent studies of Hampshire County communities are Patricia Juneau Tracy, *Jonathan Edwards, Pastor: Religion and Society in Eighteenth-Century Northampton* (New York, 1979); Russell W. Mank, Jr., "Family Structure in Northampton, Massachusetts, 1654-1725," Ph.D. dissertation, University of Denver, 1975; Tiziana Rota, "Marriage and Family Life in Northampton, Massachu-

setts: A Demographic Study, 1690-1750," M.A. thesis, Mount Holyoke College, 1975; Anne Baxter Webb, "On the Eve of Revolution:
Northampton, Massachusetts, 1750-1775," Ph.D. dissertation, Uni-
versity of Minnesota, 1976; Stephen C. Innes, *Labor in a New Land:
Economy and Society in Seventeenth-Century Springfield* (Princeton,
N. J., 1983); Alan C. Swedlund, "Population Growth and Settle-
ment Pattern in Franklin and Hampshire Counties, Massachusetts,
1650-1850," *American Antiquity*, 40 (1975): 22-33; Nancy R.
Folbre, "Patriarchy and Capitalism in New England, 1620-1900,"
Ph.D. dissertation, University of Massachusetts, 1979; and Alan H.
McArdle, "Population Growth, Out-Migration, and the Regulation of
Community Size: Hadley, Massachusetts, 1660-1730," M.A. thesis,
University of Massachusetts, 1975.

11 Robert J. Taylor, *Western Massachusetts in the Revolution* (Providence, R.I., 1954), pp. 24-44. A contemporary but less commonly
cited work is Lee N. Newcomer, *The Embattled Farmers: A Massachusetts Countryside in the Revolution* (New York, 1953).

12 Taylor, *Western Massachusetts*, pp. 175-7.

I. FAMILY POWER AND POLITICAL RELATIONS

1 Frederick Jackson Turner, *The Frontier in American History* (New
York, 1920), esp. pp. 1-66.

2 Henry M. Burt, *The First Century of the History of Springfield: The
Official Records from 1636 to 1736* (Springfield, Mass., 1898), pp.
156-8.

3 See, for instance, David Grayson Allen, *In English Ways: The Movement of Societies and the Transferal of English Local Law and Custom
to Massachusetts Bay in the Seventeenth Century* (Chapel Hill, N. C.,
1981); Paul Boyer and Stephen Nissenbaum, *Salem Possessed: The
Social Origins of Witchcraft* (Cambridge, Mass., 1974); and Kenneth
A. Lockridge, *A New England Town: The First Hundred Years, Dedham, Massachusetts, 1636-1736* (New York, 1970).

4 For a discussion of the early ecclesiastical disputes in Hampshire
County see Paul R. Lucas, *Valley of Discord: Church and Society
along the Connecticut River, 1636-1725* (Hanover, N. H., 1976) and
Ronald K. Snell, "Freemanship, Officeholding, and the Town Fran-
chise in Seventeenth Century Springfield, Massachusetts," *New England Historical and Genealogical Register* 133 (1979): 163-79. Lucas
points especially to the enduring tension between the clergy and laity,
suggesting that conflict was perhaps more inherent in Puritanism
than earlier studies allowed. In his effort to undermine the notion of
monolithic Puritanism, however, Lucas draws most of his examples of

local conflict from Connecticut, not Hampshire County. Indeed, except for the discussion of Mather's troubles in Northampton, what emerges from Lucas's study is an appreciation of the strength of the Hampshire clergy united under Solomon Stoddard. Throughout Stoddard's lifetime there was simply not the kind of anticlerical behavior in Hampshire County that existed in Connecticut or was to exist in Hampshire County in the mid-eighteenth century.

5 Patricia Juneau Tracy, *Jonathan Edwards, Pastor: Religion and Society in Eighteenth-Century Northampton* (New York, 1979), pp. 38-43; Stephen C. Innes, *Labor in a New Land: Economy and Society in Seventeenth-Century Springfield* (Princeton, N. J., 1983). Because Innes's book is in press at the time of this writing, I rely for specific reference on his earlier works. See Innes, "A Patriarchal Society: Economic Dependency and Social Order in Springfield, Massachusetts, 1636-1702," Ph.D. dissertation, Northwestern University, 1977, pp. 30-72, and "Land Tenancy and Social Order in Springfield, Massachusetts, 1652-1702," *William and Mary Quarterly*, third series, 35 (1978): 33-56.

6 During the past quarter-century, the scholarly debate over the relative degree of democracy in colonial New England has seldom suffered from a lack of participants. See, for instance, Robert E. Brown, *Middle Class Democracy and the Revolution in Massachusetts, 1691-1780* (Ithaca, N. Y., 1955); Charles S. Grant, *Democracy in the Connecticut Frontier Town of Kent* (New York, 1961); Robert J. Dinkin, "Provincial Massachusetts: A Deferential or a Democratic Society?" Ph.D. dissertation, Columbia University, 1968; Michael Zuckerman, *Peaceable Kingdoms: New England Towns in the Eighteenth Century* (New York, 1970); Kenneth Lockridge and Alan Kreider, "The Evolution of Massachusetts Town Government 1640-1740," *William and Mary Quarterly*, third series 23 (1966): 549-74; Dirk Hoerder, "Society and Government, 1760-1780: The Power Structure in Massachusetts Townships," thesis, John F. Kennedy Institute, Free University, Berlin, 1972; and Edward M. Cook, Jr., *The Fathers of the Towns: Leadership and Community Structure in Eighteenth Century New England* (Baltimore, 1976). The list could go on, and as Bruce C. Daniels suggests in *Town and Country: Essays on the Structure of Local Goverment in the American Colonies* (Middletown, Conn., 1978), pp. 10-11, it will probably grow longer in the future.

The pattern of office holding in the earliest Hampshire towns is outlined in Tables 1 and 2 in the appendix.

7 Sylvester Judd, *History of Hadley, Including the Early History of Hatfield, South Hadley, Amherst, and Granby, Massachusetts* (Springfield, Mass., 1905), pp. 78-85.

8 Two very useful studies of county government in colonial Massachusetts are David T. Konig, *Law and Society in Puritan Massachusetts: Essex County, 1629-1692* (Chapel Hill, N. C., 1979); and Ronald K. Snell, "The County Magistracy in Eighteenth-Century Massachusetts, 1692-1750," Ph.D. dissertation, Princeton University, 1971. The last two chapters of Snell's dissertation deal specifically with Hampshire County. See also Allen, *In English Ways*, pp. 223-7.

9 Kevin M. Sweeney's forthcoming study, "River Gods and Related Minor Deities: The Williamses of New England, 1637-1790," Ph.D. dissertation, Yale University, will provide a very valuable discussion of the significance of the county militia. As will become evident in this chapter, I have profited both from discussions with him and from his unpublished paper "War on the Homefront: Politics and Patronage in Hampshire County, 1754-1760," paper presented to the Historic Deerfield Colloquium on Recent Research in Western Massachusetts History, 1978.

10 Snell, in "County Magistracy," argues that probably no other Massachusetts county had "so unified and powerful a ruling elite as was present in eighteenth-century Hampshire" (p. 220). See also Robert J. Taylor, *Western Massachusetts in the Revolution* (Providence, R.I., 1954), pp. 11-33. As Robert Zemsky put it, the Hampshire leaders acted like "feudal barons" in dominating the politics of their western "preserve." See Zemsky, *Merchants, Farmers, and River Gods: An Essay in Eighteenth-Century American Politics* (Boston, 1971), pp. 32-3.

11 On the early settlement of Hampshire County see Harold R. King, "The Settlement of the Upper Connecticut River Valley to 1675," Ph.D. dissertation, Vanderbilt University, 1965. Snell, in "County Magistracy," suggests that "the authority of the leading families of the Connecticut Valley towns was reinforced by the pattern of settlement peculiar to the area, rather than being challenged by the rise of new leaders within new towns, as could conceivably have occurred had settlement been more scattered" (p. 227). As I will argue in Chapters 5 and 6, it was precisely the wider spread of settlement in the mid-eighteenth century that expanded this universe of Hampshire towns and eventually helped undermine the ability of the county leaders to rule with the same degree of effectiveness as before.

12 Innes, in "Patriarchal Society," offers a very useful discussion of the local leader as broker or mediator; see esp. pp. 78-82. See also Zemsky, *Merchants, Farmers, and River Gods*, pp. 32-3.

13 The following discussion of the power of the Hampshire elite derives in large part from Innes, "Patriarchal Society" and "Land Tenancy"; Snell, "County Magistracy"; and Sweeney, "War on the Homefront."

I want to acknowledge my debt to these writers. For comparative studies of county elites in other parts of Massachusetts, see John J. Waters, *The Otis Family in Provincial and Revolutionary Massachusetts* (Chapel Hill, N. C., 1968); and Kevin Joseph MacWade, "Worcester County, 1750-1774: A Study of a Provincial Patronage Elite," Ph.D. dissertation, Boston University Graduate School, 1974.

14 Mason A. Green, *Springfield, 1636-1886: History of Town and City* (Springfield, Mass., 1888), intro. and pp. 1-9; Innes, "Patriarchal Society," pp. 9-12.

15 Innes, "Patriarchal Society," pp. 92-3; Snell, "County Magistracy," pp. 237-9.

16 Innes, "Patriarchal Society," pp. 30-72.

17 Ibid., p. 146.

18 Green, *Springfield*, pp. 46-53; Innes, "Patriarchal Society," pp. 14-15.

19 The most detailed description of William Pynchon's theological difficulties is in Burt, *First Century*, pp. 79-88. On John Pynchon's assumption of political authority, see Snell, "County Magistracy," pp. 235, 242-5; see also Green, *Springfield*, pp. 198-200, and Innes, "Patriarchal Society," pp. 83-92.

20 Quoted in Innes, "Patriarchal Society," pp. 75-6.

21 Innes closes his study of the Pynchons by noting that with the death of John Pynchon, "the days of the titans were over" ("Patriarchal Society," p. 200). As far as Springfield was concerned, that was true: no one ever achieved the dominance that the Pynchons had held in seventeenth-century Springfield. On the county level, however, the broker's role established by the Pynchons still remained a necessity, and if—as both Innes and Snell suggest—the later Pynchons were not strong enough to assume the position, other men were. Snell, in "County Magistracy," identifies Samuel Partridge as the first inheritor of county leadership. In terms of the overall political development of the county, however, the Stoddard line became more permanent and therefore, I think, more significant. For that reason I have slighted Partridge in the following pages.

22 The most comprehensive published study of Stoddard is Ralph J. Coffman, *Solomon Stoddard* (Boston, 1978). One other book-length work is Harry Gerald Swanhart, "Solomon Stoddard, Puritan Patriarch: A Biography," Ph.D. dissertation, Boston University, 1961. There are good treatments of his theology and social thought in Lucas, *Valley of Discord*, and " 'An Appeal to the Learned': The Mind of Solomon Stoddard," *William and Mary Quarterly*, third series, 30 (1973): 257-92; James P. Walsh, "Solomon Stoddard's Open Com-

munion: A Reexamination," *New England Quarterly* 43 (1970): 97-114; and Perry Miller, *The New England Mind: From Colony to Province* (Boston, 1953), pp. 227-58. See also Edmund S. Morgan, *Visible Saints: The History of a Puritan Idea* (Ithaca, N. Y., 1965), pp. 146-50; and C. C. Goen, ed., *The Works of Jonathan Edwards: The Great Awakening* (New Haven, Conn., 1972), pp. 14-16.

23 See the works cited in the preceding note and Tracy, *Jonathan Edwards, Pastor*, pp. 13-50.

24 Coffman, *Solomon Stoddard*, pp. 114-15; Lucas, *Valley of Discord*, pp. 152-6.

25 See esp. Lucas, *Valley of Discord*, chap. 8; and Miller, *New England Mind: From Colony to Province*, chap. 17. Certainly the most detailed treatment is James A. Goulding, "The Controversy between Solomon Stoddard and the Mathers: Western versus Eastern Massachusetts Congregationalism," Ph.D. dissertation, Claremont Graduate School and University Center, 1971.

26 Coffman, *Solomon Stoddard*, p. 142

27 Lucas, *Valley of Discord*, pp. 193-5. On the organization of the Hampshire Association, see ibid.; Coffman, *Solomon Stoddard*, pp. 141-2; Swanhart, "Solomon Stoddard," pp. 300-4; and Snell, "County Magistracy," pp. 263-5.

28 On the development of ministerial associations, see David D. Hall, *The Faithful Shepherd: A History of the New England Ministry in the Seventeenth Century* (Chapel Hill, N. C., 1972); J. William T. Youngs, Jr., *God's Messengers: Religious Leadership in Colonial New England, 1700-1750* (Baltimore, 1976); David Harlan, *The Clergy and the Great Awakening in New England* (Ann Arbor, Mich., 1980); and James W. Schmotter, "The Irony of Clerical Professionalism: New England's Congregational Clergy and the Great Awakening," *American Quarterly* 31 (1979): 148-68.

29 See Chapter 2.

30 James R. Trumbull, *History of Northampton, Massachusetts from Its Settlement in 1654*, 2 vols. (Northampton, 1902), pp. 165-78; Daniel White Wells and Reuben Field Wells, *A History of Hatfield, Massachusetts* (Springfield, Mass., 1910), pp. 170-3.

31 Snell, "County Magistracy," pp. 268-9; Zemsky, *Merchants, Farmers, and River Gods*, p. 224; Trumbull, *History of Northampton*, II, 172-3.

32 Zemsky, *Merchants, Farmers, and River Gods*, pp. 99-156.

33 Trumbull, *History of Northampton*, II, 166-72; Snell, "County Magistracy," pp. 267-8, 273.

34 Zemsky, *Merchants, Farmers, and River Gods*, pp. 143-4.

35 Snell, "County Magistracy," pp. 260, 269-74.

36 Ibid., p. 283.
37 Again, Kevin M. Sweeney's forthcoming dissertation on the Williams family, "River Gods," should offer a full exploration of the many family connections among Hampshire County elites in the eighteenth century. At present the most useful sources are Harrison Williams, *The Life, Ancestors, and Descendants of Robert Williams of Roxbury, 1607-1693* (Washington, D.C., 1934); George Sheldon, *A History of Deerfield, Massachusetts*, 2 vols. (1896; reprint ed., Somersworth, N. H., 1972); George Henry Merriam, "Israel Williams, Monarch of Hampshire, 1709-1788," Ph.D. dissertation, Clark University, 1961; William Lawrence Welch, Jr., "River God: The Public Life of Israel Williams, 1709-1788," Ph.D. dissertation, University of Maine, 1975; and Snell, "County Magistracy," esp. app. 5.
38 See Williams, *Robert Williams*.
39 The political offices of Williams family kin have been gathered from various sources: Welch, "River God," pp. 32-4; Snell, "County Magistracy," chap. 8, app. 2; and William H. Whitmore, *The Massachusetts Civil List for the Colonial and Provincial Periods, 1630-1774* (Baltimore, 1969), pp. 91-4, 139-40.
40 Snell, "County Magistracy," chap. 8, app. 2; Whitmore, *Civil List*, pp. 91-4, 139-40.
41 Sweeney, "War on the Homefront."
42 See Chapter 5.

2. THE HAMPSHIRE COUNTY MINISTRY AND THE GREAT AWAKENING

1 The Public Records of the Church of Christ at Westfield, p. 193, Westfield (Mass.) Athenaeum; Clifford K. Shipton, *Sibley's Harvard Graduates: Biographical Sketches of Those Who Attended Harvard College*, 17 vols., (Boston, 1942), IX, 466.
2 *George Whitefield's Journals* (1905; reprint ed., Gainesville, Fla., 1969), pp. 475-8.
3 The Public Records of the Church of Christ at Westfield, p. 193, Westfield (Mass.) Athenaeum.
4 Ibid.; see also John H. Lockwood, *Westfield and Its Historic Influences, 1669-1919*, 2 vols., (Westfield, Mass., 1922), I, 575-8.
5 By 1741 the six ministers identified by Ralph J. Coffman (*Solomon Stoddard* [Boston, 1978], p. 142) as the original members of the Hampshire Association – Stoddard of Northampton, Daniel Brewer of Springfield, Isaac Chauncy of Hadley, Nathaniel Collins of Enfield,

John Williams of Deerfield, and William Williams of Hatfield – had died. For a list of their replacements and of the ministers in some of the newer towns and parishes in Hampshire County in the era of the Awakening, see Table 3 in the appendix.

6 The mechanics of the Breck affair involve immense detail, far too much for the present narrative. For a fuller description of the letters, statements, councils, and day-to-day events of the controversy, see *Narrative of the Proceedings of those Ministers of the County of Hampshire &c That have disapproved of the late Measures taken in order to the Settlement of Mr. Robert Breck, In the Pastoral Office in the first Church in Springfield. With a Defence of their Conduct in that Affair* (Boston, 1736); Shipton, *Sibley's Harvard Graduates*, VIII, 661-80; Mary Catherine Foster, "Hampshire County, Massachusetts, 1729-1754: A Covenant Society in Transition," Ph.D. dissertation, University of Michigan, 1967, pp. 55-78; and Charles Edwin Jones, "The Impolitic Mr. Edwards: The Personal Dimension of the Robert Breck Affair," *New England Quarterly*, 51 (1978): 64-79.

7 *Narrative of the Proceedings*, p. 4.

8 C. C. Goen, ed., *The Works of Jonathan Edwards: The Great Awakening* (New Haven, Conn., 1972), pp. 22, 152-3, 207-8.

9 Shipton, *Sibley's Harvard Graduates*, VIII, 667; Hampshire Association of Ministers meeting, Oct. 3, 1732, in Hampshire Association of Congregational Churches and Ministers Collection, Box A, Forbes Library, Northampton, Mass.

10 Ibid., Oct. 8, 1734.

11 *Narrative of the Proceedings*, pp. 13-14. The six were William Williams (Hatfield), Isaac Chauncy (Hadley), Jonathan Edwards (Northampton), Stephen Williams (Longmeadow), Samuel Hopkins (West Springfield), and Peter Reynolds (Enfield). Nehemiah Bull of Westfield was having his own troubles at the time, but he was no friend of Breck's either. See Lockwood, *Westfield*, I, 330.

12 Shipton, *Sibley's Harvard Graduates*, VIII, 661-80.

13 *Narrative of the Proceedings*, 66-7, 77-9. The *Narrative* has generally been attributed to Jonathan Edwards; certainly he had a large hand in its writing.

14 *Letter to the Author of The Pamphlet Called an Answer to the Hampshire Narrative* (Boston, 1737), quoted in Foster, "Hampshire County," pp. 77-8.

15 Jonathan Edwards MSS, Box 39, the Beinecke Rare Book and Manuscript Library, Yale University, New Haven, Conn. William Williams (Hatfield), Ebenezer Devotion (Suffield), Stephen Williams (Longmeadow), Peter Reynolds (Enfield), Nehemiah Bull (West-

field), and Samuel Hopkins (West Springfield) signed the letter. Foster, in "Hampshire County," identifies these signers, along with Edwards, as the evangelical party in Hampshire County; see pp. 97-8, 154-7.

16 See the records of the meetings in the Hampshire Association Collection, Box A. See also Foster, "Hampshire County," p. 75.

17 Shipton, *Sibley's Harvard Graduates*, VI, 25-35.

18 Stephen Williams Diary III, Jan. 29, July 15, Oct. 20, 1740, Pocumtuck Valley Memorial Association Library, Deerfield, Mass.

19 Ibid., July 13, 1741.

20 Shipton, *Sibley's Harvard Graduates*, VI, 25-35.

21 Stephen Williams Diary, III, Nov. 21, 1740.

22 Ibid., June 12, 1741.

23 The number of books and articles on the Great Awakening is immense, but the best overviews of the revival in New England are Edwin S. Gaustad, *The Great Awakening in New England* (New York, 1957); C. C. Goen, *Revivalism and Separatism in New England, 1740-1800: Strict Congregationalists and Separate Baptists in the Great Awakening* (New Haven, Conn., 1962); William Warren Sweet, *The Story of Religion in America* (New York, 1930); David S. Lovejoy, *Religious Enthusiasm and the Great Awakening* (Englewood Cliffs, N. J., 1969); William C. McLoughlin, *New England Dissent, 1630-1833: The Baptists and the Separation of Church and State*, 2 vols., (Cambridge, Mass., 1971); and Alan Heimert, *Religion and the American Mind: From the Great Awakening to the Revolution* (Cambridge, Mass., 1966).

24 *The Testimony and Advice of an Assembly of Pastors of Churches in New-England, At a Meeting in Boston, July 7, 1743. Occasion'd By the late happy Revival of Religion in many Parts of the Land* (Boston, 1743), pp. 29-30. Those who signed the *Testimony and Advice* were Stephen Williams (Longmeadow), Ebenezer Devotion (Suffield), Peter Reynolds (Enfield), Edward Billing (Cold Spring), Jonathan Edwards (Northampton), John Woodbridge (South Hadley), Chester Williams (Hadley), David Parsons (Amherst), and Timothy Woodbridge (Hatfield).

25 Jonathan Edwards, *Thoughts on the Revival of Religion* (Boston, 1742), in S. E. Dwight, ed., *The Works of President Edwards*, 10 vols., (New York, 1829), I, 122.

26 *Testimony and Advice*, p. 30.

27 See, for instance, James A. Henretta, *The Evolution of American Society, 1700-1815* (Lexington, Mass., 1973); and Richard L. Bushman, *From Puritan to Yankee: Character and the Social Order in Connecticut, 1690-1765* (Cambridge, Mass., 1967).

28 Hampshire Association of Ministers meeting, Apr. 18, 1738, Hampshire Association Collection, Box A.

29 Quoted in Perry Miller, "Jonathan Edwards's Sociology of the Great Awakening," *New England Quarterly* 28 (1948): 64-5.

30 For a fuller discussion of the question of wealth and calling during the Great Awakening, see J. E. Crowley, *This Sheba, Self: The Conceptualization of Economic Life in Eighteenth Century America* (Baltimore, 1974). Crowley sees a deviation from the Calvinist model described by Weber, arguing that the Awakening offered a new idea of the calling, one defined more by social concerns than by personal performance and accumulation of wealth.

31 Andrew Croswell, *What is Christ to Me, if He is Not Mine?* (Boston, 1745), p. 8, quoted in Heimert, *Religion and the American Mind*, p. 183.

32 Jonathan Ashley, *The United Endeavours and earnest Prayers of Ministers and People, to promote the great Design of the Ministry* (Boston, 1742).

33 Ibid., pp. 5-11.

34 Jonathan Ashley, *The Great Duty of Charity* (Boston, 1742).

35 Ibid., pp. 1-5.

36 Records of the Church in Deerfield, Pocumtuck Valley Memorial Association Library, pp. 9-12, 135-6; George Sheldon, *A History of Deerfield, Massachusetts*, 2 vols., (1896; reprint ed., Somersworth, N. H., 1972), I, 538.

37 Sylvester Judd, *History of Hadley, Including the Early History of Hatfield, South Hadley, Amherst, and Granby, Massachusetts* (Springfield, Mass., 1905), pp. 387-8; Shipton, *Sibley's Harvard Graduates*, VIII, 476-80.

38 J. H. Temple and George Sheldon, *History of the Town of Northfield, Massachusetts* (Albany, 1875), p. 230; Herbert Collins Parsons, *A Puritan Outpost: A History of the Town and People of Northfield, Massachusetts* (New York, 1937), pp. 125-7.

39 William Rand, *Ministers must preach Christ Lord, and themselves Servants* (Boston, 1736), p. 3; see also Rand, *The Ministers Duty to preach the pure Word of God* (Boston, 1739).

40 Temple and Sheldon, *History of Northfield*, pp. 231-2; Parsons, *Puritan Outpost*, pp. 125-7.

41 Hampshire Association of Ministers meeting, May 3, 1739, Hampshire Association Collection, Box A.

42 Temple and Sheldon, *History of Northfield*, pp. 231-2; Parsons, *Puritan Outpost*, p. 127.

43 Judd, *History of Hadley*, pp. 387-8; Shipton, *Sibley's Harvard Graduates*, VIII, 476-80.

44 Judd, *History of Hadley*, pp. 387-8.

45 One other Hampshire minister had in fact been dismissed just a few years prior to Rawson's expulsion. Richard Treat had fallen into a dispute with his people at Brimfield over their inability to pay him his salary, and according to Franklin B. Dexter, "after a few years some other cause seems to have arisen." He was dismissed in 1734, but there does not seem to be any evidence to suggest the existence of a conflict heated by the fires of religious revivalism. See Dexter, *Biographical Sketches of the Graduates of Yale College*, 6 vols., (New York, 1903), I, 212-3.

46 William Rand, *Ministers should have sincere and ardent Love to the Souls of their People* (Boston, 1742); Shipton, *Sibley's Harvard Graduates*, VI, 550-1; John Montague Smith, *History of the Town of Sunderland, Massachusetts* (Greenfield, Mass., 1899), pp. 60-1.

47 Charles Chauncy, *Seasonable Thoughts on the State of Religion in New England* (Boston, 1743). The Hampshire County ministers who subscribed to Chauncy's *Seasonable Thoughts* were Jonathan Ashley (Deerfield), John Ballantine (Westfield), Robert Breck (Springfield), James Bridgham (Brimfield), Ebenezer Gay (Suffield), Abraham Hill (Road Town), Samuel Hopkins (West Springfield), Samuel Kendal (New Salem), Noah Merrick (Springfield), William Rand (Sunderland), John Sergeant (Stockbridge), Edward Upham (Springfield), and Chester Williams (Hadley). Of those, none but Chester Williams signed the *Testimony and Advice*.

48 *The Testimony of the North Association in the County of Hartford, in the Colony of Connecticut, convened at Windsor, Feb. 5, 1744-5, Against the Rev. Mr. George Whitefield and his Conduct. And an Address From some of the Ministers in the County of Hampshire, to the Rev. Mr. George Whitefield* (Boston, 1745). Foster, in "Hampshire County," suggests that the letter to Whitefield might be the best indicator of anti-Awakening sentiment, just as the *Testimony and Advice* gives a fairly accurate list of pro-Awakening ministers – at least as of the mid-1740s. The anti-Whitefield signers were all those who subscribed to Chauncy's *Seasonable Thoughts*, with the exception of Chester Williams and the addition of John Norton (Falltown), Jonathan Hubbard (Sheffield), Benjamin Doolittle (Northfield), and William McClenathan (Blandford). (See Table 3 in the appendix).

49 Edwards to Joseph Bellamy, Jan. 15, 1746/7, in Edwards MSS, folder 39.

50 On the "reintegration" of Old Light and New Light ministers after the Awakening, see David Harlan, *The Clergy and the Great Awakening in New England* (Ann Arbor, Mich., 1980), pp. 74-82.

3. THE REVIVALIST REMOVED

1 The most detailed nineteenth-century works on the Edwards affair are Sereno E. Dwight, *The Life of President Edwards* (New York, 1830); and James R. Trumbull, *History of Northampton, Massachusetts, from Its Settlement in 1654*, 2 vols., (Northampton, 1902), II, 202-34. Both of these works reproduce a great deal of useful information and documentation. The two standard biographies of Edwards, Perry Miller, *Jonathan Edwards* (New York, 1949), and Ola E. Winslow, *Jonathan Edwards, 1703-1758* (New York, 1940), also give a good summary of the events and issues. Miller's book, however, is primarily intended as an intellectual biography and therefore does not contain the attention to local detail that is found in Winslow's. Two more recent works have also given considerable attention to Edwards's dismissal; see Mary Catherine Foster, "Hampshire County, Massachusetts, 1729-1754: A Covenant Society in Transition," Ph.D. dissertation, University of Michigan, 1967; and Patricia Juneau Tracy, *Jonathan Edwards, Pastor: Religion and Society in Eighteenth-Century Northampton* (New York, 1979). Tracy's work corrects a number of errors found in the earlier treatments, and she does the best job so far of connecting Edwards's theological positions with his experience as minister in Northampton. If she slights anything, it is the role of Edwards's neighboring ministers in the affair, and that question is the main point of discussion here. My account of the Edwards affair draws upon all these works, as well as on the manuscript sources, and therefore I will cite only specific references of special significance from the works at hand.

2 Quoted in Dwight, *Life of Edwards*, p. 568.

3 For a discussion of Edwards's growing dissatisfaction with his own efforts during the Great Awakening and with his people in Northampton, see Tracy, *Jonathan Edwards, Pastor*, pp. 147-76.

4 Quoted in Dwight, *Life of Edwards*, p. 313.

5 Edwards to Thomas Foxcroft, May 24, 1749, in Edwards MSS, folder 39, Beinecke Rare Book and Manuscript Library, Yale University, New Haven, Conn.

6 Dwight, *Life of Edwards*, pp. 314-15.

7 Edwards to Foxcroft, Nov. 21, 1749, in Edwards MSS, folder 39. In general, this letter to Foxcroft provides Edwards's best short summary of the events in Northampton leading up to the calling of a council.

8 Ibid.

9 The best source on Joseph Hawley's career is still E. Francis Brown, *Joseph Hawley, Colonial Radical* (New York, 1931).

10 For a year before the ecclesiastical matter became especially heated, Hawley was having to manage a private affair between his family and Edwards. Elisha Hawley had had a bastard child by Martha Root before going off to his post at Fort Massachusetts. Root wanted some money for child support, but Edwards apparently wanted young Hawley to marry the woman. Joseph Hawley, taking care of the matter for his absent brother, thought he could make a satisfactory deal with Root, but he worried about what Edwards might be able to do. Hawley's legal mind had almost assured him that "no Church on earth Can by their Censures inforce a match in Such Case, untill ye two points, viz absolute virgin[ity] and the enticement on ye mans part are fully proved," and he set about trying to show how often young Martha had made advances toward his brother. Still, the matter had to go before a council of ministers for a final decision. The council that came to Northampton – made up of some of the ministers who later sat in judgment on Edwards – admitted that Elisha was not necessarily bound to marry the woman, but it left the question of his being bound at least by conscience somewhat open and vague. In the end, with so much attention focused on his younger brother, Joseph Hawley was quite glad to see the council move on to the matter of Edwards and let the sins of his brother fade into the background. Writing to Elisha in August of 1749, Joseph noted with some relief that "latterly the conversation has almost (as far as I can observe) entirely Subsided . . . The dispute between [Edwards] and ye people on his late Sentiments engrosses most of ye Conversation. And I believe ye event will be a Separation between him and ye people." See Joseph Hawley Papers, I, 6-19, New York Public Library, New York City; see also Tracy, *Jonathan Edwards, Pastor*, pp. 164-5; and Kathryn Kish Sklar, "Culture versus Economics: A Case of Fornication in Northampton in the 1740s," in *Papers in Women's Studies* (Ann Arbor, Mich., 1978), pp. 35-6.

Hawley's motives for playing so active a role in helping prosecute the Edwards affair were perhaps also based on more than the immediate problems facing his brother. Hawley's father had committed suicide toward the end of the revival in 1736, and Hawley may well have held Edwards partly responsible for the spiritual agony that apprently led his father to take his own life. See Trumbull, *History of Northampton*, II, 79-83.

11 Brown, *Joseph Hawley*, pp. 36-7.

12 Ibid., pp. 18-39.

13 See William Lawrence Welch, Jr., "River God: The Public Life of Israel Williams, 1709-1788," Ph.D dissertation, University of Maine, 1975, pp. 19-20.

14 Edwards to Rev. Thomas Gillespie, July 1, 1751, quoted in Dwight, *Life of Edwards*, pp. 466-7. See also Edwards to Thomas Foxcroft, Feb. 19/20, 1749, May 24, 1749, and Nov. 21, 1749, in Edwards MSS, folder 39.

Departing from the earlier arguments of Dwight, Miller, and Winslow, some recent studies have tended to play down the importance of Williams's role in the ouster of Edwards. There is no doubt that Williams was hostile to Edwards, but there is some doubt about the extent to which he became *personally* involved in the proceedings. See Tracy, *Jonathan Edwards, Pastor*, pp. 185-8; and George Henry Merriam, "Israel Williams, Monarch of Hampshire, 1709-1788," Ph.D. dissertation, Clark University, 1961, pp. 18-19, 152-8. Even so, it would be impossible to ignore Israel Williams as a figure in the drama, offstage or not.

15 Dwight, *Life of Edwards*, pp. 433-43.The full title of Edwards's treatise is *An Humble Inquiry into the Rules of the Word of God Concerning the Qualifications Requisite to a Complete Standing and Full Communion in the Visible Christian Church* (Boston, 1749).

16 Unfortunately, the records dealing with the Edwards controversy are missing from the Hampshire Association of Congregational Churches and Ministers Collection, presumably removed at some point by someone wishing to avoid detailed examination of the clergy's role.

17 Edwards to Foxcroft, Nov. 21, 1749, in Edwards MSS, folder 39.

18 Dwight, *Life of Edwards*, pp. 309-10; Peter Clark to Ebenezer Pomeroy, Apr. 4, 1750, and Clark to Edwards, May 21, 1750, both in Edwards MSS, folder 39; Thomas Prince to Timothy Dwight, (n.d.), in Hawley Papers, I, 34.

19 Edwards to Foxcroft, Nov. 21, 1749, in Edwards MSS, folder 39.

20 Dwight, *Life of Edwards*, p. 327.

21 Quoted in ibid., pp. 336-7.

22 Quoted in ibid., p. 346.

23 Stephen Williams to Northampton committee, Apr. 5, 1750, in Edwards MSS, folder 39.

24 Quoted in Dwight, *Life of Edwards*, pp. 346, 352-5.

25 Quoted in ibid., pp. 348-50.

26 Report of the Council, June 22, 1750, in Edwards MSS, folder 46A. In telling Edwards of the trouble he faced in coming to the council, Billing said that his people had told him he was an "unfit Member of that Counsel, which suggestion (without doubt) was put into ye

Noddles of some weak people by some of your Chh renowned for
Superior wisdom." Billing to Edwards, June 11, 1750, in Edwards
MSS, folder 39.
27 Report of the Council, June 22, 1750.
28 Ibid.
29 For the events of Billing's dismissal, see Clifford K. Shipton, *Sibley's
Harvard Graduates: Biographical Sketches of Those Who Attended Harvard College*, 17 vols., (Boston, 1942), IX, 22-8; and Mark Doolittle,
*Historical Sketch of the Congregational Church in Belchertown, Mas-
sachusetts* (Northampton, Mass., 1852), pp. 29, 280-1; for the Williams quotation, see Stephen Williams Diary, IV, Apr. 14, 17, 1752,
Pocumtuck Valley Memorial Association Library, Deerfield, Mass.
30 Shipton, *Sibley's Harvard Graduates*, IX, 27; David Willard, *History
of Greenfield* (Greenfield, Mass., 1838), pp. 39, 99-101. Billing's new
church was Greenfield.

4. THE LEGACY OF RELIGIOUS DISSENT

1 Between 1750 and 1759 twelve Congregational ministers were ordained in Hampshire County. It is difficult to assess each man's theological position exactly, but it does seem very likely that almost all of
the new ministers fit rather comfortably into the dominant strain of
the Hampshire County clergy.

Eight of the twelve were identified by Sibley or Dexter as having
either an Old Light, anti-Edwardsean bias or some strong connection
with one of the more liberal ministers of the county. Edward Billing,
who moved from Cold Spring to Greenfield, was the only one who
had previously occupied another pulpit in the county, and he of
course had proved to be quite out of step with the sentiments of his
ministerial colleagues in 1750 and 1752. For the remaining three
newcomers there is too little information to determine a clear theological stance. See Table 4 in the appendix.

For the description of young Samuel Hopkins, see Franklin B.
Dexter, *Biographical Sketches of the Graduates of Yale College*, 6 vols.,
(New York, 1903), III, 210-12.
2 David Harlan, in *The Clergy and the Great Awakening in New England* (Ann Arbor, Mich., 1980), has argued that from the early part
of the eighteenth century, even before the Awakening, ministerial
associations "did not assume any significant power over ecclesiastical
affairs" (p. 15). He especially faults two earlier studies of associations,
J. William T. Youngs, Jr., *God's Messengers: Religious Leadership in
Colonial New England, 1700-1750* (Baltimore, 1976); and James W.
Schmotter, "The Irony of Clerical Professionalism: New England's

Congregational Clergy and the Great Awakening," *American Quarterly* 31 (1979): 148-68, for overemphasizing the self-conscious professionalism of the associations and therefore for overemphasizing the effects of the Great Awakening in changing ministers' perceptions of their collective role and of their individual relationships with their people.

Although I think Harlan's argument is a useful one – especially in reminding us to look at the associations' record of failure, their general inability to intervene effectively in local ecclesiastical disputes – I also think it underplays (as do the Youngs and Schmotter works) the continuing attempts of ministerial associations to maintain at least some semblance of collective authority. To be sure, the Awakening gave a serious blow to ministerial confidence; indeed, the surviving records suggest that the Hampshire Association ceased meeting on a regular basis after 1747 and divided into northern and southern branches. But as should become evident from the narrative that follows in this chapter, the ministers still came together occasionally on an ad hoc basis to deal with particular cases and crises. Though for the most part the Association proved to be no more successful than it had been before the Awakening – and here one must give Harlan his due – the point remains that the ministers never gave up altogether their self-proclaimed status as a collective source of regional authority. At the very least, one must realize that the decline of the Association was not an immediate result of the Awakening but stemmed more from a recurrence of fecklessness and failure in the post-Awakening years.

3 *Memoirs of Doctor Seth Coleman, A.M.* (New Haven, Conn., 1817), pp. 18-19, 53.

4 Ibid., p. 101.

5 James R. Trumbull, *History of Northampton, Massachusetts, from Its Settlement in 1654*, 2 vols. (Northampton, 1902), II, 235-42. See also E. Francis Brown, *Joseph Hawley, Colonial Radical* (New York, 1931), pp. 39-41.

6 Quoted in Trumbull, *History of Northampton*, II, 548.

7 Quoted in ibid., p. 232; and in Sereno E. Dwight, *The Life of President Edwards* (New York, 1830), pp. 422-27.

8 For brief sketches of Parsons and Hooker see Clifford K. Shipton, *Sibley's Harvard Graduates: Biographical Sketches of Those Who Attended Harvard College*, 17 vols. (Boston, 1942), VIII, 610-15; and Dexter, *Graduates of Yale College*, II, 254-6 and Trumbull, *History of Northampton*, II, 410-11.

9 In addition to Edwards and Billing, twelve other ministers were dismissed for reasons other than poor health. See Table 5 in the appen-

dix. Here again, the reasons for dismissal in these cases tend to be vague and elusive and do not lend themselves to airtight conclusions. In some towns the people rejected their ministers for either unacceptable conduct or unacceptable doctrine; both New Light and Old Light ministers were dismissed. In some cases the people and the minister quarreled over money, perhaps a sign of some deeper antagonism, perhaps merely a sign of real poverty. It would be impossible to relate all these cases to a single clear cause. What does seem evident, however, is that forbearance did not always prove to be the rule, and that increasingly disagreement or difficulty could lead to separation.

10 Petition to Hampshire Association from Pelatiah Webster, Feb. 5, 1754, and Minutes of Hampshire Association meeting, May 4, 1754, both in Letters of Robert Breck, Connecticut Valley Historical Museum, Springfield, Mass.

11 Journal of the Reverend John Ballantine, Oct. 17, 23, 1765, June 3, 1767, Westfield (Mass.) Athenaeum; Dexter, *Graduates of Yale College*, II, 97-9.

12 Mason A. Green, *Springfield, 1636-1886: History of Town and City* (Springfield, Mass., 1888), pp. 253-4, 267.

13 "Letter written by Samuel Hopkins, pastor of the Church in Hadley, Jan. 19, 1760," in Porter and Phelps Correpondence to 1795, Amherst College Library, Amherst, Mass.

14 Ballantine Journal, Apr. 20-24, 1762, May 2, 1765, May 3, 1767.

15 Ibid., Jan. 17, 1768.

16 Ibid., Apr. 18, 1753, May 2, 1765.

17 Quoted in William C. McLoughlin, *New England Dissent, 1630-1833: The Baptists and the Separation of Church and State*, 2 vols. (Cambridge, Mass., 1971), I, 225-6.

18 For Upham's subscription to Chauncy's *Seasonable Thoughts*, see n. 47 to Chapter 2; and also McLoughlin, *New England Dissent*, I, 422.

19 Boston *News-Letter*, Feb. 17, 1762, quoted in Grace M. Clark and Naida H. King, *History of the Feeding Hills Congregational Church, 1762-1962* (Feeding Hills, Mass., 1962), pp. 5-7.

20 Ballantine Journal, Feb. 10, 1762.

21 McLoughlin, *New England Dissent*, I, 454-5. McLoughlin's work is especially important in making clear the distinction between pre-Awakening Baptists and post-Awakening Separate-Baptists, and I have drawn much from his analysis. At various points throughout his narrative he also discusses the most pertinent cases from Hampshire County, and although I do not always agree with his interpretation of particular cases, I have included in the following pages references to his work where applicable. See also C. C. Goen, *Revivalism and*

Separatism in New England, 1740-1800: Strict Congregationalists and Separate Baptists in the Great Awakening (New Haven, Conn., 1962).

Perhaps the most provocative treatment of the Baptist and Separate question lies in the briefer works of Rhys Isaac, especially "Religion and Authority: Problems of the Anglican Establishment in Virginia in the Era of the Great Awakening and the Parsons' Cause," *William and Mary Quarterly*, third series, 30 (1973): 3-36, and "Evangelical Revolt: The Nature of the Baptists' Challenge to the Traditional Order in Virginia, 1765 to 1775," *William and Mary Quarterly*, third series, 31 (1974): 345-68. As the title of the second article makes clear, Isaac focuses on the religious dissenters as threats to the whole fabric of society, secular as well as religious. Although he deals with a special and possibly even extreme case in colonial Virginia, I think the general terms of his argument can apply equally well to New England.

22 Massachusetts Archives, XIV, 376-8, State House, Boston.

23 Ibid., pp. 379-82. The incident is described in McLoughlin, *New England Dissent*, I, pp. 468-474, but McLoughlin fails to note the *mutual* accusations by east- and west-side Congregationalists regarding the association of their opponents with the Baptists. In viewing the controversy as one of successful collaboration between Congregationalists and Baptists he obscures the way in which supposed involvement with Baptists could be used rather easily and even rather carelessly as a form of slander. For the complete series of petitions, see Massachusetts Archives, XIV, 126-7, 376-8, 379-82, 402, 443-6.

24 Stephen Williams Diary, VIII, Sept. 4, 1772, Pocumtuck Valley Memorial Association Library, Deerfield, Mass.

25 McLoughlin, *New England Dissent*, I, 531-46.

26 Massachusetts Archives, XIV, 596-608.

27 Ibid.

28 Ibid.

29 Goen, *Revivalism and Separatism*, pp. 188-93; see also McLoughlin, *New England Dissent*, I, 347-9.

30 The Ashfield Baptists' petition is in Massachusetts Archives, XIV, 512-13; the 1771 valuation is in ibid., CXXXII, 57-8.

31 See the Deerfield valuation in ibid., pp. 225-7.

32 See especially McLoughlin, *New England Dissent*, I, 402-5.

33 Granville Church Records, Folder "Church Covenants, Reports, Constitutions, Reports of Councils, 1755-1885," Granville (Mass.) Library. Alfred M. Copeland, in *A History of Hampden County, Massachusetts*, 3 vols. (Springfield, Mass., 1902), notes that the first Granville church was formed in 1754 "as a result of the preaching of Whitefield and Jonathan Edwards" (III, 260).

34 Reply to complaints of David Rose and Nathan Barlow, Oct., 1757, in Granville Church Records, Folder "Church Covenants, Reports . . . "; see also Timothy Mather Cooley, *Sketches of the Life and Character of the Rev. Lemuel Haynes, A.M.* (New York, 1837), pp. 42-3. The biographical material on Smith in Dexter, *Graduates of Yale College*, II, 240-1, seems to have been drawn largely from Cooley's book.

35 Reply to complaints of David Rose and Nathan Barlow, Oct. 1757; and reply to complaints of Thomas Gillet, Mar. 27, 1760(?) and Elisabeth Gillet, Mar. 26, 1761(?) in Granville Church Records, Folder "Church Covenants, Reports . . . "

36 Untitled report, Apr. 1761, in Granville Church Records, Folder "Church Covenants, Reports . . . "

37 "First Admonition Sent to Separates," May 1763, in Granville Church Records, Folder "The Church and the Separatists, 1763-1769."

38 "Second Admonition to Separates," and "Method of Dissolving the Union Between us & the Separates," May 1763, in Granville Church Records, Folder "The Church and the Separatists, 1763-1769."

39 Undated letter in Granville Church Records, Folder "The Church and the Separatists, 1763-1769."

40 Granville Church Records, "The Doings of the Church and Committee."

41 Ibid.

42 Ibid.

43 Albion B. Wilson, *History of Granville, Massachusetts* (n.p. n.d.), pp. 174-5. Smith was not the only Hampshire County minister accused of both thelogical and political heterodoxy in the early years of the Revolution. At Charlemont the Reverend Jonathan Leavitt fell into a dispute with the people of his town, partly because of his Arminian views, partly because of his "suspected lukewarmness towards the Revolution." See Dexter, *Graduates of Yale College*, II, 543-5. Also see Chapter 7.

44 Sylvester Judd MSS, "Miscellaneous 18," p. 53, Forbes Library, Northampton, Mass.

45 William Lawrence Welch, Jr., "River God: The Public Life of Israel Williams, 1709-1788," Ph.D. dissertation, University of Maine, 1975, pp. 134-5; Thomas Hutchinson to Israel Williams, January 8, 1773, in Israel Williams Papers II, Massachusetts Historical Society, Boston.

46 Josiah G. Holland, *History of Western Massachusetts*, 2 vols., (Springfield, Mass., 1855), I, 184-5.

5. NEW SETTLEMENTS IN AN UNSETTLED SOCIETY

1 The works of Kenneth Lockridge and Philip Greven have made this story of land pressure and population a very familiar one. See Lockridge, *A New England Town: The First Hundred Years*, Dedham, Massachusetts, *1636-1736* (New York, 1970), chap. 8; "The Population of Dedham, Massachusetts, 1636-1736," *Economic History Review*, second series, 19 (1966): 318-44; and "Land, Population, and the Evolution of New England Society, 1630-1790," *Past and Present* no. 39 (1968), pp. 62-80; and Greven, *Four Generations: Population, Land, and Family in Colonial Andover, Massachusetts* (Ithaca, N.Y., 1970), chaps. 6-8. In the case of Dedham, Edward M. Cook, Jr., points out further that most young men did not move away in substantial numbers until after around 1740, suggesting that the mid-century was the time when conditions began to be most severe. See Cook, "Social Behavior and Changing Values in Dedham, 1730-1775," *William and Mary Quarterly*, third series, 27 (1970): 546-80; for a discussion of similar conditions in Concord, see also Robert A. Gross, *The Minutemen and Their World* (New York, 1976), chap. 4.

For population growth elsewhere there are several other recent works that are important studies of eastern Massachusetts towns. See Susan L. Norton, "Population Growth in Colonial America: A Study of Ipswich, Massachusetts," *Population Studies* 25 (1971): 433-52; Daniel Scott Smith, "Population, Family, and Society in Hingham, Massachusetts, 1635-1880," Ph.D. dissertation, University of California at Berkeley, 1973; John Demos, *A Little Commonwealth: Family Life in Plymouth Colony* (New York, 1970); Douglas L. Jones, *Village and Seaport: Migration and Society in Eighteenth-Century Massachusetts* (Hanover, N. H., 1981); and Richard Joseph Martin, "Revolutionary Salem: Stratification and Mobility in a Massachusetts Seaport, 1759-1799," Ph.D. dissertation, New York University, 1975. For the situation in Connecticut see Bruce C. Daniels, *The Connecticut Town: Growth and Development, 1635-1790* (Middletown, Conn., 1979).

On the general question of population increase province-wide, see Henretta, *The Evolution of American Society, 1700-1815* (Lexington, Mass., 1973); Robert V. Wells, *The Population of the British Colonies in America before 1776* (Princeton, N.J., 1975); Stella Sutherland, *Population Distribution in Colonial America* (New York, 1966); David H. Flaherty, *Privacy in Colonial New England* (Charlottesville, Va., 1972); and Evarts B. Green and Virginia D. Harrington, *American*

Population before the Federal Census of 1790 (New York, 1932). By 1765, Hampshire and Berkshire Counties had by far the lowest population densities in the province. See Table 6 in the appendix.

Yet despite all the attention given to population pressure, it is important to keep in mind Christopher Clark's suggestion that the crisis of the agrarian economy stemmed from "inequalities in access to land, rather than a general problem of 'overcrowding.'" In general, I think his point is well taken, and it certainly serves as a useful warning against the implicit Malthusianism that often creeps into the land-scarcity argument. See Clark, "The Household Economy, Market Exchange and the Rise of Capitalism in the Connecticut Valley, 1800-1860," *Journal of Social History* 13 (1979): 169-90.

2 The recent work of Douglas L. Jones has provided useful information on migration in eighteenth-century Massachusetts. See especially "The Strolling Poor: Transiency in Eighteenth Century Massachusetts," *Journal of Social History* 9 (1975): 28-54.

For a discussion of the settlement of Hampshire County see Harold R. King, "The Settlement of the Upper Connecticut River Valley to 1675," Ph.D. dissertation, Vanderbilt University, 1965; and Alan C. Swedlund, "Population Growth and Settlement Pattern in Franklin and Hampshire Counties, Massachusetts, 1650-1850," *American Antiquity* 40 (1975): 22-33.

Using the 1690 militia list figures in Greene and Harrington, *American Population*, one can make rough estimates of town population by using a multiplier of 5. Accordingly, the 1690 population figures would be Springfield, 815; Northampton, 550; Hadley, 310; Hatfield, 410; Westfield, 280; Deerfield, 255; and Northfield, 170.

The first provincial census was not until 1765, but again, it is possible to provide estimates for the growth of the population by mid-eighteenth century. A Springfield tax list for 1738, for instance, lists 360 taxpayers (excluding widows and heirs also on the list). Assuming that a tax list does not include all polls and would therefore tend to be more limited than a militia list, one could use a multiplier of between 5 and 6. In that case, the 1738 Springfield population would be between 1,800 and 2,160.

3 Two recent studies have provided estimates for population growth in Northampton and Hadley; both suggest that out-migration was an important factor in regulating population. Tiziana Rota, in "Marriage and Family Life in Northampton, Massachusetts: A Demographic Study, 1690-1750," M.A. thesis, Mount Holyoke College, 1975, shows a steady rise in Northampton population between 1690 and 1749, from around 550 to 1,040. She notes, however, that the Northampton population increased at less than an exponential rate of

growth and concludes that "even if the natural increase of the population was remarkable, the effect of migration must have had a dramatic effect [on limiting the net population increase]" (p. 20).

Similarly, Alan H. McArdle gives figures for Hadley population of 97 in 1659, 461 in 1720, and 358 in 1733. Periodic declines in the population, he argues, resulted as much from out-migration as from drops in the birth rate. In the early years people leaving Hadley returned to Connecticut, but after 1680 most moved to other Hampshire County towns. See McArdle, "Population Growth, Out-Migration, and the Regulation of Community Size: Hadley, Masschusetts, 1660-1730," M.A. thesis, University of Massachusetts, 1975, pp. 30-2, 36-7.

See also Herbert Collins Parsons, *A Puritan Outpost: A History of the Town and People of Northfield, Massachusetts* (New York, 1937); Mark Doolittle, *Historical Sketch of the Congregational Church in Belchertown, Massachusetts* (Northampton, Mass., 1852); James R. Trumbull, *History of Northampton, Massachusetts, from Its Settlement in 1654*, 2 vols. (Northampton, 1902), II, 183-90; Mason A. Green, *Springfield, 1636-1886: History of Town and City* (Springfield, Mass., 1888), pp. 208-10; and Sylvester Judd, *History of Hadley, Including the Early History of Hatfield, South Hadley, Amherst, and Granby, Massachusetts* (Springfield, Mass., 1905), pp. 387-8, 404-6.

4 John Williams's *The Redeemed Captive Returning to Zion* (Boston, 1707) was a best-seller throughout the early eighteenth century. For a sampling of incidents and alarms throughout Hampshire County, see Sylvester Judd MSS, "Massachusetts Vol. I" and "Massachusetts Vol. II," Forbes Library, Northampton, Mass.

5 "Of the Settlement and Increase of New England," in Nathanial Ames, *An Astronomical Diary, or Almanack for the Year of our Lord Christ, 1763* (Boston, 1763).

6 See especially Greven, *Four Generations*.

7 Nathan Birdsey to Joseph Hawley, Feb. 18, 1767, in Joseph Hawley Papers, II, n. pag., New York Public Library, New York City.

8 Jones, in "The Strolling Poor," p. 33, has pointed to a "phenomenal increase" of 248% in the number of official warnings for transiency in Hampshire County from the period 1750-4 to 1760-4. Indeed, for the period 1760-9 I have counted a total of 585 warnings issued by some thirty Hampshire towns. Though Springfield, Northampton, and Westfield alone accounted for 37.8% of the total, five other older towns – Brimfield, Hadley, Hatfield, Deerfield, and Northfield – issued another 24.4%. Of the newer towns in the county, only Amherst and South Hadley, valley towns recently separated from Hadley, issued over twenty warnings each (thirty-five and thirty-one,

respectively, or 11.2% of the total). The remaining twenty towns accounted for just over a quarter of all official warnings issued during the decade. See Hampshire County Court Records: Inferior Court of Common Pleas and Court of General Sessions, Forbes Library (microfilm).

9 Journal of the Reverend John Ballantine, Feb. 13, 1763, Jan. 12, 1764, Westfield (Mass.) Athenaeum.

10 The figures for 1765 and 1776 given in Greene and Harrington, *American Population*, are 17,298 and 32,701, respectively, an increase of 15,403, or 89%. The Greene and Harrington figures for 1776, however, contain gaps for a few Hampshire County towns. Working from a manuscript list in the Massachusetts Archives, CCCXXII, 99, State House, Boston, I have added figures for those towns to the total, making it 34,947 (see Table 7 in the appendix). According to Greene and Harrington (pp. 17, 21-40), the total population of Massachusetts rose from 245,627 in 1765 to 338,667 (blacks included) in 1776, for a net increase of 37.8%. For Connecticut in roughly the same period (1760-70), Bruce C. Daniels has figured a growth rate of 25%. See Daniels, *Connecticut Town*, pp. 46-7.

11 See Table 7 in the appendix. In "The Strolling Poor," (pp. 29-32), Douglas Jones points out that between 1741 and 1790, 90% of the new towns founded in Massachusetts were in the western counties (Worcester, Hampshire, and Berkshire). Many of these new towns, of course, were subdivisions of older towns, and that phenomenon will be discussed in more detail in Chapter 6.

12 See Chapter 4.

13 Alfred M. Copeland, *A History of the Town of Murrayfield* (Springfield, Mass., 1892), pp. 28-35.

14 The best analysis of the collective values of town life is Michael Zuckerman, *Peaceable Kingdoms: New England Towns in the Eighteenth Century* (New York, 1970). In a very perceptive review of Zuckerman's book, ("The Morphology of New England Society in the Colonial Period," *Journal of Interdisciplinary History* 2 [1973]: 379-98), James A. Henretta has suggested that even in the face of changing economic and religious conditions in the middle of the eighteenth century, "men would continue to invoke the old precepts of uniformity, harmony, and community" (p. 395). In a similar vein, Theodore M. Hammett ("The Revolutionary Ideology in Its Social Context: Berkshire County, Massachusetts, 1725-1785," Ph.D. dissertation, Brandeis University, 1976) has argued that people in frontier towns in Berkshire County, Mass., tried to "synthesize the ideal and reality of life in their towns," and developed "a commitment to a transitional ideal of reconciliation. This concept accepted the fact of

dissension and disagreement while working for a basic peace, harmony, and decency in town relations. Increasing conflict called forth
intensified effort to restore unity" (pp. 210-11).

15 For Joseph Burnal's political offices see Chesterfield Town Records,
I, n. pag., Forbes Library (microfilm); and *Town Records of Dudley,
Massachusetts, 1732-1794* (Pawtucket, R.I., 1893), pp. 13-62.

16 On the variety and proliferation of town offices and their importance
in involving the citizens of the towns, see Bruce C. Daniels, "Connecticut's Villages Become Mature Towns: The Complexity of Local
Institutions," *William and Mary Quarterly*, third series, 34 (1977):
83-103; and Edward M. Cook, Jr., *The Fathers of the Towns: Leadership and Community Structure in Eighteenth Century New England*
(Baltimore, 1976), pp. 24-34.

In selecting their leaders the voters of the new settlements followed
a number of patterns or, more accurately, no real pattern at all. At
Granville only fourteen men served as selectmen over a twenty-two-
year period, and four of them served for more than eight terms each.
But at Pelham, by comparison, a total of fifty-four men shared the
office of selectman over a thirty-three-year period, and no one served
more than seven terms. In the towns settled in the 1740s and 1750s,
some men managed to keep themselves and their families in office
over the years. Seth Shaw of Palmer was a selectman seventeen times
between 1752 and 1772, and other Shaws accounted for six more
terms. Similarly, four members of the Boies family of Blandford held a
selectman's post a total of thirty times over a thirty-four-year period,
each of them serving at least four terms. To some extent the patterns
of office holding in some of the newer towns were not unlike those in
the older towns; see Tables 1 and 8 in the appendix. The differences
in the lengths of time for which figures are available, however, make a
close comparison difficult. For a more general discussion of office
holding in small towns and frontier towns, see Cook, *Fathers of the
Towns*, esp. pp. 59-60, 179-82.

17 Judd MSS, "Hatfield-Deerfield," II, 170. Judd interviewed Joseph
Burnal, Jr. (born 1756) in 1833.

18 Peter Gibbon, "A short narrative of my life," typescript, Granville
(Mass.) Library. I am very grateful to Ted Hammett for bringing this
document to my attention.

19 Timothy Dwight, *Travels in New England and New York*, ed. Barbara
Miller Solomon, 4 vols. (Cambridge, Mass., 1969), II, 238, 25,
261-2, III, 271.

20 C. O. Parmenter, *History of Pelham from 1738 to 1898* (Amherst,
Mass., 1898), pp. 9-18.

21 The 1745 tax list is in the set of manuscript records collected as

Pelham Town Record, 1743-1779, University of Massachusetts Library, Amherst (microfilm). For the distribution of landholdings, see Table 9 in the appendix.

22 Charles S. Grant, *Democracy in the Connecticut Frontier Town of Kent* (New York, 1961), pp. 31-9; Gross, *Minutemen*, pp. 213-4 n. For a refinement of Grant's estimates, see his doctoral dissertation, "A History of Kent, 1738-1796: Democracy on Connecticut's Frontier," Columbia University, 1957, app. 3, pp. 323-31.

23 In *History of Pelham*, pp. 102-10, Parmenter lists forty-two individual assessment returns for 1760, not a complete listing for the whole town but a good proportion. The totals are summarized in Table 10 in the appendix.

24 The distribution of acres of improved land per Pelham household is shown in Table 9 in the appendix.

25 Massachusetts Archives, CXXXIII, 209, CXVIII, 44. See Table 11 in the appendix.

26 In an important article on the values of rural farm families, James A. Henretta has questioned the extent to which people actively engaged in profit seeking and market production, and his argument is a useful corrective to the emphasis on economic expansion that infuses Charles Grant's study of the Connecticut frontier town of Kent. See Henretta, "Families and Farms: *Mentalitè* in Pre-Industrial America," *William and Mary Quarterly*, third series, 25 (1978): 3-33. Recent studies of the more established Hampshire towns, however, have suggested a wide range of economic activity. Peter Bolles Hirtle, in "Agrarian Economy in Flux: The Agricultural History of Deerfield, 1670-1760," paper prepared for the Historic Deerfield Summer Fellowship Program, 1973, argues that by 1760 the farmers of Deerfield had become involved in commercial farming to a considerable degree, sending beef to Boston and selling surplus grain and produce. See also J. Ritchie Garrison, "Tradition and Change in the Agriculture of Deerfield, Massachusetts, 1760-1860," paper presented to the Historic Deerfield Colloquium on Recent Research in Western Massachusetts History, 1978. Sylvester Judd offers similar evidence for other towns in the valley; see Judd MSS, "Miscellaneous II," pp. 84, 203. Although it would be a mistake to argue that all farmers in the older towns were primarily involved in large-scale farming for a profit, some did apparently engage in a certain amount of commercial farming by the middle of the eighteenth century. See also Howard S. Russell, *A Long, Deep Furrow: Three Centuries of Farming in New England* (Hanover, N. H., 1976), pp. 112-81 ff.

27 On the nature of rural exchange see Clark, "Household Economy"; and Michael Merrill, "Cash is Good to Eat: Self-Sufficiency and Ex-

change in the Rural Economy of the U.S.," *Radical History Review* 3 (1977): 42-71.

28 Elisha Alvord Account Book, Northampton Historical Society, Northampton, Mass.

29 David P. Szatmary, in *Shays' Rebellion: The Making of an Agrarian Insurrection* (Amherst, Mass., 1980), discusses the "chain of debt" that involved rural merchants and farmers in western Massachusetts. Though his emphasis is on the 1780s, much of his evidence pertains to the pre-Revolutionary era as well. See esp. pp. 19-36.

30 The Inferior Court of Common Pleas generally met four times a year, twice in Northampton (February/March and November) and twice in Springfield (May and August). The February/March and the August sessions, which occurred during seasonal lulls for farmers, were by far the busiest. For that reason I have examined all cases from these sessions for two two-year periods, 1762-3 and 1772-3 – a total of 1,373 cases. During the 1762-3 period (667 cases), residents of new towns – i.e., those towns incorporated after 1740 – appeared as defendants in 244 cases and as plaintiffs in 122, for a ratio of 2:1. A decade later the ratio was slightly lower (1.79:1), or 341 cases as defendants and 191 as plaintiffs. Put differently, residents of the new towns appeared as defendants in 36% of the cases in the 1762-3 period and 49% of those in 1772-3; their appearances as plaintiffs ranged from 18% to 27% in the same periods. For a more complete breakdown of plaintiffs and defendants by status and town, see Table 12 in the appendix.

William Lawrence Welch, Jr., in "River God: The Public Life of Israel Williams, 1709-1788," Ph.D. dissertation, University of Maine, 1975, offers an interesting observation on the role of the county elite in court proceedings. The court, he notes, was a jury court, "and hence decisions there . . . were by jury and not by directives handed down from the bench . . . Still, for many westerners this did not change a basic image. For them judges not juries constituted courts, and the Williams 'clan' . . . symbolized an oppressive legal system" (pp. 137-8).

31 Parmenter, *History of Pelham*, pp. 410-12.

32 Roy H. Akagi, *The Town Proprietors of the New England Colonies* (New York, 1924), still provides the best overall description of the policies and restrictions surrounding land grants. For the terms of local grants see Josiah G. Holland, *History of Western Massachusetts*, 2 vols. (Springfield, Mass., 1855), I, 76; Allan Healy, *Charlemont, Massachusetts: Frontier Village and Hill Town* (Brattleboro, Vt., 1965), pp. 12-13; Jonathan Blake, *History of the Town of Warwick, Massachusetts, From its First Settlement to 1854* (Boston, 1873), p. 12.

33 Blake, *History of Warwick*, pp. 22-3; James C. Rice, *Secular History of the Town of Worthington From its First Settlement to 1854* (Springfield, Mass., 1854), pp. 24, 94. As Akagi points out, however, the record of proprietors in fulfilling the terms of their grants was not generally a good one; see Akagi, *Town Proprietors*, pp. 219-29.

34 Massachusetts Archives, CXVI, 339-40, 352-3, 381-3, 421-3, CXVII, 265-6, 707-9, XCVIII, 178-80; Chesterfield Town Records, vol. I.

Though the petitions were no doubt somewhat overstated, it is true that delayed settlement was a common feature. For most frontier towns in Hampshire County, the time lag between the original grant and formal incorporation generally proved to be substantial. Incorporation, of course, might be preceded by years of partial settlement, and it is impossible to say with any certainty how "full" the townships were. But as a general standard, the date of incorporation should serve as the best indicator of the point at which the townships could be fully independent and ready to stand on their own (see Table 13 in the appendix). Certainly the dates of incorporation for Hampshire County towns tell a much different story from that described by Charles S. Grant for auction towns in eighteenth-century Connecticut. In the new towns in Connecticut, incorporation often took place the same year as the original grant or sale, and usually no more than two or three years later. In Hampshire County two years seemed to be the bare minimum. Some of the delay would have to be ascribed to threatening conditions along the frontier of Massachusetts during the 1740s and 1750s, but some blame would also have to be laid at the feet of proprietors and speculators. In general, the happy conditions of harmony and good will that Grant found existing between Connecticut proprietors and settlers did not seem so much in evidence in Massachusetts. See Grant, *Democracy in Kent*, p. 24. See also Daniels, *Connecticut Town*, pp. 181-5.

35 The extensive holdings of Israel Williams, for instance, are discussed in Welch, "River God," pp. 30-1; and in George Henry Merriam, "Israel Williams, Monarch of Hampshire, 1709-1788," Ph.D. dissertation, Clark University, 1961, pp. 11-14.

36 Massachusetts Archives, CXVII, 32-3.

37 Kevin M. Sweeney, "War on the Homefront: Politics and Patronage in Hampshire County, 1754-1760," paper presented to the Historic Deerfield Colloquium on Recent Research in Western Massachusetts History, 1978, pp. 2-3, 11; Welch, "River God," pp. 45-46. The friction with Joseph Hawley over Hawley's exclusion from defense planning is also discussed in Merriam, "Monarch of Hampshire," pp.

45-6; and in E. Francis Brown, *Joseph Hawley, Colonial Radical* (New York, 1931), pp. 75-9.
38 Sweeney, "War on the Homefront," pp. 3-11. See also Arthur L. Perry, *Origins of Williamstown*, (New York, 1894), pp. 245-8.
39 Massachusetts Archives, CXVII, 113-16, 208-9, 374-5.
40 Holland, *History of Western Massachusetts*, I, 190-2; Brown, *Joseph Hawley*, pp. 80-4; Sweeney, "War on the Homefront," pp. 11-12. See, for example, the muster lists for Williams's troops sent to serve with General Amherst in Canada, 1759, in Judd MSS, "Massachusetts 5," pp. 197-9.
41 For a discussion of the varied and shifting attitudes toward Colonel Williams's military performance, see Sweeney, "War on the Homefront"; and Welch, "River God," pp. 88-9.
42 See Chapter 6.

6. THE POLITICS OF PAROCHIALISM

1 Although this process of settlement and separation has been touched upon in a number of sources, the best brief description for a single town is Kenneth A. Lockridge, *A New England Town: The First Hundred Years, Dedham, Massachusetts, 1636-1736* (New York, 1970), chap. 6; and for a whole region, Richard L. Bushman, *From Puritan to Yankee: Character and the Social Order in Connecticut, 1690-1765* (Cambridge, Mass., 1967), chap. 4; and Bruce C. Daniels, *The Connecticut Town: Growth and Development, 1635-1790* (Middletown, Conn., 1979), chap. 1. Both Lockridge and Bushman are dealing with events in the early part of the eighteenth century, preceding by some years the history of Hampshire County separations described in this chapter; Daniels's work deals with the Revolutionary era in Connecticut.

For a discussion of the geographical perspective on New England settlement, see Bonnie Barton, "New England Settlement: An Inquiry into the Comparability of Geographical Methodologies," Ph.D. dissertation, University of Michigan, 1972. See also Alan C. Swedlund, "Population Growth and Settlement Pattern in Franklin and Hampshire Counties, Massachusetts, 1650-1850," *American Antiquity* 40 (1975): 22-3.
2 The exchange between David Grayson Allen and Michael Zuckerman in "The Zuckerman Thesis and the Problem of Legal Rationalization in Provincial Massachusetts," *William and Mary Quarterly*, third series, 29 (1972): 443-68, offers a very useful discussion of the

political significance of town separations. For earlier examples of conflict, see Lockridge, *New England Town*, chap. 6; Paul Boyer and
Stephen Nissenbaum, *Salem Possessed: The Social Origins of Witchcraft* (Cambridge, Mass., 1974), pp. 80-109; and Robert A. Gross,
The Minutemen and Their World (New York, 1976), pp. 15-18.

3 Douglas L. Jones, in "The Strolling Poor: Transiency in Eighteenth
Century Massachusetts," *Journal of Social History* 9 (1975): 29-32,
points out that by the middle of the eighteenth century very few
town divisions took place in the eastern half of Massachusetts; they
were confined to the western half of the province. The divisions of
Hampshire County towns before 1775 are shown in Table 14 in the
appendix.

4 Massachusetts Archives, XII, 665-7, State House, Boston.

5 Springfield Church Records, Connecticut Valley Historical Museum,
Springfield, Mass.

6 Massachusetts Archives, CXVI, 640-3. New England law and custom provided for several levels of corporate structure. A *parish* or
precinct was generally a section of town having its own meetinghouse
and minister; the members of the parish had their own yearly meetings to take care of certain local matters, but they remained members
of the larger town meeting and were thus subject to decisions made
by the whole town. *District* status conferred a greater degree of independence, as the residents conducted their own affairs and had all the
rights of a *town* except that of sending a representative to the General
Court. In 1753 Governor Shirley, fearful of the increasing number of
representatives, began to limit the granting of town status, and from
then until 1775, most newly separated areas could have only district
status. But in general, the step from parish to district was the most
significant, because it accorded the greatest change in opportunities
for self-government and independence; in the discussion that follows,
therefore, district and town status should be considered to mean essentially the same thing. See Josiah G. Holland, *History of Western
Massachusetts*, 2 vols. (Springfield, Mass., 1855), I, 202-3.

7 Massachusetts Archives, XII, 671-8; 126-30.

8 Sylvester Judd MSS, "South Hadley 7," p. 9, Forbes Library, Northampton, Mass.; see also Sylvester Judd, *History of Hadley, Including
the Early History of Hatfield, South Hadley, Amherst, and Granby,
Massachusetts* (Springfield, Mass., 1905), pp. 387-91.

9 Judd MSS, "South Hadley 7," pp. 116, 118.

10 South Hadley Town Records, pp. 11, 12, South Hadley Town
Clerk's Office.

11 Judd, *History of Hadley*, pp. 402-3. Judd lists the residents of each
section roughly by their settlement. His list, he admits, is "not per-

fect," and the actual numbers in each category may vary slightly. Still, even with some allowance for error, the lists of residents show an expansion of the east side that far exceeded that of the west.

12 Of the office holders named in the precinct records between 1744 and 1760, most were west-siders, who served more frequently and for longer terms than east-siders.

No. men elected	Total no. terms served	Avg. no. terms per office holder	No. men serving 5 terms or more
West 17	81	4.7	8
East 10	24	2.4	1

See Judd MSS, "South Hadley 7."

13 It is worth noting that throughout the whole controversy regarding the meetinghouse, nothing seems to have been said on either side about religion. Despite all the ill feeling and bickering that enveloped the people for over a decade, neither side recorded any overt slur against the orthodoxy or spiritual health of the opposition. The loss of South Hadley church records makes it impossible to distinguish the identities of church members, but within each side were men who had opposed each other during the Great Awakening. Judd records the names of fifteen men who, during the controversy surrounding the Reverend Grindall Rawson in 1741, dissented from the votes taken against the minister (See Chapter 2.) Such dissent, of course, does not necessarily imply that the dissenters either held an Old Light stance or gave total support to the minister; they may have registered their objections for reasons other than doctrine – procedure, for instance, i.e., the way the action against Rawson was being carried out. Still, given the religious situation at the time, it seems just as likely that their dissent was a reflection of doctrinal position. Whatever the case, the dissenters came from both sides of town, and five from the east, some of the earliest residents of that part, signed the 1760 petition. See Judd, *History of Hadley*, p. 389.

14 South Hadley Town Records, pp. 9-26.

15 South Hadley Town Records, pp. 11-14; Judd, *History of Hadley*, p. 392; see also Judd MSS., "South Hadley 7," pp. 118-19.

16 Massachusetts Archives, XIV, 204-5.

17 Ibid., pp. 177-8; see also Judd, *History of Hadley*, pp. 402-3 and app., "Genealogies of Hadley Families."

18 Massachusetts Archives, XIV, 177-8.

19 Ibid., pp. 204-5.

20 Ibid.

21 Judd, *History of Hadley*, pp. 392-3.
22 Ibid.
23 Ibid.; Judd MSS, "South Hadley 7," pp. 121-2. In Nov. 1761, thirty South Hadley men – three from the west side, the others from the east – were bound by recognizance to appear at the county court, and were discharged after making appearance. There is no record of any further legal action against them. All but four of the men arrested described themselves as yeomen – the four exceptions being a cordwainer, a blacksmith, a physician, and a gentleman.
24 Judd MSS, "South Hadley 7," p. 13; South Hadley Town Records, p. 26; Judd, *History of Hadley*, p. 393.
25 On the rising level of division controversies, see James A. Henretta, "The Morphology of New England Society in the Colonial Period," *Journal of Interdisciplinary History* 2 (1973): 395-6.
26 Springfield Town Records, p. 388, City Clerk's Office; Stephen Williams Diary, VIII, Mar. 23, 30, 1773, Pocumtuck Valley Memorial Association Library, Deerfield, Mass.
27 Springfield Town Records, pp. 389-98. Henretta, in "Morphology of New England Society," makes a very perceptive point about the values expressed during division controversies: "The system of values, upon which this communal culture was based, was enunciated most frequently precisely at the moment at which they were not accepted as binding by a significant number of inhabitants. It is not accidental, therefore, that most of the affirmations of consensus and community which [Michael] Zuckerman cites [in *Peaceable Kingdoms: New England Towns in the Eighteenth Century* (New York, 1970)] come from the 1750s or later, for it was then that the changed economic and religious conditions of New England had undermined the traditional foundations of town life. An increasingly diverse and rapidly growing society needed a new ethic; until this new system of values was found, men would continue to invoke the old precepts of uniformity, harmony, and community" (p. 395).
28 Bushman, *Puritan to Yankee*, pp. 60-2.
29 Bushman's argument about land values (*Puritan to Yankee*, pp. 61-2), though not altogether invalid, still seems rather one-dimensional. Although he does offer evidence to indicate that land close to the town center and meetinghouse was more desirable or valuable than outlying parcels – a finding that should hardly be surprising – he offers no evidence whatsoever that people actually sought town division specifically *in order to* raise the price of their land. As one might expect, there are no explicit statements of such a desire. Moreover, Bushman does not provide any evidence of subsequent economic activity undertaken by people who successfully built or relocated a meetinghouse.

The main benefit of having higher-priced land comes from selling it for a profit; indeed, for people who held onto land with rising value, the immediate economic result could be negative, in the form of higher taxes. The economic motivation may have influenced some people, but probably not to the degree Bushman suggests.

In general Bushman is so anxious to turn his people into Yankees in the 1760s that he denies their Puritan side, their sense of the church as an important source of communal identity and order. Unless one assumes that outlivers were dissembling in their meetinghouse petitions, it is impossible to ignore the emphasis they put on having their own preaching and especially on being able to provide adequate religious education for their children. Quite naturally they felt uneasy about being distant from the meetinghouse, for physical distance might also lead to a certain psychological distance. To reduce the location of the meetinghouse simply to a function of the real estate market is to miss the full meaning of the "centrality" of the church in rural society – both in the eighteenth century and, indeed, in the nineteenth and twentieth centuries as well.

30 For a discussion of the appeal of old norms and values in a period of rapid social change, see the passage from Henretta's "Morphology of New England Society" cited in n. 27 to this chapter; and Kenneth A. Lockridge, "Social Change and the Meaning of the American Revolution," *Journal of Social History* 7 (1973): 403-39.

31 Israel Williams to Francis Bernard, Aug. 19, 1761, in Israel Williams Papers, II, Massachusetts Historical Society, Boston.

32 Hatfield Town Records, 1741-1813, p. 187, Forbes Library (microfilm).

33 Massachusetts Archives, XII, 56-7; George Sheldon, *A History of Deerfield, Massachusetts*, 2 vols. (1896; reprint ed., Somersworth, N. H., 1972), I, 570-6; and Francis M. Thompson, *History of Greenfield, Shire Town of Franklin County* (Greenfield, Mass., 1904), pp. 172-82.

34 Hatfield Town Records, pp. 188, 191, 205-8, 219-20. For the actions of the Williamsburg people against Israel Williams during the first months of the Revolutionary crisis, see Chapter 7. Joseph B. Felt, in *Collections of the American Statistical Association* (Boston, 1847), pt. I, 37, notes that Williamsburg was one of a handful of towns that petitioned the General Court in 1779 to have its name changed because of the local hostility to the person for whom it was named. The petition was apparently not granted or pursued further.

35 *Records of Hadley Third and Second Precinct*, in Carpenter and Morehouse, *The History of the Town of Amherst, Massachusetts* (Amherst, 1896), pt. II, pp. 63, 66.

36 Massachusetts Archives, XIV, 684-96. See also Carpenter and More-house, *History of Amherst*, pt. I, pp. 103-7; and Judd MSS, "Massachusetts 5," pp. 288-91.

37 Judd MSS, "Massachusetts 5," pp. 106-8; Judd, *History of Hadley*, p. 410; Carpenter and Morehouse, *History of Amherst*, pt. I, p. 107.

38 Throughout the 1760s and early 1770s, most of the political leaders in Amherst were residents of the center part of town and signers of the petition in opposition to the plan to divide the town. Only a few of the town's major officials came from the faction that sought division. In 1773, however, the pro-division forces established a clear dominance that they maintained for several years. The pattern of office holding in Amherst (for the positions of selectman, moderator, treasurer, and clerk) is shown in this table:

Years	No. positions held by petitioners	No. positions held by non-petitioners
1760-72	71 (69.6%)	31 (30.4%)
1773-9	11 (19.6%)	45 (80.4%)

39 For population figures see Table 7 in the appendix; for the distribution of new towns in all Massachusetts counties see Table 15 in the appendix.

7. REVOLUTION IN THE NEIGHBORHOOD

1 Sylvester Judd MSS, "Northampton I," p. 333, and "Miscellaneous 15," p. 348, Forbes Library, Northampton, Mass.

2 The best accounts of the violence and mob activity in Boston are in Edmund S. Morgan and Helen M. Morgan, *The Stamp Act Crisis: Prologue to Revolution* (New York, 1962), chap. 9; and Dirk Hoerder, *Crowd Action in Revolutionary Massachusetts, 1765-1781* (New York, 1977), chaps. 2 and 3.

3 Josiah Pierce Diary, 1766, n. pag., Jones Library, Amherst, Mass.

4 Journal of the Reverend John Ballantine, Nov. 11, 1765, Westfield (Mass.) Athenaeum; Hoerder, *Crowd Action*, pp. 133-5; and "People and Mobs: Crowd Action in Massachusetts During the American Revolution, 1765-1780," Ph.D. dissertation, Free University, Berlin, 1971, p. 128. For the history of the Pine Laws and the resistance to them, see Joseph J. Malone, *Pine Trees and Politics: The Naval Stores and Forest Policy in Colonial New England, 1691-1775* (Seattle, 1964), esp. p. 62.

5 Between 1760 and 1768, inclusive, only eight Hampshire County towns (Brimfield, Deerfield, Hadley, Hatfield, Northampton, Spring-

field, Sunderland, and Westfield) consistently sent representatives to the General Court. The new town of Wilbraham, incorporated in 1763, sent its own representative in 1764; after that, however, it joined with Springfield to share the expenses. Other small towns quite often joined with neighboring towns to send a representative (e.g., Southampton with Northampton, Greenfield with Deerfield, South Hadley and Amherst with Hadley); in those cases, however, the representative almost always came from the older and larger town. See *Journals of the House of Representatives of Massachusetts* (Boston, 1919-78), esp. XXXVII and XLIV. For a summary of the voting records of Hampshire representatives between 1726 and 1765, see William Pencak, *War, Politics and Revolution in Provincial Massachusetts* (Boston, 1981), p. 245.

6 James R. Trumbull, *History of Northampton, Massachusetts, from Its Settlement in 1654*, 2 vols. (Northampton, 1902), II, 324-6; for a general discussion of the Convention of Towns, see Richard D. Brown, "The Massachusetts Convention of Towns, 1768," *William and Mary Quarterly*, third series, 26 (1969): 94-104, or *Revolutionary Politics in Massachusetts: The Boston Committee of Correspondence and the Towns, 1772-1774* (Cambridge, Mass., 1970), pp. 28-31.

7 Daniel White Wells and Reuben Field Wells, *A History of Hatfield, Massachusetts* (Springfield, Mass., 1910), p. 181.

8 For a list of delegates to the Convention see Brown, "Convention of Towns," pp. 103-4.

9 For the period from Jan. 1773 through Jan. 1774 – the time when most towns would have responded to the first appeals from the Boston Committee of Correspondence – I have found evidence of correspondence from seven Hampshire towns (Amherst, Brimfield, Colrain, New Salem, Pelham, South Hadley, and Wilbraham), or around 17% of the towns in the county. There may be one or two elusive letters from other towns, but it is doubtful that there are many. Brown, in *Revolutionary Politics*, reports that by Sept. 1773, some 22% of Hampshire towns had corresponded with Boston. The point here is not to quibble over percentages; whatever the exact figure, it seems clear that Hampshire County lagged behind the eastern half of the province in responding to Boston's first appeals. For Brown's estimates and samples from all Massachusetts counties see pp. 97, 251-3.

10 Pelham Town Records, 1743-1816, pp. 145-7, Forbes Library (microfilm). This letter is also included in C. O. Parmenter, *History of Pelham from 1738 to 1898* (Amherst, Mass., 1898), pp. 125-7; the Parmenter version has the virtue of being published but the vice of being inaccurately transcribed.

11 For a discussion of the effect of the British policies in 1774, see David Ammerman, *In the Common Cause: American Response to the Coercive Acts of 1774* (Charlottesville, Va., 1974).

12 Brown, *Revolutionary Politics*, pp. 178-9; see also L. Kinvin Wroth, "Province in Rebellion: An Interpretive Essay," in Wroth, ed., *Province in Rebellion: A Documentary History of the Founding of the Commonwealth of Massachusetts, 1774-1775* (Cambridge, Mass., 1975), p. 36.

As already noted, seven Hampshire towns had written to Boston by Jan. 1774; another thirteen made their first communication with the Committee of Correspondence between June and Sept. 1774; see Wroth, *Province in Rebellion*, "Detailed Table of Contents of Microfiche Texts," pp. 164-6. Brown counts twenty-two towns in Hampshire County that eventually corresponded with Boston; he failed to count West Springfield, which would bring the total to twenty-three. See Brown, *Revolutionary Politics*, endpaper map. There were always the slower towns to be remembered, too. The people of Chesterfield, for instance, never got around to corresponding at all, and it was not until Jan. 1775 that they finally decided "to take into Consideration Some of ye Resolves of ye Provintial Congress heretofore Neglected." See Chesterfield Town Records, 1762-1815, Forbes Library (microfilm).

The specific references to the role of Silent Wilde are in the letter from Colrain to the Boston Committee and a letter from Montague to Thomas Cushing, in Wroth, *Province in Rebellion*, document 236, p. 741, and document 270, pp. 801-2. (Hereafter all letters exchanged between towns and the Boston Committee of Correspondence [BCC] will be followed by the microfiche citation for the *Province in Rebellion* collection.)

13 Ammerman, *Common Cause*, p. 7.

14 See Brown, *Revolutionary Politics*, pp. 120-136. The main point here is not simply, as Brown suggests, that "towns met to consider and formulate their basic political beliefs," a process leading to "the elements of a consensus" throughout Massachusetts, a "general agreement about basic political principles" (pp. 93-4, 121). It is important to understand the particularism of many of these responses, as the towns expressed general political principles in terms of their own local situation.

15 Williamsburg to BCC, Aug. 25, 1774, document 287, p. 819.

16 Murrayfield to BCC, July 28, 1774, document 248, p. 762; Wilbraham to BCC, Aug. 4, 1774, document 256, pp. 780-8; Granville to BCC, July 11, 1774, document 233, pp. 727-38, and Aug. 31, 1774,

document 253, pp. 774-6; Granby to BCC, July 11, 1774, document 232, pp. 735-7.

As Richard Brown points out, the town responses to the Boston Committee covered the whole range from "silent repudiation to admiring applause." That variety of opinion "suggests an independence of action which cannot be described as either domination or manipulation by the Boston Committee." The important result of the Boston Committee in the early months was to spur towns into thinking about these issues and thereby to force them to develop a local political response. Again, see Brown, *Revolutionary Politics*, pp. 120-36.

17 Colrain to BCC, July 12, 1774, document 236, p. 741.

18 BCC to Colrain, July 18, 1774, document 238, p. 745. Note the quickness of the reply.

19 Wilbraham to BCC, Aug. 4, 1774, document 256, pp. 780-3.

20 Colrain to BCC, Aug. 8, 1774, document 259, pp. 786-7. On the "more particular, confidential relationship between Boston and the towns," see Brown, *Revolutionary Politics* pp. 136 ff.

21 The account is rendered in Trumbull, *History of Northampton*, II, 345-8. There is also a narrative description in Hoerder, "People and Mobs," pp. 497-8.

22 Judd is quoted in Trumbull, *History of Northampton*, II, 346. The literature on crowd action in preindustrial Europe is quite extensive. See especially Natalie Zemon Davis, *Society and Culture in Early Modern France* (Stanford, Calif., 1975); George Rudé, *The Crowd in History: A Study of Popular Disturbances in France and England, 1730-1848* (New York, 1964); and E. P. Thompson, "The Moral Economy of the English Crowd in the Eighteenth Century," *Past and Present* no. 50 (1971), pp. 76-136.

One of the first American historians to focus attention on the comparative history of crowd action was Pauline Maier, whose "Popular Uprisings and Civil Authority in Eighteenth Century America," *William and Mary Quarterly*, third series, 27 (1970): 3-35, provided an important beginning for the recent emphasis on crowd behavior in the Revolutionary era. Maier portrayed pre-Revolutionary mobs as fairly representative of a cross-section of colonial society, more middle-class than their European counterparts. Moreover, she argued that mob action was generally not an attack on established institutions or political and social elites; indeed, she has stressed a kind of harmony between the political goals of colonial leaders and those of colonial mobs. Those leaders, she suggests, were often successful in "focussing popular exuberance" in order to "work with long-established tendencies in the mob toward purposefulness and responsibility" (p. 28).

241

Though Maier offers a useful analysis of the cultural legitimcy of crowd action in an American context, her discussion of the relationship between crowds and elites gives a rather limited view of the common people themselves, underestimating their autonomy from – and occasional antipathy toward – the established political leaders. For a view giving more emphasis to the distinct political values and goals of pre-Revolutionary crowds, see Hoerder, *Crowd Action*. Also important are Charles Tilly, "Collective Action in England and America, 1765-1775," and Richard Maxwell Brown, "Back Country Rebellions and the Homestead Ethic in America, 1740-1799," both in Richard Maxwell Brown and Don E. Fehrenbacher, eds., *Tradition, Conflict, and Modernization: Perspectives on the American Revolution* (New York, 1977), pp. 45-99; and Edward Countryman, " 'Out of the Bounds of the Law': Northern Land Rioters in the Eighteenth Century," in Alfred F. Young, ed., *The American Revolution: Explorations in the History of American Radicalism*, (DeKalb, Ill., 1976), pp. 37-70.

23 Trumbull, *History of Northampton*, II, 345-8.

24 George Sheldon, *A History of Deerfield, Massachusetts*, 2 vols. (1896; reprint ed., Somersworth, N. H., 1972), II, 681-700; Judd MSS, "Massachusetts 5," p. 348, and "Revolutionary Matters," p. 169; Trumbull, *History of Northampton*, II, 373-4.

25 Joseph Hawley to Theodore Sedgwick, May 10, 1775, in Joseph Hawley Papers, II, n. pag., New York Public Library, New York City; Trumbull, *History of Northampton*, II, 350-1, 374; Mark Doolittle, *Historical Sketch of the Congregational Church in Belchertown, Massachusetts* (Northampton, Mass., 1852), p. 46.

26 Trumbull, *History of Northampton*, II, 372.

27 The depositions of Benjamin Read, James Hunt and William Read, and Seth Tubbs are in the Israel Williams Papers, II, Massachusetts Historical Society, Boston.

28 "James Hunt & William Read's testimony relating to a mob – Sept. 15, 1775," and "Benj Read to all people, Williamsburgh – Sept. 14, 1774," in Israel Williams Papers, II.

29 Benjamin Read deposition, in Israel Williams Papers, II. Hoerder, in *Crowd Action*, p. 343, suggests that the Hatfield people "lost interest" in the plans of the Williamsburg mob, apparently because the outsiders seemed too orderly to suit the desires of Williams's Hatfield neighbors.

30 Deposition of Seth Tubbs, in Israel Williams Papers, II.

31 William Lawrence Welch, Jr., "River God: The Public Life of Israel Williams, 1709-1788," Ph.D. dissertation, University of Maine, 1975, pp. 150-1.

32 See Edward M. Cook, Jr., *The Fathers of the Towns: Leadership and Community Structure in Eighteenth Century New England* (Baltimore, 1976), p. 117.

33 See Chapter 5.

34 Sheldon, *History of Deerfield*, II, 677-8.

35 John Dickinson to Israel Williams, May 23, 1775, and James Easton to Israel Williams, [1775], in Israel Williams Papers, II.

36 House of Representatives, Apr. 15, 1777, order for Israel Williams and son to be jailed, in Israel Williams Papers, II.

37 Hatfield Committee of Correspondence to Provincial Council, Mar. 29, 1777, in Israel Williams Papers, II.

38 Israel Williams to Provincial Council, Dec. 1779, in Israel Williams Papers, II.

39 Mason A. Green, *Springfield, 1636-1886: History of Town and City* (Springfield, Mass., 1888), pp. 275-87; see also ibid., chap. 14.

40 Bruce G. Merritt, "Loyalism and Social Conflict in Revolutionary Deerfield, Massachusetts," *Journal of American History* 57 (1970): 277-89. Sheldon, *History of Deerfield*, II, 674-6, 680-1.

41 Isaac Chauncy et al. to Northampton Committee, Apr. 28, 1775, in Hawley Papers, II, n. pag. See Chapter 5.

42 Clifford K. Shipton, *Sibley's Harvard Graduates: Biographical Sketches of Those Who Attended Harvard College*, 17 vols. (Boston, 1942), VI, 32-3.

43 Sheldon, *History of Deerfield*, II, 710-11.

44 Shipton, *Sibley's Harvard Graduates*, X, 199-200.

45 Franklin B. Dexter, *Biographical Sketches of the Graduates of Yale College*, 6 vols. (New York, 1903), II, 119-20, 240-1, 443-54, 543-5, 548-9; Shipton, *Sibley's Harvard Graduates*, VIII, 614-15, IX, 55-7; Judd MSS, "Northampton I," p. 334.

46 Stephen Williams Diary, IV, Sept. 11, 1742, Pocumtuck Valley Memorial Association Library, Deerfield, Mass.

47 Ibid., VIII, June 20, July 4, Aug. 8, 1774.

48 For a discussion of mob action throughout Massachusetts in the early months of the Revolution, see Hoerder, *Crowd Action*, pp. 271-352; see also Kevin Joseph MacWade, "Worcester County, 1750-1774: A Study of a Provincial Patronage Elite," Ph.D. dissertation, Boston University Graduate School, 1974.

BIBLIOGRAPHICAL ESSAY

One of the benefits of working on the history of early Hampshire County is the richness of the local records and manuscript materials. A very valuable – albeit voluminous and somewhat idiosyncratically organized – source is the Sylvester Judd Manuscript in the Forbes Library in Northampton, Massachusetts; the Judd papers include a large number of reasonably accurate transcriptions or summaries of local and provincial records and, even more valuable, numerous personal reflections and oral histories collected by Judd in the early nineteenth century. Also at the Forbes are microfilm copies of the town records for several Hampshire towns, including Chesterfield, Cummington, Hatfield, Northampton, Pelham, Ware, Williamsburg, and Worthington. The Town Clerk's Office in South Hadley and the City Clerk's Office in Springfield have the manuscript records for their respective communities. Moreover, the early records for Springfield are printed in Henry M. Burt, *The First Century of the History of Springfield: The Official Records from 1636 to 1736* (Springfield, 1898); those for Amherst are given in Carpenter and Morehouse, *The History of the Town of Amherst, Massachusetts* (Amherst, 1896). The records of the Hampshire County Inferior Court of Common Pleas and Court of General Sessions of the Peace are in the Hampshire County Court House in Northampton or on microfilm at the Forbes Library. Petitions and other papers relating to Hampshire towns are in the collections of the Massachusetts Archives in the State House in Boston or on microfilm at the University of Massachusetts Library, Amherst. The Revolutionary era letters from the Hampshire towns to the Boston Committee of Correspon-

244

dence are included in the microfiche collection edited by L. Kinvin Wroth, *Province in Rebellion: A Documentary History of the Founding of the Commonwealth of Massachusetts, 1774-1775* (Cambridge, Mass.: Harvard University Press, 1975).

An important source for the ecclesiastical history of Hampshire County is the Hampshire Association of Congregational Churches and Ministers Collection at the Forbes Library. Unfortunately, the records end in the late 1740s, just on the eve of the Edwards controversy. Various other bits of material pertaining to the Hampshire Association of Ministers are in the Letters of the Reverend Robert Breck at the Connecticut Valley Historical Museum in Springfield; the Breck collection also contains some very useful records of the First Church in Springfield. Other manuscript church records are available for Deerfield at the Pocumtuck Valley Memorial Association Library in Deerfield; for Granville at the Granville Library; for Northampton at the Forbes Library; and for Westfield at the Westfield Athenaeum. The Westfield Athenaeum also has a typescript copy of the Journal of the Reverend John Ballantine, 1737-74, one of the most valuable (and entertaining) journals of a Hampshire clergyman who lived during the period under study here. Likewise of interest are the diaries of the Reverends Edward Billing and Stephen Williams, both available at the Pocumtuck Valley Memorial Association Library. The Jonathan Edwards Manuscripts at the Beinecke Rare Book and Manuscript Library at Yale University are, of course, critical to an understanding of ecclesiastical affairs in the county.

The two most prominent secular leaders of the county, Joseph Hawley and Israel Williams, also left extensive collections of personal papers. Hawley's papers are in the New York Public Library, and Williams's are in the Massachusetts Historical Society, Boston; other Williams family papers are in the Pocumtuck Valley Memorial Association Library and the Williams College Library, Williamstown.

Almost every town in the county has a published history, generally the work of a nineteenth-century antiquarian. Whatever these local historians lacked in detachment they usually made up in detail, and many of the town histories are especially valuable because they draw extensively on local records and reproduce a great deal of documentary material. In addition to the books on Amherst and Springfield already cited, some of the better town histories are Mason A. Green, *Springfield, 1636-1886: History of Town and City* (Springfield, 1888); John H. Lockwood, *Westfield and Its Historic Influences 1669-1919* (Westfield, 1922); George Sheldon, *A History of Deerfield, Massachusetts*, 2 vols. (1896; reprint ed., Somersworth, N.H., 1972); James Russell Trumbull, *History of Northampton, Massachusetts, from Its First Settlement in 1654*, 2 vols. (Northampton, 1902); Daniel White Wells and Reuben Field Wells, *A History of Hatfield, Massachusetts* (Springfield, 1910); David Willard, *History of Greenfield* (Greenfield, 1838); and Albion B. Wilson, *History of Granville, Massachusetts* (n.p., n.d.).

A very valuable introduction to the region as a whole is provided by Josiah G. Holland, *History of Western Massachusetts*, 2 vols. (Springfield, 1855). The ecclesiastical history of the northern part of the region is covered in Theophilus Packard, Jr., *A History of the Churches and Ministers, and of Franklin Association, in Franklin County, Mass.* (Boston, 1854), which is a helpful companion to the indispensable volumes produced by Clifford K. Shipton, *Sibley's Harvard Graduates: Biographical Sketches of Those Who Attended Harvard College*, 17 vols. (Boston, 1942); and Franklin Bowditch Dexter, *Biographical Sketches of the Graduates of Yale College*, 6 vols. (New York, 1903).

SECONDARY SOURCES

Scholarly writing is as much a cumulative as a creative process, and every historian builds upon the work of others. Although I hope I have given adequate acknowledgement of all my debts in the notes to each chapter, I would like to draw special attention here to those secondary works I found particularly stimulating or useful. Two works that provided important models for the study of political and social change on the regional level were Richard L. Bushman, *From Puritan to Yankee: Character and the Social Order in Connecticut, 1690-1765* (Cambridge, Mass.: Harvard University Press, 1967); and Robert J. Taylor, *Western Massachusetts in the Revolution* (Providence, R.I.: Brown University Press, 1954). Any conceptual or interpretive disagreements I have with either author are far overshadowed by my admiration for their works.

Several unpublished doctoral dissertations also contributed greatly to my understanding of western Massachusetts as a region: Mary Catherine Foster, "Hampshire County, Massachusetts, 1729-1754: A Covenant Society in Transition," Ph.D. dissertation, University of Michigan, 1967; Theodore M. Hammett, "The Revolutionary Ideology in its Social Context: Berkshire County, Massachusetts, 1725-1785," Ph.D. dissertation, Brandeis University, 1976; and Ronald K. Snell, "The County Magistracy in Eighteenth-Century Massachusetts, 1692-1750," Ph.D. dissertation, Princeton University, 1971. Snell's work offers an especially valuable study of regional elites, a topic also discussed in Robert Zemsky, *Merchants, Farmers, and River Gods: An Essay on Eighteenth-Century American Politics* (Boston: Gambit Press, 1971); David T. Konig, *Law and Society in Puritan Massachusetts: Essex County, 1629-1692* (Chapel Hill: University of North Carolina Press, 1979); and John J. Waters, *The Otis Family in Provincial and Revolutionary Massachusetts* (Chapel Hill: University of North Carolina Press, 1968). Of the several works dealing with particular political leaders in Hampshire County, I found Stephen C. Innes's "A Patriarchal Society: Economic Dependency and Social Order in Springfield, Massachusetts, 1636-1702," Ph.D. dissertation, Northwestern University, 1977, to be the most conceptually stimulating.

The historiography of New England towns has become extremely rich in recent years, and like most early American social historians, I have been influenced by what are now several of the standard works in the field: Kenneth A. Lockridge, *A New England Town: The First Hundred Years, Dedham, Massachusetts, 1636-1736* (New York: W. W. Norton, 1970); Philip Greven, *Four Generations: Population, Land, and Family in Colonial Andover, Massachusetts* (Ithaca, N.Y.: Cornell University Press, 1970); and Robert A. Gross, *The Minutemen and Their World* (New York: Hill and Wang, 1976). Lockridge's "Land, Population, and the Evolution of New England Society, 1630-1790," *Past and Present*, no. 39 (1968), pp. 62-80, also contributed to my general understanding of the recurring patterns of development of New England towns. Other, more recent, works that provide a detailed analysis of New England towns are David Grayson Allen, *In English Ways: The Movement of Societies and the Transferal of English Local Law and Custom to Massachusetts*

Bay in the Seventeenth Century (Chapel Hill: University of North Carolina Press, 1981); Douglas Lamar Jones, *Village and Seaport: Migration and Society in Eighteenth-Century Massachusetts* (Hanover, N.H.: University Press of New England, 1981); and Bruce C. Daniels, *The Connecticut Town: Growth and Development, 1635-1790* (Middletown, Conn.: Wesleyan University Press, 1979). The best general work on the social values of New England town life is still Michael Zuckerman, *Peaceable Kingdoms: New England Towns in the Eighteenth Century* (New York: Alfred A. Knopf, 1970). Given the nature of my particular focus here, however, I have taken special notice of the refinement of Zuckerman's argument offered by David Grayson Allen, "The Zuckerman Thesis and the Problem of Legal Rationalization in Provincial Massachusetts," *William and Mary Quarterly*, third series, 29 (1972): 443-68; and James A. Henretta, "The Morphology of New England Society in the Colonial Period," *Journal of Interdisciplinary History* 2 (1973): 379-98.

In studying the religious values and behavior of the people in Hampshire County towns I found Paul R. Lucas's *Valley of Discord: Church and Society along the Connecticut River, 1636-1725* (Hanover, N.H.: University Press of New England, 1976), to be a useful introduction to the early history of the region, as was Ralph J. Coffman's *Solomon Stoddard* (Boston: Twayne Publishers, 1978). Because of its focus on the relationship between the minister and his people, Patricia Juneau Tracy's *Jonathan Edwards, Pastor: Religion and Society in Eighteenth-Century Northampton* (New York: Hill and Wang, 1979) proved to be the most intriguing of all the books on Edwards, at least for my purposes. For a more general view of the Great Awakening and its aftermath, I began (as so many other historians have) with Alan Heimert's classic *Religion and the American Mind: From the Great Awakening to the Revolution* (Cambridge, Mass.: Harvard University Press, 1966). I also drew heavily on William G. McLoughlin, *New England Dissent, 1630-1833: The Baptists and the Separation of Church and State*, 2 vols. (Cambridge, Mass.: Harvard University Press, 1971). But of all the works dealing with the Great Awakening, probably the most important to my understanding of the popular uses of evangelical religion were two articles by Rhys Isaac focusing not on New England but on Virginia: "Religion and Authority: Problems of the Anglican Establishment in Vir-

ginia in the Era of the Great Awakening and the Parsons' Cause,"
William and Mary Quarterly, third series, 30 (1973): 3-36; and
"Evangelical Revolt: The Nature of the Baptists' Challenge to the
Traditional Order in Virginia, 1765 to 1775," *William and Mary
Quarterly*, third series, 31 (1974): 345-68.

Likewise, my appreciation of popular political behavior was in-
fluenced by a number of studies of crowd activity outside colonial
New England. Several of the essays in Natalie Zemon Davis,
Society and Culture in Early Modern France (Stanford: Stanford
University Press, 1975), suggested a valuable analytical approach,
as did George Rudé, *The Crowd in History: A Study of Popular
Disturbances in France and England, 1730-1848* (New York:
John Wiley and Sons, 1964), and E. P. Thompson, "The Moral
Economy of the English Crowd in the Eighteenth Century," *Past
and Present*, no. 50 (1971), pp. 76-136. Two important studies of
popular politics in eighteenth-century Massachusetts are Dirk
Hoerder, *Crowd Action in Revolutionary Massachusetts, 1765-
1781* (New York: Academic Press, 1977); and Gary B. Nash, *The
Urban Crucible: Social Change, Political Consciousness, and the
Origins of the American Revolution* (Cambridge, Mass.: Harvard
University Press, 1979). In looking at the political transformation
of the rural countryside, I was especially influenced by Kenneth
A. Lockridge, "Social Change and the Meaning of the American
Revolution," *Journal of Social History* 7 (1973): 403-39; and Edward Countryman, " 'Out of the Bounds of the Law': Northern
Land Rioters in the Eighteenth Century," in Alfred F. Young,
ed., *The American Revolution: Explorations in the History of American Radicalism* (DeKalb: Northern Illinois University Press,
1976).

INDEX

251

Index

Index

Dwight, Timothy, on hilltowns, 116–17
Dwight, Timothy, Judge, 32–3
Dwight, Timothy, II, 33

Eastman, William, 138
economic inequality
  in early Hampshire towns, 14, 15, 21
  in Great Awakening, 47–9
  land grants and, 14, 15, 110
  in new settlements, 95, 115
  reflected in town politics, 15–16
Edwards, Jonathan, 7, 28, 32, 57–8, 59–75, 78, 94
  admission standards of, 61–3
  on baptism, 61–2, 65
  in Breck controversy, 42, 43, 53
  on choice of ministerial council, 67–72
  difficult personality of, 59–60, 62
  dismissal of, 59, 72–3, 79, 81, 82
  eastern ministers' view of, 67
  economic self-interest as viewed by, 48
  effect of his dismissal, 79–80
  emotional force of, 36–7, 45
  extremist practices rejected by, 68, 72–3
  isolation of, 67–9, 72
  and Joseph Hawley, 63–5, 79–80
  in ministerial rift, 39, 42
  on "neighbourhood" of Hampshire County, 7, 28, 71
  open communion rejected by, 60–1, 94
  in revivalist movement, 36–7, 38, 40–1, 45, 46
  Separates and, 94
  Williams family opposition to, 32, 65–6, 68
elites
  decline of, 161–2
  early emergence of, 20
  mob action and, 166–75
  new settlers' attitudes toward, 125–30
  patronage for, 19–20, 28–35
  River Gods as, 7–8, 9, 18–19
  see also kinship networks
Enfield, Mass., John Pynchon's role in, 23
enthusiastic religion, see Great Awakening

family size
  population dispersal and, 132
  subsistence farming and, 118–19
farming
  amount of land necessary for, 118–19
  crops raised in, 119
  land scarcity and, 110–11
  livestock and, 119
  soil quality and, 117
  subsistence, 118–19, 120
  tenant, 21–2

Fort Henry, 128
Fort Massachusetts, 127
Forward, Justus, 75
frontier towns
  as American creation, 12–13
  Indian warfare and, 109, 125–6, 128
  as military outposts, 13
  nonresident proprietors of, 123–6
  Puritanism recreated in, 13–14
  rate of migration to, 109–10, 112
  Seven Years' War and, 110, 125–8
  see also settlements

Gibbon, Peter, 116, 117, 120
Gillet, Elizabeth, 98
Gillet, Thomas, 97–8
governors, royal
  patronage of, 7–8, 19–20, 29–30
  political legitimacy of, 19
  River Gods' relationship with, 7–8
Granby, Mass., formation of, 143
Grant, Charles, 118, 119
Great Awakening, 9, 36–58
  ambivalent view of, 44–7
  Ashley's criticism of, 50–3
  backlash against, 57–8
  Baptists in, 86
  class conflict and, 48–9
  compared to the Revolution, 183, 185
  continuing revivalism after, 77–80
  as disruptive event, 45–6
  dual perception of, 37
  economic self-interest in, 48
  economic stratification in, 47–9
  excessive behavior in, 45–7, 51–2, 68, 72–3, 74
  family bonds in, 51
  heightened sense of purity in, 49–50, 56, 76
  individuals vulnerable to attack in, 47–50
  ministerial authority undermined in, 15, 37, 49–57, 76
  ministerial rift in, 38–40
  spiritual distinctions in, 47, 49–50, 61, 76
Griswold, Sylvanus, 86
Gross, Robert, 118, 119

Hadley, Mass.
  division of, 16, 133
  John Pynchon's role in, 23
  soil quality in, 117
  spread of population in, 109
  vulnerability of, 13
Hall, David, 71, 79–80
Hampshire Association of Ministers, 9, 32, 102

253

Index

Index

Louisburg expedition (1746), 64
Lyman, Gideon, 149–50, 153

Massachusetts General Court
  Ashfield's anti-Baptist letter to, 91–2
  county courts established by, 17
  land sale restrictions of, 123
  ministerial associations and, 27
  Pynchon family in, 23
  religious dissenters tolerated by, 85–6, 87
  rural representatives to, 8
  South Hadley's status and, 136
  John Stoddard in, 28
  in township incorporations, 124
  Williams family in, 32
Massachusetts Government Act, 161
Massachusetts Proposals (1705), 27
Mather, Cotton, 26, 27, 28
Mather, Eleazar, 24
Mather, Increase, 26, 27, 28
meetinghouse controversies, 113, 134–43, 151–2
  between Baptists and Congregationalists, 88
  democratic process in, 139–40
  destructive approach in, 141–3
  population growth and, 137, 138
  property values considered in, 147, 148
  see also division controversies
Merrick, Noah, 57
migrants, migration, 107–17
  conservatism retained in, 13–14
  land improvements by, 117–18
  out-, 107, 109, 112–13
  patterns of, 112–13
  physical obstacles to, 115–17
  rate of increase in, 107, 112
  town size regulated by, 10, 109
  of transient poor, 111–12
  see also settlements
military
  county, 18
  kinship network in, 31, 33–4
  private profits reaped from, 33–4, 127
  in Seven Years' War, 126–9
  western forts and, 110
ministerial associations, 27–8
  legal status of, 27
  need for, 27
  see also Hampshire Association of Ministers
ministerial authority
  in Congregationalist churches, 26
  in Great Awakening, 50–6
  in post-Awakening era, 76, 103–6
  in seventeenth century, 14–15, 27
ministry, 36–58

  anti-Awakening backlash in, 57–8, 72–3, 76
  Ashley's view of, 50–3
  in Ballantine's ordination, 38–40
  in Breck controversy, 40–4, 54
  changed role of, 46
  dismissals in, 52–6, 59, 72–3, 81–2
  disorder first felt by, 36
  economic self-interest as viewed by, 47–9
  in Edwards controversy, 66–73
  growing rift in, 38–40
  land grants to, 123
  as legal requirement, 14
  in post-Awakening conflicts, 81–4
  post-Awakening revivalism and, 80–1
  post-Awakening self-defense of, 37, 76–7
  post-Awakening unity in, 74
  punished in Revolutionary era, 180–3
  revivalist attacks on, 49
  as source of order, 105
  standards of, 41
  vulnerability of, 50, 51, 52–7, 103
mob action, 166–76
  behavior in, 168
  as European heritage, 167–8
  opposition expressed to, 170
  outbreak of, 169–70
  in Springfield, 166–7, 168
  by Williamsburg people, 171–6
Montague, Mass., in 1768 convention, 158–9
Moody, John, 138
Moody, Samuel, 138
Morton, James, 81–2
Murrayfield, Mass.
  division controversy in, 143–4
  meetinghouse controversy in, 113

New Jersey, tenant uprisings in, 185
news, slow transmission of, 156
New Salem, Mass., tax burden of, 124
Newton, Roger, 183
New York, land riots in, 185
Northampton, Mass.
  division of, 143
  division of land in, 109
  economic stratification in, 15
  focus of authority shifted to, 24
  jail in, 180
  John Pynchon's role in, 23
  mob action in, 169–70
  out-migration from, 109
  reaction to 1768 convention in, 158
  religious controversy in, 15, 59–73
  soil quality in, 117
  transients in, 112, 115
  vulnerability of, 13

255

Index

North Carolina, local conflicts in, 185
Northfield, Mass., abandonment of, 109–10

office holding
  in early Hampshire towns, 16
  in new settlements, 114–15
Otis, James, 158

Parsons, David, 77–8, 80
  in Revolutionary crisis, 183
Partridge, Oliver, 122
  as object of mob action, 169
  in Williams kinship network, 30, 32, 33
Partridge, Samuel, 30
patronage
  of county elite, 19–20, 30, 33–4, 127
  of royal governors, 7–8, 19–20, 29–30
Peebles, Robert, 118
Pelham, Mass.
  mob action in, 122, 169
  in response to Boston Committee, 159–60
  settlement and development in, 118–19
Pennsylvania, frontiersmen's protest in, 185
Phelps, Charles, 82–3, 84–5, 105
Phips, William, 19
Pierce, Josiah, 157
Pine Laws, 157
Pontiac's Rebellion, 185
population
  division controversies and, 133, 137, 144
  increased by migration, 107
  land scarcity and, 110–11
  office holding and, 115
  patterns of, 112–13
  rapid growth of, 10, 11, 112
  transient poor in, 111–12
Porter, Eleazar, 32
Prince, Thomas, 67, 68
proprietors, nonresident, 123–6
Puritans
  covenants of, 13–14
  religious tensions of, 14–15, 25–6, 78
  waning communalism of, 17–18
Pynchon, John, 20–4, 31, 35
  death of, 23–4
  increased stratification under, 21
  land holdings of, 20–1
  network of dependence on, 22–3
  offices held by, 23
  pervasive influence of, 21–3
Pynchon, John, II, 24, 32
Pynchon, William, 20–3, 35
  background of, 20
  increased stratification under, 21
  judicial powers of, 23
  land holdings of, 20–1

offices held by, 20, 22–3
  pervasive influence of, 21–3
  as political link with Boston, 22–3
Pynchon, William, II, 32

Rand, William, 39, 52–3, 56, 57
Rawson, Grindall, 52–3, 54–6
Read, Benjamin, 171–3
"Regulator" movement, 185
revivalism, see Great Awakening
Revolutionary era, 155–87
  Bicentennial commemoration of, 3
  Coercive Acts (Intolerable Acts) in, 8, 160, 161
  compared to Great Awakening, 183, 185
  distrust of political elite heightened in, 164–6
  growing exchange of correspondence in, 159–65
  Hampshire County's isolation in, 156–60, 186
  as ideological struggle, 3–4
  local autonomy threatened in, 161–2
  local leaders threatened in, 166–7, 169–80
  Massachusetts Government Act in, 161
  ministry challenged in, 104, 180–3
  parochial disputes as preparation for, 155–6
  political emergence of new towns in, 162–5
  restrictive British legislation in, 160–2
  violent uprisings before, 185–6
Reynolds, Peter, 39, 71
River Gods
  dominance of, 7–8, 9
  political system of, 18–19

Seasonable Thoughts on the State of Religion in New England (Chauncy), 57, 58, 86
Separates, 84–5, 91–102
  antielitist viewpoint of, 95–6
  Baptists distinguished from, 87
  churches established by, 56, 84
  as disruptive force, 85
  Edwards's post-Awakening position and, 94
settlements, 107–31
  county leaders' relationship with, 125–30
  disputes in, 113–14
  greater political equality in, 115
  incorporation of, 123–4
  increased number of, 107–8
  indebtedness in, 120–2
  land grants and, 123
  land scarcity and, 110–11
  migration and, 107, 109, 112–13

256

Index